Canada's Constitutional Law in a Nutshell

Bernard W. Funston

B.A. (Trent), M. Litt (Cambridge), LL.B. (Alberta)

A member
of the Bars of Alberta and
the Northwest Territories

and

Eugene Meehan

LL.B. (Edinburgh), LL.B. (Ottawa), LL.M. (McGill), D.C.L. (McGill)

A practising member
of the Bars of Ontario and Alberta

CARSWELL
Thomson Professional Publishing

The publisher is not engaged in rendering legal, accounting or other professional advice. If legal advice or other expert assistance is required, the services of a competent professional should be sought. The analysis contained herein represents the opinions of the authors and should in no way be construed as being official or unofficial policy of any governmental body.

This work reproduces official English language versions of federal statutes and/or regulations. As this material also exists in official French language form, the reader is advised that reference to the official French language version may be warranted in appropriate circumstances.

The paper used in this publication meets the minimum requirements of the American National Standard for Information Sciences — Permanence of Paper for Printed Library Materials, ANSI X39.48-1984.

Canadian Cataloguing in Publication Data

Funston, Bernard W., 1956-
    Canada's constitutional law in a nutshell

ISBN 0-459-55823-4

1. Canada — Constitutional law. I. Meehan,
Eugene, 1952-   . II. Title.

KE4219.F85 1994   342.71   C94-931434-X
KF4482.F85 1994

CARSWELL
Thomson Professional Publishing

One Corporate Plaza, 2075 Kennedy Road, Scarborough, Ontario M1T 3V4
Customer Service:
Toronto 1-416-609-3800
Elsewhere in Canada/U.S. 1-800-387-5164
Fax 1-416-298-5094

As a country's Constitution is the foundation
on which that country's future is built,
this book is dedicated to our children:
Clare, Gregory and John Funston; and
Marc, Mélanie and Morgan Meehan.

The next year Cartier returned and this time sailed on beyond Gaspé, entering the mouth of the St. Lawrence river. While he voyaged upstream in the early autumn of 1535, he might well have thought that here at last was the passage to India, as the river stretched its mighty length into the hazy distance, and days of sailing along a shore crowned with golden ash, reddening maples and wild grapes brought no sign of the channel's end. At length he reached narrows in the river, between a bold promontory and a broad, beautiful island, where he stopped to visit the Iroquois Indian village of Stadacona.... And Cartier, misunderstanding an Iroquois word, perhaps a reference to the Indian corn fields, thought that the country's name was Canada.

J.M.S. Careless, *Canada: A Story of Challenge*

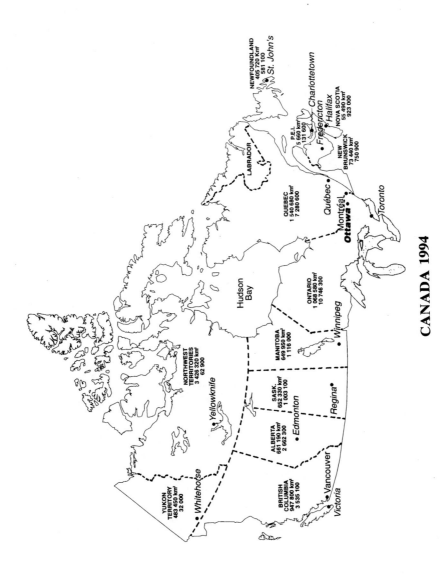

CANADA 1994

YUKON TERRITORY
483 450 km²
32 000

NORTHWEST TERRITORIES
3 426 320 km²
62 900

BRITISH COLUMBIA
947 800 km²
3 535 100

ALBERTA
661 190 km²
2 662 300

SASK.
652 330 km²
1 003 100

MANITOBA
649 950 km²
1 116 000

ONTARIO
1 068 580 km²
10 746 300

QUÉBEC
1 540 680 km²
7 280 600

NEWFOUNDLAND
405 720 km²
581 100

LABRADOR

P.E.I.
5 660 km²
131 600

NOVA SCOTIA
55 490 km²
923 000

NEW BRUNSWICK
73 440 km²
750 900

Whitehorse

Yellowknife

Edmonton

Regina

Winnipeg

Victoria

Vancouver

Toronto

Ottawa

Montréal

Québec

Fredericton

Charlottetown

Halifax

St. John's

Hudson Bay

Preface

This book is a Nutshell only — a nutshell is small — therefore this book is only a summary overview of this area of law, and nothing more.

Readers are directed to the references footnoted in the text of this Nutshell and the Selected Bibliography at the end for a detailed review and analysis of constitutional law in Canada.

Acknowledgments

We wish to thank the following for the research and other work they have assisted us with in the writing of this Nutshell:

- Moira Dillon (now articling at Fraser & Beatty in Ottawa)
- Asha Gosein (now articling at Simpson Wigle in Hamilton)
- Patricia Pledge (now articling at Gowling Strathy & Henderson in Ottawa)
- Catherine Markson (now in third year at University of Ottawa Law School)
- Karen M. Cuddy (lawyer with Lang Michener in Ottawa)
- Laura Nelson (of the Bars of Alberta and the Northwest Territories)
- Ken Tyler (Legal Counsel, Manitoba Department of the Attorney General)

We also thank legal secretaries Erin Smith and Rachel Avon for transforming illegible handwriting into legible type, and for their continuing encouragement and assistance to Eugene Meehan to become (computer) literate.

A special thanks goes to David Keeshan, Acquisitions Editor, and Kimberly Aiken, Production Editor, at Carswell for their exceptional professional assistance.

Bernard Funston would like to particularly thank his wife Laura and his parents Katherine and Bernie Sr. for their constant encouragement over the years.

Table of Contents

PART II — DIVISION OF POWERS

PART III — THE CHARTER

Chapter 9 — Charter of Rights and Freedoms — The Main Provisions 153

PART IV — AMENDING THE CONSTITUTION

Chapter 10 — The Constitutional Amending Procedures 197

Illustrations

* Reprinted from J.A. Lower, *Canada: An Outline History*, 2d ed. (McGraw-Hill Ryerson, 1991).
** Maps 3 to 10 are reprinted from N.L. Nicholson, *The Boundaries of the Canadian Confederation* (MacMillan, 1979). Special thanks is given to The Institute of Canadian Studies, Carleton University, Ottawa, and to Mrs. N.L. Nicholson.

Table of Cases

[All cases are referenced to page numbers of the text.]

*Authors' Note: The correct style of cause for this case is actually *Sibbeston v. Canada (Attorney General)*, as appears in D.L.R. (4th) and N.R., not *Sibbeston v. Northwest Territories (Attorney General)* as appears in N.W.T.R. and W.W.R. Sibbeston was the Attorney General for the Northwest Territories at the time he brought this action against Canada.

PART I

AN OVERVIEW OF
THE CONSTITUTION

1

Canada's Legal Framework — Then and Now

1. Introduction

For generations British law students have begun their inquires into the intricacies of legal learning by turning to Glanville Williams' lucid book *Learning the Law*. He opens by saying, "This is not a textbook."[1]

We adopt the same claim: This is not a textbook. It is designed to prepare the student of law or politics for reading textbooks about the Constitution of Canada. Many of the ideas and principles underlying the Constitution are quite simple. The relationships governed by our Constitution, however, are often very complex. As a result, constitutional law, like all branches of the law, contains subtleties and nuances which would require a much lengthier book than this to describe and explain. It is our purpose here to describe some basic ideas and relationships so that the student has a broad overview or "mental map" of the Constitution before proceeding into the more detailed texts and case reports.

There is no magic in the word "constitution". Most clubs, associations, societies and companies have some form of constitution.

The *Concise Oxford Dictionary* defines a constitution as a "body of fundamental principles according to which a State or other organization is governed." This is a starting point, but it inevitably leads to further questions.

The study of the Constitution involves not only the fundamental principles, but also the form of government, the nature of the institutions, the machinery by which it is carried out, and how governments operate in practical situations. A few important questions are:

1. Where did our Constitution come from?
2. What comprises the Constitution?
3. How are fundamental principles articulated in the Constitution?
4. What does the Constitution say about the machinery of government?
5. How, and by whom, are our governments chosen?
6. How are governments dismissed?
7. Who really makes decisions and runs our system of government?

---

[1] G. Williams, *Learning the Law*, 9th ed. (Stevens & Sons, 1973) at 1.

8. What can governments do and not do?
9. How do the levels of government in Canada interrelate?
10. How are the constitutional rules that govern the governments changed?

This book contains a general examination of these questions and takes a cursory look at the purposes and functions served by various constitutional rules.

2. The Constitution and Canada: House and Home

As you proceed through this book keep this in mind: A group of people (Canadians) drew up the blueprints (*Constitution Act, 1867*[2]) and built a four-room house (Ontario, Quebec, Nova Scotia, New Brunswick). Provision was made in the blueprints for additions. Over the years rooms have been added (six provinces and two territories).

The rules of this house provide for a division of powers. The people who occupy a particular room (province/territory) will decide what goes on in that room unless it directly affects another room or the people in it. The occupants of a room elect a team of interior decorators/caterers (provincial/territorial governments) to decorate and maintain their room and cater to their needs.

Being democratic, the occupants of the entire house together elect a larger team of decorators/caterers (federal government) to attend to matters that generally affect the whole house, its occupants, and the yard. This team also manages relations with the neighbours.

Over the years the occupants of the house have hired and fired a number of teams of decorators/caterers, for each room and for the house generally. Each new team of decorators/caterers has brought different tastes and skills to bear. So while the basic structure of the house has, for the most part, remained unchanged and there are still 12 rooms, each new team has brought changes in the look (political philosophy) given to each room and to the house generally. Furnishings (laws) and colour preferences (policies) have run the gamut.

Various decorator/caterer teams have had some impressive ideas about major renovations (constitutional amendments) from time to time, but the original blueprints for the house left lots of space to grow and so far have not been significantly redrawn, except for a recent addition to the rules of the house which reminds decorators/caterers that the occupants have rights too (*Charter of Rights and Freedoms*[3]). It is a fact of life that there are strains within the house from time to time: unpaid bills are

---

[2] (U.K.), 30 & 31 Vict., c. 3 [now R.S.C. 1985, App. II].

[3] Part I of the *Constitution Act, 1982*, being Schedule B to the *Canada Act 1982* (U.K.), 1982, c. 11.

accumulating; some occupants believe affairs would run more smoothly if the house were a duplex; the original occupants of the lands on which the house was built want to enjoy the comforts and influence that other people in the house have enjoyed over the years.

Our point: The blueprint for the old house has a very important but subtle influence on daily life in each room and within the house generally. Although it defines the spaces or areas within which the occupants interact, the life of the house is not in its blueprint; it springs from the occupants and their interactions which emerge from shared or differing values and interests.

It is easy to forget that "constitutionalism", that is the organization of our political and legal systems according to a constitution, is a relatively recent development in an historical sense. Today we take for granted the "rule of law"[4] which, unlike "might is right" governance in dictatorships, prevents arbitrary behaviour by governments and citizens.[5]

The laws which now govern behaviour in our society are established by duly elected representatives operating in democratically sanctioned institutions. By contrast, in the early years of settlement the colonies were governed by Prerogative of the Crown.[6] The Governors of the colonies made and enforced laws in the name of the Monarch. Even where provision was made for assemblies to be elected by the people to assist the Governor, the Governor was not bound to follow their advice or even to call elections. In the case of Quebec in the mid-1700s, for example, Governors Murray and Carleton decided not to institute assemblies because they feared it would lead to bothersome demands from various interest groups.[7]

Some writers have described the Constitution as "a mirror which reflects the soul of the nation". However, to the average reader the constitutional statutes may seem more "smoke" than "mirror". The written, legal part of the Constitution contains few ringing phrases and is far less poetic than this description would suggest. A person does not obtain a clear understanding of how the Constitution actually works in practice by simply reading the constitutional statutes. These documents do not say anything about the Prime Minister or Premiers, their ministers or cabinets,[8] or political parties. Nor can the written Constitution reflect how

---

[4] The Preamble to the *Canadian Charter of Rights and Freedoms* says: "Whereas Canada is founded upon principles that recognize the supremacy of God and the rule of law."

[5] See, for a general discussion of the rule of law, R. Van Loon & M. Whittington, *The Canadian Political System* (McGraw-Hill Ryerson, 1987) at 166-170.

[6] See J.E. Read, "The Early Provincial Constitutions" (1948) 26 Can. Bar Rev. 621.

[7] See C. Nish, "The 1760s" in J.M.S. Careless, ed., *Colonists and Canadiens 1760 to 1867* (MacMillan, 1968) at 1-19.

[8] Note, however, that s. 63 of the *Constitution Act, 1867* did name, "in the first instance", the portfolios for the initial executive councils for Ontario and Quebec, but not for New Brunswick or Nova Scotia. Subsequently, executive councils and their composition have been provided for in provincial legislation.

the courts have interpreted the rules and practices that ultimately shape Canadian society. In addition, there are political or "conventional" rules of the Constitution which one must strain to perceive in the mists of tradition.

The Constitution has also been described as a "living tree". This is probably closer to the mark. Constitutional statutes represent only the trunk and branches. As our society has developed over the years, "foliage" has been added by evolving political traditions and practices, and by the changing interpretations given to constitutional statutes by the courts.

3. What Constitutes the Constitution

There are three important points to remember about what constitutes "the Constitution":

(a) The Constitution is not a Single Document, nor Entirely Written

Not all aspects of the Constitution are in written form and the written portions are not contained in a single document or statute.

Most Canadians have some impressions about what the Constitution is and what it says. We have had a steady diet of constitutional issues in the media for much of the past 30 years. For many people, the Constitution conjures up something written and definite. However, the Constitution is not really something you can hold in your hand.

(b) The Constitution Includes Both Legal and Political Rules

The Constitution is not entirely a body of law. Most experts consider the Constitution to include both *legal* and *political rules*.

The *legal rules*, contained for the most part in constitutional statutes and court decisions, are interpreted and enforced by the courts. When a dispute arises the parties go to court, argue their points of view, and when a decision is handed down by the court, the parties treat it as binding and act accordingly.

Simply reading constitutional statutes to obtain an understanding of the Constitution may initially tend to confuse rather than enlighten. For example, the *Constitution Act, 1867* supposedly describes our system of government. However, what it describes may not seem, at first glance, to conform to our understanding of current institutions and existing political realities. Some provisions, read too literally, would leave a complete misconception about how Canada is governed. Section 9 of the *Constitu-*

tion Act, 1867 gives the impression that the Queen is the head of, and runs, the government of Canada. As related above, the 1867 Act does not mention the Prime Minister or the federal cabinet. Clearly the Constitution is not a complete code for government. It is only a broad outline for our system.

Can we take the Constitution seriously if we cannot take it literally? The answer is ''Yes''. It was never the purpose of the various Constitution Acts to set down Canada's Constitution in its entirety, nor were these Acts intended to provide a highly detailed rule or guide book for Canadian government and society. In fact, it would be impossible to write such a document.

The *political rules* of the Constitution, called ''conventions'', arise from fundamental political traditions. Constitutional conventions are political rather than legal in nature and do not appear in any legally binding documents. Conventions are not directly enforced through the courts. If observed at all,[9] it is through various political institutions or by the self-discipline of our politicians. Conventions have been described as the code of ethics that governs our political processes.

Although the legal rules of the Constitution are the ''supreme law of Canada'',[10] the importance of the political or conventional rules cannot be minimized. The relationship between these legal and non-legal rules is central to the operation of the Constitution. For example, a Royal Commission recently described some conventional elements of the Constitution as being more important than the legal elements:

> Although a written constitution is an important component of a modern state like Canada, what predominates in the end are certain ways of doing and looking at things, ways of relating to our fellow citizens and our governmental institutions, — all of which are animated by a sense of social purpose, and a feeling for justice and injustice. In a word, what counts ultimately are our traditions. They not only provide flesh to the bare bones of the written constitution, they are in fact the living structure of the constitution itself, which the text only imperfectly articulates.[11]

---

[9] Note: Some conventions carry more authority than others. Some are fundamental to our system of government, some are peripheral. Non-observance of a fundamental convention would not be done lightly.

[10] This phrase is contained in s. 52(1) of the *Constitution Act, 1982*, being Schedule B to the *Canada Act 1982* (U.K.), 1982, c. 11.

[11] Judge R. Dussault & G. Erasmus, Co-Chairs of Royal Commission on Aboriginal Peoples, ''Notes for A Speech delivered to Federal-Provincial-Territorial Meeting of Ministers Responsible for Aboriginal Affairs and Leaders of the National Aboriginal Organizations'', Toronto, Ontario, February 1, 1994.

Conventions are regularly analyzed and commented upon by political scientists but court analysis and commentary on conventions is actually quite rare. *Re Resolution to Amend the Constitution*[12] (1981) is the most notable case containing a discussion of the role of conventions in our Constitution.

(c) The Constitution is Evolving

The legal and conventional constitutional rules evolve and change, sometimes quickly, often subtly.

Conventional constitutional rules, because they are based in our political traditions, inevitably change or evolve as changes occur in Canadian society. On the other hand, many of the legal rules of the Constitution are modified in the course of interpretation by the courts and may be difficult to articulate with precision. Therefore, identifying accepted rules or principles that underlie the Constitution presents a moving target.

To summarize, the Constitution is not concise, legalistic and static, rather it is voluminous, flexible and evolving.

4. The Functions of the *Constitution Act, 1867*

Among the main functions of Canada's Constitution are:

1. to establish a political and economic union based on federal and democratic principles;
2. to outline a framework for the machinery of government and establish governmental institutions (*e.g.*, Parliament, courts);
3. to distribute legislative powers and executive powers between the provincial and national levels of government, thereby imposing legal limits on what a particular level of government can do and not do in relation to other governments;
4. since 1982, to guarantee certain individual and collective rights and place limits on the powers of governments and legislators respecting these matters; and
5. to provide the rules and procedures for changing the Constitution itself.

It is worthwhile to keep in mind, as one constitutional scholar has noted, that "laws and constitutions are not so much extracted from ideal

---

[12] *Manitoba (Attorney General) v. Canada (Attorney General)*, [1981] 1 S.C.R. 753.

forms, but chosen to accommodate interests."[13] The reader is encouraged, therefore, to look beyond what the Constitution says, and beyond what the courts say about the Constitution, to the more difficult question as to why the Constitution and courts say what they do.

The management of relationships laid the functional basis for our Constitution. The relationships which had shaped events leading up to 1867 had been developing for almost 200 years. These included:

1. the early relationships between French and British settlers and aboriginal peoples in North America;
2. the relationships among Britain, France, aboriginal peoples and American colonists resulting from their respective commercial and military policies in North America;
3. the relationship between British colonies in what would become the United States and those in what would become Canada;
4. the relationship of Canadian and American colonies to the Imperial governments in London, England; and
5. the relationship between Francophones and Anglophones and between Catholics and Protestants.

Some relationships which were central to the dynamics of evolving Canadian nationhood after 1867 can be briefly and simply listed:

1. a new relationship among former colonial governments (*i.e.*, provinces) and a new national government in Ottawa;
2. the relationship between Canadian citizens and their two levels (federal, provincial) of government (Canada's federation was unique being based on the supremacy of parliaments within defined spheres of power, unlike the American republic which was based on sovereignty of the people, who delegated power to their state and federal governments to exercise subject to a system of checks and balances that governed the exercise of authority);
3. the relationship between French-speaking and English-speaking residents of the new country;
4. the relationships between the regions and their differing economic, social, cultural and linguistic circumstances;
5. the relationship between Canada and other nations, particularly the United States of America and the United Kingdom; and
6. the relationship between the emerging Canadian society and the aboriginal peoples.

---

[13] J. Whyte, "A Melbourne Diary" *The Literary Review of Canada* (November 1993) vol. 2:10.

5. How the Canadian Federation was Formed: The External Forces

In the years after 1763, leaders of the colonies and provinces of British North America had tried, and failed, to achieve lasting political union. Our present federal union had its origins in a series of colonial conferences in the 1860s. Delegates of the colonial governments met in Charlottetown and Quebec City in 1864, and in London, England in 1866 to work out the plans for a new union. Upper and Lower Canada (Ontario and Quebec), New Brunswick, Nova Scotia, Prince Edward Island and Newfoundland were represented. The original blueprint for Canada did not spring directly from the demands of the people, but rather from the aspirations of colonial government leaders. A set of 72 resolutions was eventually adopted at the Quebec City conference.

The governments of Prince Edward Island and Newfoundland were not initially sold on the merits of a union with the other provinces. Implementing the Quebec City Agreement proved more difficult than some representatives to the conference had anticipated. Opposition to the scheme from constituents and opposition parties, and from the United States, came near to uprooting the plan. In New Brunswick, for example, the Premier would not risk putting the Confederation plan before the legislative assembly for a vote.[14] Finally, on December 4, 1866, delegates from Upper and Lower Canada, Nova Scotia and New Brunswick met at the Westminster Palace Hotel in London, England and adopted a slightly revised agreement comprised of 69 numbered paragraphs. Paragraph 2 concisely spelled out the grand scheme:

> In the Confederation of the British North American provinces the system of government best adapted under existing circumstances to protect the diversified interests of the several provinces and secure efficiency, harmony, and permanence in the working of the Union is a General Government charged with matters of common interest to the whole country and Local Governments for each of the Canadas, and for the provinces of Nova Scotia and New Brunswick, charged with the control of local matters in their respective sections, provision being made for the admission into the Confederation on equitable terms of Newfoundland, Prince Edward Island, the North-West Territory, and British Columbia.

These resolutions acted as drafting instructions for preparation of the *British North America Act, 1867.* When the Act was passed by the British Parliament and came into force on July 1, 1867, the original 69 paragraphs had been rendered into 147 statutory provisions.

---

[14] See W.L. Morton, *The Kingdom of Canada,* 2d ed. (McClelland & Stewart, 1969) at 320.

The *Constitution Act, 1867*,[15] as the Act is now called, built on traditions and already existing colonial constitutions. The preamble to the Act states, without further explanation, that the new Dominion would have "a Constitution similar in Principle to that of the United Kingdom." Furthermore, in that part of the Act coming under the heading "Provincial Constitutions", it provided that:

> **88.** The Constitution of the Legislature of each of the Provinces of Nova Scotia and New Brunswick shall, subject to the Provisions of this Act, continue as it exists at the Union until altered under the Authority of this Act.

One historian has described the London resolutions in the following terms:

> It was a strictly practical and wholly conservative document in both content and spirit. It neither professed to enshrine an ideal nor claimed to advance a principle. It added not one voter to the electorate, and secured no right, old or new, to the subject. The reasons for this austere practicality are plain. The union of British America was proposed, not to achieve sought-after privileges and liberties, but to preserve an inheritance of freedom long enjoyed and a tradition of life valued beyond any promise of prophet or of demagogue. Confederation was to preserve by union the constitutional heritage of Canadians from the Magna Carta of the barons to the responsible government of Baldwin and Lafontaine, and, no less, the French and Catholic culture of St. Louis and Laval.[16]

The external forces which gave impetus to the Canadian union are revealed by another prominent historian:

> The Confederation drama was one play where the offstage noises were a vital part of the action. Those noises where largely echoes from the bloody battlefields of the American Civil War. They often threatened to drown the voices of the Canadian performers, the Macdonalds, the Browns, the Cartiers, as they spoke their dignified lines. Armies greater than Napoleon's were locked in conflict on the soil of North America; and as the statesmen of the British provinces strove to make plans for their countries' future, the gunfire of Bull Run and Antietam and Fredericksburg rattled the windows of their offices.[17]

George Brown, who was alive in 1867 and played a significant role in Canada's formation, described the motivating factors this way:

---

[15] The *British North America Act, 1867* was renamed the *Constitution Act, 1867* in 1982; see Chapter 2, *infra.*, under the heading "Terminology" for further details.

[16] Morton, *supra*, note 14.

[17] C.P. Stacey, "Confederation: The Atmosphere of Crisis" in E. Firth, ed., *Profiles of a Province* (Ontario Historical Society, 1967) at 74-75 and 78.

The civil war . . . in the neighbouring republic; the possibility of war between Great Britain and the United States; the threatened repeal of the Reciprocity Treaty; the threatened abolition of the American bonding system for goods in transit to and from these provinces; the unsettled position of the Hudson's Bay Company; and the changed feeling of England as to the relation of great colonies to the parent state; — all combine at this moment to arrest earnest attention to the gravity of the situation, and unite us all in one vigorous effort to meet the emergency.[18]

It was not inevitable that Canada would succeed in 1867 after constitutional experiments on a far smaller scale had failed in 1763, 1774, 1791 and 1840.

6. The Study of the Constitution

The Constitution can be analyzed on many practical and theoretical levels. There is much written on the legal, political, economic and social aspects of government, democracy and rights. Courts regularly examine questions such as these in the cases brought before them.

When sections of the *Canadian Charter of Rights and Freedoms* are in issue, for example the right to life, liberty and security of the person (s. 7), or freedom of thought, belief, opinion and expression (s. 2(*b*)), or the right to vote (s. 3), the courts try to determine the thinking behind these provisions, and what purposes these rights are intended to serve in the larger society. Understanding the "purpose" of any given constitutional provision requires a thoughtful study of history, political and constitutional theory, and the circumstances of the case in the context of current affairs in Canadian society. It is obviously not an exact science and conclusions, once reached, are rarely agreed upon by everyone.

7. Canada: A Brief Historical Chronology

The study of Canadian history is important, if not essential, to an understanding of political and constitutional issues in Canada today. An outline of periods in Canadian history of importance to the development of the country, its governments and the Constitution, might go something like this:[19]

---

[18] Quoted in Stacey, *ibid.* at 78.

[19] This section only provides a very rough outline. For brief histories of Canada, see: J.M.S. Careless, *Canada: A Story of Challenge* (Stoddart, 1991), and J.A. Lower, *Canada: An Outline History*, 2d ed. (McGraw-Hill Ryerson, 1991); for a survey history of the period from 1760 to 1867, see: Careless, ed., *Colonists and Canadiens 1760 to 1867, supra,* note 7; for the period 1867 to 1967, see: J.M.S. Careless & R.C. Brown, eds., *The Canadians 1867-1967* (MacMillan, 1968).

- *Pre-1497: Aboriginal Government:* "[W]hen the settlers came, the [aboriginal peoples] were there, organized in societies and occupying the land as their forefathers had done for centuries."[20]
- *1497-1535:* Exploration and settlement of the Atlantic provinces, Eastern Arctic and St. Lawrence Valley and eastern United States by Europeans.
- *1535-1663: Outposts of European Empires:* Development of settlements in New France in the valley of the St. Lawrence River.
- *1663-1702: Emergence of Colonial Governments:* Royal Government in New France; the emergence of the Hudson's Bay Company and England's commercial interests; and building alliances with the aboriginal peoples.
- *1702-1763: Struggle for Control of North America:* Military and commercial struggles in North America between French and British empires and their aboriginal allies.
- *1763-1774: Growing Dissatisfaction with Remote Control:* British North American policy under the Royal Proclamation of 1763.
- *1774-1791: Experimenting with Unions:* A change in British policy: the *Quebec Act, 1774*; the emergence of American independence and the United States of America; and a first attempt at Canadian union (the *Constitutional Act, 1791*).
- *1791-1860: Attempts to Reconcile Differences:* Experimenting with English/French coexistence in Canada and the emergence of responsible government in the provinces and colonies that would eventually form Canada.
- *1861-1867: The American Civil War and Fenian Threat:* an impetus for Canadian union.
- *1864-1867: Federalism and Respecting Minorities:* The Charlottetown, Quebec City and London conferences lead to the Confederation experiment and the self-governing Dominion of Canada.
- *1868-1912: Expansion of Canada:* Extending the Canadian federation east, west and north: acquisition of territories, settlement, and the admission/creation of new provinces.
- *1914-1931: Canadian Independence:* The First World War; Canada becomes an independent nation within the British Commonwealth.
- *1931-1949:* The Great Depression; the 1937 Rowell-Sirois Royal Commission on fiscal and constitutional problems; the emergence of fiscal federalism; and the Second World War.
- *1949:* Newfoundland and Labrador join the federation.
- *1950-1980: The Strengthening of Provincial Governments:* Canada in the modern era: the search for prosperity and unity.

---

[20] This statement was made by Mr. Justice Judson in relation to "Indians" in *Calder v. British Columbia (Attorney General)*, [1973] S.C.R. 313 at 328.

- *1980-1982: Patriation:* The patriation of Canada's Constitution: a new *Charter of Rights and Freedoms* and new amending formulae.
- *1983-1993: Searching for a New Federation:* The decade of constitutional debate; aboriginal and treaty rights; aboriginal self-government; Quebec's demands for reform; the Meech Lake Accord; the multilateral "Canada Round" of negotiations; the Charlottetown Accord; growing concerns with fiscal federalism; the threat of Quebec separation.

NORTH AMERICA IN 1800

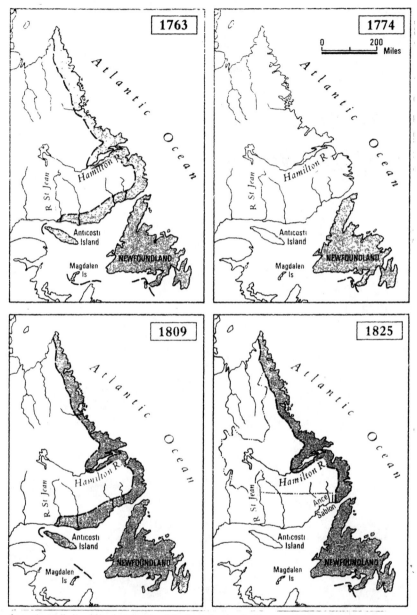

Approximate limits of Newfoundland and its dependencies, in diagrammatic form only   — — — —
Approximate landward boundary between Canada and Newfoundland after 1927   —..—..—..

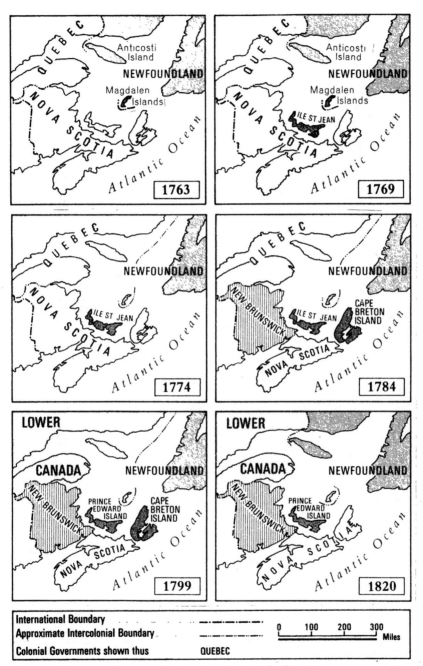

Figure 17. Boundary evolution in the Gulf of St. Lawrence region.

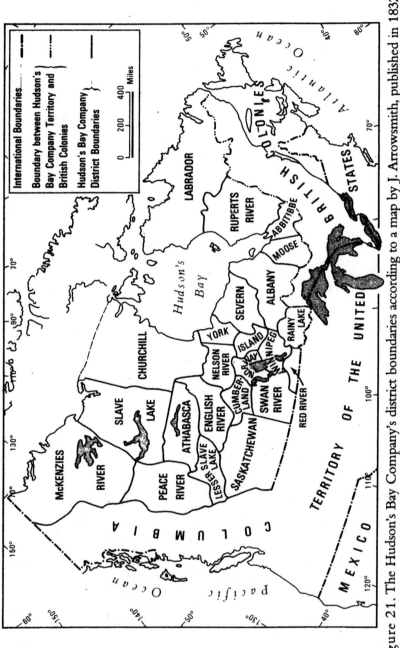

Figure 21. The Hudson's Bay Company's district boundaries according to a map by J. Arrowsmith, published in 1832.

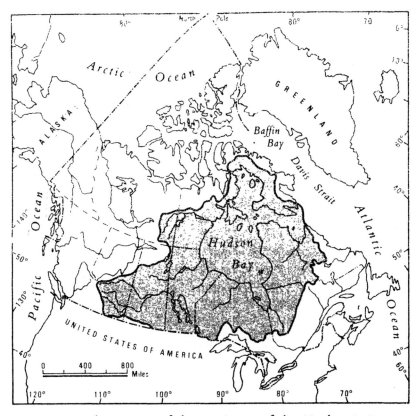

Figure 10. The extent of the territory of the Hudson's Bay
    Company according to a map by J. Arrowsmith,
    published in 1857.

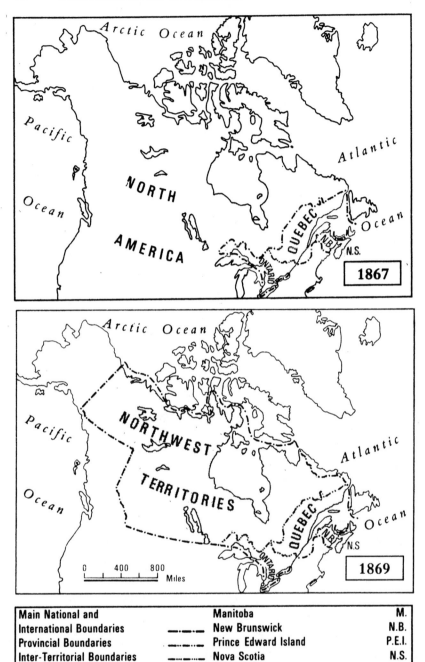

Figure 13. The major political boundaries of Canada, 1867-1869.

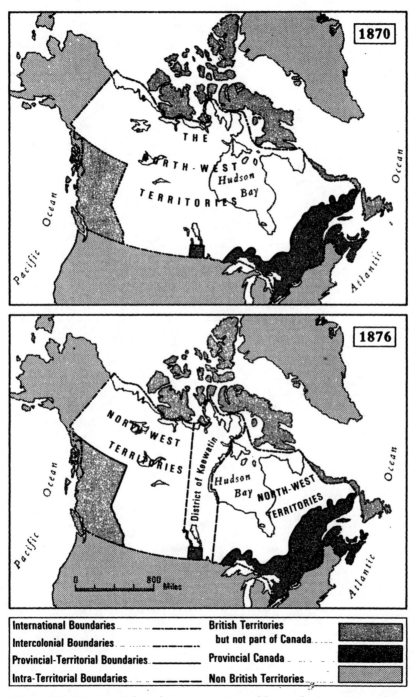

Figure 25. Territorial and intra-territorial boundaries, 1870-1876.

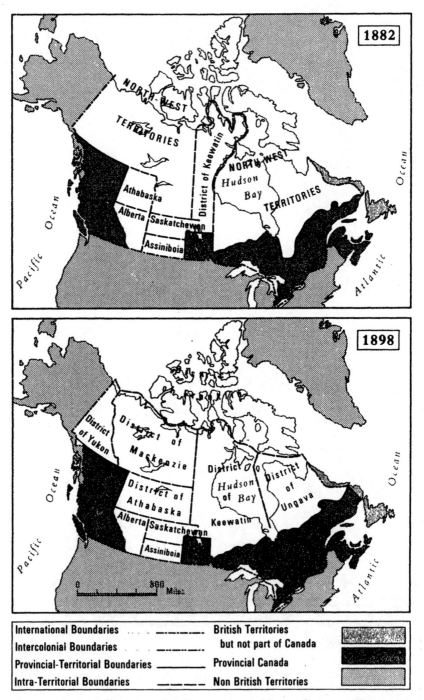

Figure 26. Territorial and intra-territorial boundaries, 1882-1898.

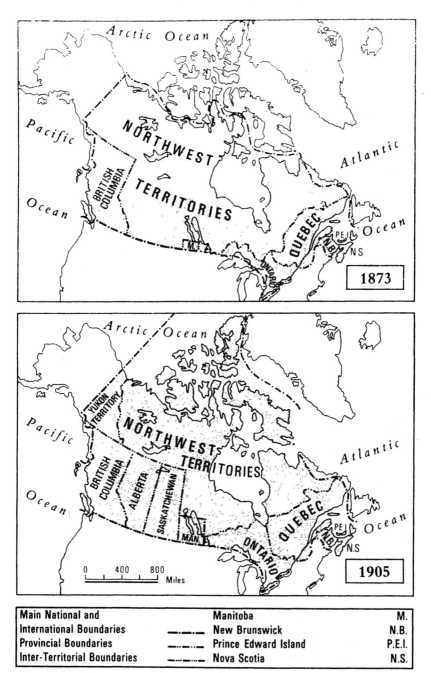

Figure 14. The major political boundaries of Canada, 1873-1905.

8. Recent Developments: Pressures From Within

While the establishment of the Canadian federation may have been driven by external forces, as related above, internal forces are now more likely to influence the future of the country. Issues with potential for major impact on the Canadian federation are:

1. the movement for Quebec's independence and separation from Canada;
2. the recognition and implementation of an inherent right of self-government for aboriginal peoples;[21] and
3. the strains on the Canadian economic union arising from national and provincial debt loads and shifting trade patterns, in a rapidly changing national, continental and global economy.

These and other issues dominated constitutional reform negotiations for much of the 1980s and the first two years of the 1990s. The decade began with a referendum in Quebec on sovereignty-association. Then federal-provincial relations were strained by the federal government's intention to patriate the Constitution through unilateral federal action. In 1982, the Constitution was patriated after a compromise package of reforms was reached with all provinces, except Quebec.

In 1983, the constitutional conferences on aboriginal constitutional matters began. Aboriginal issues dominated the constitutional agenda until 1986 when the governments decided, at Quebec's request, to give Quebec's constitutional demands priority. The constitutionally required conferences on aboriginal issues were completed by April 1987 without agreement on major reforms.

The Prime Minister and Premiers then signed the Meech Lake Accord at the end of April 1987 to meet Quebec's constitutional demands. Over the next three years opposition to the Accord grew. To alleviate opposition, a "companion Accord" was negotiated by First Ministers in a marathon session in June 1990. However, the Meech Lake package of reforms was never approved by the required number of legislative assemblies. No constitutional amendments were made.

Following the demise of the Meech Lake Accord, Quebec boycotted intergovernmental meetings. The federal government initiated studies and public hearings to look at the amending formula and to seek the public's views as to which shared values were most important to Canadians. In September 1991, the federal government tabled a set of proposals for constitutional reform and set up a Parliamentary committee to hold public hearings on this package. A series of constitutional conferences involving

---

[21] See Chapter 8 for a discussion of aboriginal self-government.

the public, academics, governments and interest groups were also held in January and February 1992 to examine the proposals.

In March 1992, a multilateral process of constitutional negotiation began involving federal, provincial (except Quebec) and territorial governments, and four national aboriginal organizations. On July 7, 1992, a constitutional package was agreed to by all participants. In August 1992, Quebec joined the negotiations and changes were made to the package. Negotiations culminated on August 28, 1992, where it had all begun in 1864, in Charlottetown, Prince Edward Island. The agreement reached by the participants in 1992 was commonly known as the "Charlottetown Accord". This Accord contained the most extensive set of constitutional reforms since 1867. By October 8, 1992, those parts of the Accord calling for constitutional amendments had been rendered into legal language.

On October 26, 1992, two referenda were held, one in Quebec and the other in the rest of Canada, to obtain the support of Canadians for the reforms contemplated by the Charlottetown Accord. The package was rejected in many provinces and therefore was abandoned.

The three issues listed at the beginning of this section remain unresolved. It is an open question as to whether constitutional amendments or some other means can resolve them.

Respect for the legitimacy and workability of the Constitution has to be built on realistic expectations as to what the Constitution can and cannot do. In recent years, Canadians and their governments may have placed too much emphasis on constitutional reform to provide solutions to economic, social, cultural, linguistic and political problems. Too much talk of reform may trivialize that which is extraordinary and fundamental and may destabilize that which is relied on for stability.

To summarize, our Constitution is mainly about government. Government, in its broadest sense, is simply the organization of people in pursuit of common purposes. Those purposes can include political and economic stability and advantage, law and order, and social and cultural development. The role governments play in furthering the goals of Canadians is not static. In modern times it has become difficult to define and agree upon what governments should and should not do. Government permeates virtually every activity in our lives through regulation of public and private activities, businesses and industries, programs and services.[22] The Constitution, however, does not dictate the degree of government intervention in our lives.

During efforts to reform the Constitution during the late 1980s and early 1990s, it was common to hear in political speeches statements such

---

[22] See Van Loon & Whittington, *supra*, note 5 at 166-170.

as: "Constitutions don't make countries, countries make constitutions."[23] These statements were generally a call for unity of purpose to achieve constitutional reform, but they also imply that we perhaps should not expect too much from our Constitution, nor blame it too much for the challenges we face as a society.

---

[23] Joe Clark, the Minister responsible for constitutional affairs in the Conservative Government of Brian Mulroney, made this statement in several public speeches during protracted constitutional negotiations in 1992.

2

Canada's Constitutional Documents and Conventions

1. Introduction

The Constitution is composed of two main bodies of rules or principles:

1. legal rules found in the formal Constitution as defined by the *Constitution Act, 1982*[1] and in statutes, orders-in-council, and court decisions relating to the executive, judicial and legislative branches; and
2. informal rules, called conventions, that stem from political practices.[2]

Throughout this book we use the word "Constitution" in a general sense to include its legal and conventional aspects. Where a specific legal rule or provision is discussed, the relevant Act and section number will be provided in the text as appropriate.

2. Terminology

Most of the statutes that make up the core of the formal Constitution were renamed in 1982. For example, *The British North America Act, 1867*, passed in 1867 by the United Kingdom Parliament to create the Canadian federation, was renamed the *Constitution Act, 1867* in 1982.

Many other constitutional Acts also bearing the name "British North America Act" have been passed by both the British and Canadian Parliaments in the years since 1867. Some directly amended provisions in the 1867 Act while others stand as supplements to it. (When referring to one of these Acts, the year of passage is added after the name.) Many, but not all, of these Acts were also renamed "Constitution Act", provided they were still in force. An example of an Act which did not follow this

---

[1] Being Schedule B to the *Canada Act 1982* (U.K.), 1982, c. 11.

[2] A. Heard, *Canadian Constitutional Conventions, The Marriage of Law and Politics* (University of Toronto Press, 1991) at 1. This is a readable and comprehensive book on the subject of conventions from which much of the information on conventions in this Chapter is taken.

pattern is the *British North America Act, 1949* which was renamed the *Newfoundland Act* because it admitted the province of Newfoundland and Labrador to the federation.[3]

In addition, s. 53(2) of the *Constitution Act, 1982* provides that wherever any Act refers to a constitutional statute by its old name, it is amended by substituting for the old name the new name listed in the Schedule to the *Constitution Act, 1982*.

One must remember, therefore, that books, articles and case reports from the courts published prior to 1982 will still refer to British North America Acts while those published after 1982 will usually use the new names.

3. The Main Constitution Acts

Prior to 1982 there was no definition of "the Constitution of Canada" in any of the constitutional Acts.[4] A definition is now found in s. 52(2) of the *Constitution Act, 1982* which says:

> The Constitution of Canada includes
> (a) the *Canada Act 1982*, including this Act;
> (b) the Acts and orders referred to in the schedule; and
> (c) any amendment to any Act or order referred to in paragraph (a) or (b).

It should be noted that because s. 52(2) says "includes", the definition is not necessarily exhaustive. The "schedule" referred to in subs. (b) above is a table attached to the *Constitution Act, 1982*. It lists 30 documents, both statutes and orders-in-council. Twenty-four of these are still in force, the remaining six having been repealed by the *Constitution Act, 1982*.

Two Acts receive most attention in literature on the Constitution and in court proceedings: the *Constitution Act, 1867* and the *Constitution Act, 1982*. Later Chapters of this book will go into more detail on their specific provisions and how they have been interpreted by the courts. In this Chapter, the basic structure and content of these two main Acts is examined.

---

[3] See the Schedule to the *Constitution Act, 1982* for the new names of the various Acts.
[4] The *British North America Act (No. 2), 1949*, 13 Geo. 6, c. 81, characterizes The *British North America Act, 1867*, as it was then called, as "the Constitution of Canada": *Hogan v. R.*, [1975] 2 S.C.R. 574 at 583-584, 18 C.C.C. (2d) 65, quoted in L. Davis, *Canadian Constitutional Law Handbook* (Canada Law Book, 1985) at 70-71.

4. The Structure and Content of the *Constitution Act, 1867*

The names of the Parts and the headings found in the *Constitution Act, 1867* and the *Constitution Act, 1982* are listed below. They give some indication of the content and purpose of the Acts.

The *Constitution Act, 1867* has, in addition to its Preamble, eleven Parts and six Schedules:

Preamble

I. Preliminary (ss. 1, 2 [s. 2 was repealed])
II. Union (ss. 3-8)
III. Executive Power (ss. 9-16)
IV. Legislative Power (ss. 17-20)
— The Senate (ss. 21-36)
— The House of Commons (ss. 37-52)
— Money Votes; Royal Assent (ss. 53-57)
V. Provincial Constitutions
— Executive Power (ss. 58-68)
— Legislative Power (ss. 69-90)
VI. Distribution of Legislative Powers
— Powers of the Parliament (s. 91)
— Exclusive Powers of Provincial Legislatures (s. 92)
— Non-Renewable Natural Resources, Forestry Resources and Electrical Energy (s. 92A)
— Education (s. 93)
— Uniformity of Laws in Ontario, Nova Scotia and New Brunswick (s. 94)
— Old Age Pensions (s. 94A)
— Agriculture and Immigration (s. 95)
VII. Judicature (ss. 96-101)
VIII. Revenues; Debts; Assets; Taxation (ss. 102-126)
IX. Miscellaneous Provisions
— General (ss. 127-133)
— Ontario and Quebec (ss. 134-144)
X. Intercolonial Railway (s. 145 [now repealed])
XI. Admission of Other Colonies (ss. 146, 147)
— The First Schedule: [Original] Electoral Districts of Ontario
— The Second Schedule: Electoral Districts of Quebec specially fixed
— The Third Schedule: Provincial Public Works and Property to be the property of Canada
— The Fourth Schedule: Assets to be the Property of Ontario and Quebec conjointly
— The Fifth Schedule: Oath of Allegiance

— The Sixth Schedule: Primary Production from Non-Renewable Natural Resources and Forestry Resources [added in 1982]

5. The Structure and Content of the *Constitution Act, 1982*

The *Constitution Act, 1982* has, in addition to a short Preamble, seven Parts and one Schedule. Some of its Parts are probably better known than the Act itself:

PART I   Canadian Charter of Rights and Freedoms
           — Guarantee of Rights and Freedoms (s. 1)
           — Fundamental Freedoms (s. 2)
           — Democratic Rights (ss. 3-5)
           — Mobility Rights (s. 6)
           — Legal Rights (ss. 7-14)
           — Equality Rights (s. 15)
           — Official Languages of Canada (ss. 16-22)
           — Minority Language Educational Rights (s. 23)
           — Enforcement (s. 24)
           — General[5] (ss. 25-31)
           — Application of Charter (ss. 32, 33)
           — Citation (s. 34)
PART II   Rights of the Aboriginal Peoples of Canada (ss. 35, 35.1)
PART III   Equalization and Regional Disparities (s. 36)
PART IV   Constitutional Conference (s. 37 [now repealed])
PART IV.1 Constitutional Conferences (s. 37.1 [now repealed])
PART V   Procedure for Amending the Constitution of Canada (ss. 38-49)
PART VI   Amendment to the Constitution Act, 1867 (s. 50 [added s. 92A and Sixth Schedule to *Constitution Act, 1867*])
PART VII   General[6] (ss. 52-61)
           — Schedule: Modernization of the Constitution [lists and renames many constitutional documents]

---

[5] Sections 25-31 provide, among other things, that aboriginal, treaty or other rights and freedoms of aboriginal peoples of Canada are not abrogated or derogated by the Charter; the multicultural heritage of Canada shall be preserved and enhanced; Charter rights are guaranteed equally to male and female persons; rights respecting denominational schools are preserved; references to provinces in the Charter include the territories; and legislative powers are not extended by the Charter.

[6] Among the provisions under this heading are s. 52(1), which says that the Constitution is the supreme law of Canada and any law inconsistent with it is, to the extent of the inconsistency, of no force or effect, and s. 52(2) which defines the "Constitution of Canada".

Listed below are other constitutional Acts and Orders-in-Council. Some of the Acts listed are now spent or have been repealed or amended; however, this list will give some indication as to where the original *Constitution Act, 1867* and *Constitution Act, 1982* have been amended or supplemented. These other constitutional documents have been organized roughly under the major headings used in the *Constitution Act, 1867* and *Constitution Act, 1982* provided above.

6. Some Constitutional Documents Related to the *Constitution Act, 1867*

1. Preamble/Title of Act
   - *Statute Law Revision Act, 1893* (U.K.), 56-57 Vict., c. 14 [spent]
   - *Constitution Act, 1982*, Schedule, Item 1
2. Union
   - *Statute Law Revision Act, 1893*
3. Executive Power
   - 1947 Letters Patent Constituting Office of Governor General (U.K.)[7]
4. Legislative Power
   - *Parliament of Canada Act, 1875* (U.K.), 38-39 Vict., c. 38
   - *Constitution Act, 1982*
5. Senate
   - *Constitution Act, 1886* (U.K.), 49-50 Vict., c. 35
   - *Statute Law Revision Act, 1893*
   - *Constitution Act, 1915* (U.K.), 5-6 Geo. 5, c. 45
   - *Newfoundland Act* (U.K.), 12-13 Geo. 6, c. 22
   - *Constitution Act, 1965* (Can.), 14 Eliz. 2, c. 4, Part I
   - *Constitution Act (No. 2), 1975* (Can.), 23-24 Eliz. 2, c. 53
6. House of Commons
   - *Constitution Act, 1886* (U.K.), 49-50 Vict., c. 35
   - *Constitution Act, 1915* (U.K.), 5-6 Geo. 5, c. 45
   - *Statute Law Revision Act, 1927* (U.K.), 17-18 Geo. 5, c. 42 [spent]
   - *British North America Act, 1943* (U.K.), 6-7 Geo. 6, c. 30 [repealed]
   - *British North America Act, 1946* (U.K.), 9-10 Geo. 6, c. 63 [repealed]
   - *British North America Act, 1952* (Can.), 1 Eliz. 2, c. 15 [repealed]
   - *Constitution Act, 1974* (Can.), 23 Eliz. 2, c. 13, Part I
   - *Constitution Act (No. 1), 1975* (Can.), 23-24 Eliz. 2, c. 28, Part I
   - *Canadian Charter of Rights and Freedoms* (1982), ss. 3-5

---

[7] See also the *Governor General's Act*, R.S.C. 1985, c. G-9, which is ordinary federal legislation.

- *Constitution Act, 1985 (Representation)*, S.C. 1986, c. 8, Part I[8]
7. Provincial Constitutions[9]
    - *Rupert's Land Act, 1868* (U.K.), 30-31 Vict., c. 105 [spent]
    - *Temporary Government of Rupert's Land Act* (Can.), 32-33 Vict., c. 3 [repealed]
    - *Rupert's Land and North-Western Territory Order* (U.K.), 23 June 1870
    - *Manitoba Act, 1870* (Can.), 33 Vict., c. 3 and (Can.), 32-33 Vict., c. 3
    - *Constitution Act, 1871* (U.K.), 34-35 Vict., c. 28
    - *British Columbia Terms of Union*, (U.K.), 16 May 1871
    - *Prince Edward Island Terms of Union* (U.K.), 26 June 1873
    - *Adjacent Territories Order* (U.K.), 31 July 1880
    - *Canada (Ontario Boundary) Act, 1889* (U.K.), 52-53 Vict., c. 28
    - *Statute Law Revision Act, 1893*
    - *Manitoba Boundary Extension Act* (Can.), S.C. 1912, c. 32
    - *Alberta Act* (Can.), 4-5 Edw. 7, c. 3
    - *Saskatchewan Act* (Can.), 4-5 Edw. 7, c. 42
    - *Ontario Boundaries Extension Act* (Can.), S.C. 1912, 2 Geo. 5, c. 40
    - *Quebec Boundaries Extension Act, 1912* (Can.), S.C. 1912, 2 Geo. 5, c. 45
    - *Constitution Act, 1930* (U.K.), 20-21 Geo. 5, c. 26
    - *Newfoundland Act* (U.K.), 12-13 Geo. 6, c. 22
    - *Constitution Amendment Proclamation, 1987 (Newfoundland Act)* (Can.), SI/88-11
8. Distribution of Legislative Powers
    - *Constitution Act, 1871* (U.K.), 34-35 Vict., c. 28
    - *Constitution Act, 1886* (U.K.), 49-50 Vict., c. 35
    - *Statute of Westminster, 1931* (U.K.), 22 Geo. 5, c. 4
    - *Constitution Act, 1940* (U.K.), 3-4 Geo. 6, c. 36
    - *British North America (No. 2) Act, 1949* (U.K.), 13 Geo. 6, c. 81 [repealed]
    - *British North America Act, 1951* (U.K.), 14-15 Geo. 6, c. 32 [repealed]

---

[8] See also the *Electoral Boundaries Readjustment Act*, R.S.C. 1985, c. E-3.

[9] This is not a complete list of constitutional Acts affecting provincial constitutions. For example, the *Constitution Act, 1867* originally provided for certain matters relating to the executive, and to electoral districts of Quebec and Ontario. These provisions have been replaced by provincial legislation. Constitutions of the northern territories are ordinary legislation provided for under the *Constitution Act, 1871*. Parliament has enacted the *Northwest Territories Act*, R.S.C. 1985, c. N-27 [the original version was enacted in 1875]; the *Yukon Act*, R.S.C. 1985, c.Y-2 [the original version was enacted in 1898]; and the *Nunavut Act*, S.C. 1993, c. 28 [to come into force April 1, 1999 or earlier by order of the Governor in Council].

- *Constitution Act, 1964* (U.K.), 12-13 Eliz. 2, c. 73
- *Constitution Act, 1982*, see s. 50

9. Judicature[10]
   - *Constitution Act, 1960* (U.K.), 9 Eliz. 2, c. 2

10. Revenues; Debts; Assets; Taxation
    - *British Columbia Terms of Union* (U.K.), 1871
    - *Prince Edward Island Terms of Union* (U.K.), 1873
    - *Constitution Act, 1907* (U.K.), 7 Edw. 7, c. 11
    - *Constitution Act, 1930* (U.K.), 20-21 Geo. 5, c. 26
    - *Newfoundland Act* (U.K.), 12-13 Geo. 6, c. 22

11. Miscellaneous
    - *Statute Law Revision Act, 1893* (U.K.)
    - *Statute of Westminster, 1931* (U.K.)

12. Intercolonial Railway
    - *Statute Law Revision Act, 1893* (U.K.)

13. Admission of other Colonies
    - See above under Provincial Constitutions

7. Some Constitutional Documents Related to the *Constitution Act, 1982*

1. Canadian Charter of Rights and Freedoms
   - *Constitution Amendment Proclamation, 1983* (Can.), SI/84-102 (re: s. 25)
   - *Constitution Amendment Proclamation, 1993* (Can.), SI/93-54 (*New Brunswick Act*) (re: s. 16)

2. Rights of Aboriginal Peoples of Canada[11]
   - *Constitution Amendment Proclamation, 1983* (Can.), SI/84-102 (re: ss. 35 and 37.1)
   - *James Bay and Northern Quebec Native Claims Settlement Act*, S.C. 1977, c. 32
   - *Western Arctic Inuvialuit Claims Act*, S.C. 1984, c. 24
   - *Gwich'in Land Claim Settlement Act*, S.C. 1992, c. 53
   - *Nunavut Land Claims Agreement Act*, S.C. 1993, c. 29

3. General
   - *Constitution Amendment Proclamation, 1983* (Can.), SI/84-102 (re: ss. 54.1 and 61)

---

[10] See also the *Supreme Court Act*, R.S.C. 1985, c. S-26, which is an ordinary Act of Parliament.

[11] The aboriginal land claims agreements listed here are examples of some modern day treaties. Numerous other treaties are protected by s. 35.

8. Conventions[12]

As related in Chapter 1, many vital details about federal and provincial government are not stated or even hinted at in the Constitution Acts.[13] A literal reading of the provisions on "Executive Power" found in Part III of the *Constitution Act, 1867* might lead to the conclusion that Canada is a virtual dictatorship run by the Queen through the office of the Governor General.[14] Also, the elected House of Commons would appear to meet only when the Governor General asks it to; considers financial legislation only when he/she wants; and is dissolved at his/her command to force a general election.[15] This did occur in some colonies prior to 1848 when the principle of responsible government took hold;[16] however, conventions have now modified these and many other aspects of the Constitution Acts. In fact, major parts of the Constitution depend on conventions.[17]

Conventions can be described as rules of constitutional behaviour that ought to be considered binding by those who operate the Constitution, assuming they have correctly interpreted the precedents and relevant constitutional principles.[18]

Conventions are central to the operation of the Constitution and are often referred to as the "unwritten rules" of the Constitution. More accurately, they cover parts of the Constitution lying outside the fundamental legal documents, but they may still be written down.[19]

9. Responsible Government: Some of the Main Conventions

A thorough study of conventions "would involve numbers of volumes without end."[20] The principle of responsible government involves some of the most important conventions which operate on the exercise of powers by the executive branch. Responsible government has two main components: (1) the responsiblity of individual ministers for their activities and

---

[12] Heard, *supra*, note 2.

[13] R.M. Dawson, *The Government of Canada*, 5th ed. (University of Toronto Press, 1970) at 58.

[14] *Ibid.* at 59.

[15] *Ibid.*

[16] *Ibid.*

[17] Heard, *supra*, note 2 at 1.

[18] This definition is based on our interpretation of the analysis found in Heard, *ibid.* at 3 and 12 which examines definitions contained in G. Marshall & G. Moodie, *Some Problems of the Constitution* (Hutchison, 1959).

[19] Dawson, *supra*, note 13 at 59.

[20] Heard, *supra*, note 2 at vii.

those of their departments; and (2) the responsibility or accountability of the executive as a whole to a majority of members in the elected House of Commons.[21]

Some of the main conventions involved in responsible government at the national level can be summarized as follows:

1. the Governor General only acts on the advice of the Privy Council;
2. this Privy Council is not the full Council described in s. 13 of the *Constitution Act, 1867*, but rather is a much smaller subset, the Cabinet;
3. the Cabinet is chosen by the Prime Minister, and the number of ministers in it is up to him/her;
4. the Prime Minister, although mentioned nowhere in the *Constitution Act, 1867*, is the head of government;
5. the Prime Minister and his/her Cabinet must have the support of a majority of members in the House of Commons;
6. the Prime Minister and his/her Cabinet must have seats in the House of Commons or Senate;
7. House of Commons support for Prime Ministers and Cabinets is rallied by means of political parties; and
8. a failure to command the support of a majority of members in the House of Commons results in the government stepping down and, usually, the calling of a general election.[22]

Conventions vary in importance and authority:

Some will represent merely acceptable procedures while others are explicit and well-recognized practices; one may be trifled with on occasion or even, if necessary, ignored, while another may in its extreme form partake of the same rigidity as the written constitution itself. The number of members in the Canadian cabinet, for example, though largely customary, can be readily altered; representation of the different provinces in the cabinet, can be somewhat modified, but not abandoned; while the responsibility of the cabinet to Parliament is a custom more firmly entrenched than most of the [*Constitution Act, 1867*].[23]

---

[21] *Ibid.* at 50. The principle of responsible government operates on federal, provincial and territorial cabinets.

[22] Most of these conventions are taken from Dawson, *supra*, note 13 at 59-60. Also see G. Tardi, *The Legal Framework of Government, A Canadian Guide* (Canada Law Book, 1992) Chapter 11, "The Electoral Process", 109-121, and Chapter 12, "The Legislative Process", 122-130, for statutory provisions relating to political institutions of government.

[23] Dawson, *supra*, note 13 at 67; also see Chapter 7, "The Variety and Character of Conventions" in Heard, *supra*, note 2, 140-156.

10. Other Conventions

There are many other conventions, too many to describe here, which relate to:[24]

1. the exercise of prerogative powers by the Crown;
2. the operation of Parliament and the legislatures generally, including political parties and, at the national level, the relationship between the elected House of Commons and the appointed Senate;
3. the operation of the federal and provincial cabinets, ministers and civil services and the relationships among them;
4. federalism generally, aside from the formal division of powers, including reservation and disallowance of federal and provincial Acts, and the role of the federally appointed Lieutenant Governors in provincial matters;
5. the role of judges and courts in the governmental process and the independence of judges and courts from interference by the executive and legislative branches; and
6. until 1982, the roles of federal and provincial governments in the amendment of the Constitution.[25]

Conventions are extremely important, therefore, because they clothe the legal framework of the formal Constitution and provide a large measure of flexibility: the operation of the Constitution can be significantly changed without having to directly amend the Constitution Acts or other legal aspects of the Constitution.[26]

---

[24] This information is taken from Heard, *supra*, note 2 at 2-15. This list is not exhaustive.

[25] The amending procedures are now legally prescribed in Part V of the *Constitution Act, 1982*.

[26] Heard, *supra*, note 2 at 5.

3

The Constitution and the Courts

1. How Courts in Canada are Established and Organized

The *Constitution Act, 1867*, provides for a judicial system in Canada consisting of federally (s. 101) and provincially (s. 92(14)) constituted courts.

(a) Federal Courts

Pursuant to s. 101 of the *Constitution Act, 1867*, the federal government was granted authority to establish and maintain the courts required to better administer the laws of Canada. The Parliament of Canada has created by statute the Supreme Court of Canada,[1] the Federal Court of Canada[2] and the Tax Court of Canada.[3] The specific functions of these courts are set out in their enabling statutes, and may be further defined in other federal statutes.[4]

Implied in s. 101 is the power of the federal government to appoint judges to these federally constituted courts. The salaries are paid for by the federal government and are established by the *Judges Act.*[5]

(i) *Supreme Court of Canada*

The Supreme Court of Canada, the highest appellate court in the nation, is not specifically provided for in the *Constitution Act, 1867*. The federal government relied upon its authority under s. 101 to enact the *Supreme Court Act* which established this Court. Even though the Supreme Court is established by ordinary statute, the amending formulae in ss. 41

---

[1] *Supreme Court Act*, R.S.C. 1985, c. S-26.
[2] *Federal Court Act*, R.S.C. 1985, c. F-7.
[3] *Tax Court of Canada Act*, R.S.C. 1985, c. T-2.
[4] G.L. Gall, *The Canadian Legal System*, 3d ed. (Carswell, 1990) at 149.
[5] R.S.C. 1985, c. J-1; Gall, *ibid.* at 106.

and 42 of the *Constitution Act, 1982* seem to have given a constitutional status to some aspects of the Court.[6]

The *Supreme Court Act* outlines the Court's composition, authority, functions and jurisdiction. The Court is composed of one Chief Justice and eight other Justices who together exercise jurisdiction over appeals from the provincial courts in both criminal and civil matters. The Supreme Court will hear cases that raise issues of national importance or appeals on issues of law.[7] The Court also hears reference cases which specifically deal with constitutional or other outlined issues referred to them by the federal government and upon which they will give their opinion.

(ii) *Federal Court of Canada*

The Federal Court is also established pursuant to s. 101 of the *Constitution Act, 1867*. The *Federal Court Act* provides for 14 federally appointed judges and one Chief Justice.[8]

The Federal Court is divided into a Trial Division and an Appellate Division. The Trial Division has exclusive jurisdiction over some areas of intellectual property, certain actions concerning members of the Canadian Armed Forces, and actions for equitable relief against any federal board, commission or tribunal.[9] It also exercises original concurrent jurisdiction over claims against the federal Crown; shares jurisdictions with other courts on specific matters such as aeronautics, interprovincial works and undertakings; and adjudicates disputes between provincial legislatures or between provincial and federal legislatures.[10]

The judges in the Appellate Division will hear appeals from the Trial Division, appeals under certain federal statutes, and applications regarding decisions of federal boards, commissions or tribunals on specific grounds.[11] This Court will also hear matters referred by these federal boards, commissions and tribunals.

(iii) *Tax Court of Canada*

The Tax Court was also established under the authority of s. 101 by a federal statute. It consists of 15 federally appointed judges whose sala-

---

[6] Gall, *ibid.* at 82. See also Chapter 10 on the amending formulae.

[7] *Ibid.* at 107.

[8] *Ibid.* at 153.

[9] *Ibid.*

[10] *Ibid.*

[11] *Ibid.*

ries are determined and provided for by the federal government.[12] These judges specifically hear appeals regarding assessments made under both the *Income Tax Act*[13] and the *Canada Pension Plan Act*.[14]

(b) Provincial Courts

Provinces establish the "superior courts" of the province pursuant to the "administration of justice" power in s. 92(14) of the *Constitution Act, 1867*. Their powers are defined by statutes such as the provincial Judicature Acts and by the rules of court or rules of practice within each province.

(i) *Federally Appointed Judges*

Although the "superior courts" are established and administered by the provinces, the federal government is vested, pursuant to s. 96, with the power to appoint the judges to these courts which include the District and County Courts in the province.[15] Sections 97 to 100 of the *Constitution Act, 1867* also relate to federally appointed judges, and provide that judges are to be selected from among lawyers practicing in the province where the judge is to preside.

These judges preside over the intermediate and highest trial courts and Courts of Appeals of the provinces and territories. The Superior Courts established in each province consist of the Trial Division or Court of Queen's Bench, and the Appellate Division or Court of Appeal.

Judges maintain office "during good behavior", until age 75, and can only be removed from office by the Governor General on address of the Senate and House of Commons. The Parliament of Canada is responsible under s. 100 for the determination and provision of salaries, allowances and pensions of the judges of the provincially constituted Superior Courts.

The highest Superior Courts of each province (going from west to east) are the British Columbia Supreme Court, the Alberta Court of Queen's Bench, Saskatchewan Court of Queen's Bench, Manitoba Court of Queen's Bench, Ontario Court of Justice (General Division), Quebec

---

[12] *Ibid.*

[13] R.S.C. 1952, c. 148.

[14] R.S.C. 1985, c. C-8; Gall, *supra*, note 4 at 153.

[15] *Ibid.* at 154. The District or County Courts and Surrogate Courts have merged or amalgamated with the provincial Superior Courts and their functions are now being performed by the Superior Courts.

Superior Court, New Brunswick Court of Queen's Bench, Prince Edward Island Supreme Court, Nova Scotia Supreme Court, Newfoundland Supreme Court, and, in the Territories, the Yukon Supreme Court and Northwest Territories Supreme Court.

The Trial Division level of these provincially and territorially constituted courts has a very broad jurisdiction that includes most criminal matters, appeals from summary offences, civil matters over a certain monetary amount, divorces, separations and certain administrative law matters.[16]

The Appellate Division hears appeals from the Trial Division.[17]

(ii) *Provincially Appointed Judges*

The provinces also appoint judges, but for a different level of court. Pursuant to s. 92(14) of the *Constitution Act, 1867*, each province is granted the exclusive legislative power over the administration of justice in the province, including the constitution, maintenance and organization of provincial courts. Furthermore, these provincial courts are granted jurisdiction over civil matters and procedure, and criminal matters. These trial courts are constituted under provincial statutes and the judges within these courts are appointed by their respective provincial government. Their salaries are set by the enabling provincial statute and are paid for by the respective provincial government. The judges within these courts cannot exercise the same functions as federally appointed judges.[18] The two territories have also established territorial courts and territorial governments appoint judges to these courts.

Provincially appointed judges have a limited (but very important) jurisdiction which consists of the Small Claims Court or Provincial Court (Civil Division), the Provincial Court (Criminal Division), the Family Court or Provincial Court (Family Division) and the Youth Court or Provincial Court (Youth Division). The judges presiding over the Small Claims Courts exercise jurisdiction over the smallest civil cases and the statutory and monetary jurisdiction varies for each province.[19] The presiding judges within the Provincial Court (Criminal Division) have jurisdiction over specified and less serious criminal cases, all preliminary hearings and all summary convictions. In the Family Court or Division, these judges will hear matters relating to children, maintenance and custody under

---

[16] *Ibid.*
[17] *Ibid.*
[18] *Ibid.* at 147.
[19] *Ibid.* at 155.

provincial statutes, and some criminal offences.[20] The Youth Court or Division presides over matters involving children and welfare, neglected children, and young offenders.[21]

Due to each province's own authority to establish these courts, the structure may vary in each province and some judges will have the authority to deal with one or more of these matters in the appropriate division or court established by the province.[22]

2. Different Types and Sources of Law

(a) Types of Law

Positive law sets out the various legal sources of law and is divided into public international law and domestic law. Public international law is concerned with the international community whereas domestic law refers to the positive law governing a sovereign, independent country such as Canada.[23] A further subdivision of the domestic law of Canada is substantive law and procedural law. Substantive law refers to the legal principles set out in statute and case law.[24] Procedural law is concerned with the law of civil procedure or the rules of the court, such as the rules of evidence. A further subdivision of the substantive law is made between public and private law. Public law involves those areas in which the public interest is primarily involved and includes criminal, administrative, constitutional and taxation law. Private law consists of those areas of the law in which private interests are concerned and includes contract, tort, and property law.[25]

(b) Sources of Law

The two main sources of law are statute and case law.

---

[20] *Ibid.*
[21] *Ibid.*
[22] *Ibid.* at 151.
[23] G.L. Gall, *The Canadian Legal System*, 2d ed. (Carswell, 1983) at 19.
[24] *Ibid.*
[25] S.M. Waddams, *Introduction to the Study of Law*, 3d ed. (Carswell, 1987) at 77.

(i) *Statutes*

The *Constitution Act, 1867* allocates powers to the federal Parliament and the provincial legislatures to enact statutes in certain areas as listed primarily in s. 91 and s. 92 respectively. Legislation that is created by either level of government is referred to as primary legislation. In addition, subordinate legislation, which is enacted by a person, body or tribunal that is subordinate to a primary legislative body, is another source of law.[26] Authority is delegated to the person, body or tribunal pursuant to the governing legislation of the primary legislative body. This delegation of authority permits the subordinate body to make by-laws, ordinances, orders in council, rules and regulations.

Some provisions in statutes are complex and ambiguous. Rules of statutory interpretation have been developed to assist the courts in interpreting these provisions. There are also various presumptions recognized in law which aid the courts. The process of statutory interpretation is somewhat subjective, as a judge may choose to use one method or aid over another.[27] One rule of statutory interpretation is to look to the legislative intent of the provision. This can be done by resorting to one of three major canons of construction. The "literal" or "plain meaning" rule requires that if the precise words used are plain and unambiguous the judge is bound to construe them in their ordinary sense.[28] The "golden" rule requires that the grammatical and ordinary sense of the words should be adhered to unless that would lead to absurdity or inconsistency with the rest of the statute. Finally, the "mischief" rule requires the judge to consider what the common law was before the making of the Act; what the mischief and defect was for which the common law did not provide; what remedy the legislature resolved to cure the defect; and what the true reason for the remedy was.[29]

The judges can also use certain aids to assist them in determining legislative intent. Some are intrinsic to the statute while others are purely extrinsic in nature.[30] Some examples of the aids to interpretation are: interpretation statutes which contain general rules for interpreting statutes and also define specific words; definition sections in certain statutes; other statutes; legislative history of a particular statute; and treatises and dictionaries.

Finally, there are various presumptions regarding statutory interpre-

---

[26] Gall, *supra*, note 23 at 31.
[27] *Ibid.* at 252.
[28] *Ibid.* at 254.
[29] *Ibid.*
[30] *Ibid.* at 255.

tation which have been derived through pronouncements made in the various case law and through the operation of custom and convention at common law.[31] A point should be made, however, that some of these presumptions are no longer of use to the modern judge. Examples of presumptions include the presumption against alteration of the law; presumption against strict criminal liability; presumption against retroactivity; and presumption of Crown immunity.

(ii) *Case Law*

The second major legal source of law is comprised of judge-made decisions, referred to as case law. When a case is decided the judge sets out the material facts, the issues of law and the *ratio decidendi*, or the reason for the decision. The *ratio decidendi* serves as a precedent which develops into a body of case law and is referred to as common law.[32] The common law is comprised of the principles which derive from precedents over the centuries and which become broadened or modified as the courts decide new cases. The doctrines of precedent and *stare decisis* direct the court to follow the precedent set by the case law when adjudicating future cases with similar facts.

The common law legal system which is adopted in all of the provinces and territories except Quebec is based on the British tradition. The province of Quebec adopts a civil law system based on the Napoleonic and French Civil Code which is a codification of the law.

3. How Constitutional Issues Get Before the Courts

In Canada, the judicial system has traditionally been a forum for clarifying constitutional ambiguities and for resolving constitutional conflicts. Although the elected governments are responsible for drafting and implementing legislation, the judiciary has become the body which subsequently examines these statutes and determines their constitutionality.[33] While this capacity of the judiciary is both criticized and defended, it is indisputable that it has shaped Canadian constitutional law.

There are multiple ways for constitutional challenges to come to the courts; as a result, the judiciary deals with issues in a variety of contexts.

---

[31] *Ibid.* at 259.

[32] *Ibid.*

[33] D. Gibson, *The Law of the Charter: General Principles* (Carswell, 1986) at 43.

(a) Methods of Raising Constitutionality Before the Courts

(i) *Factual Disputes*

Governments in conflict over the validity of a statute may challenge its constitutionality during trial within a factual dispute. A government, for example, may argue that the statute, which is potentially applicable to the facts in a dispute before the court,[34] is unconstitutional because it is *ultra vires*,[35] or outside the authority of the enacting government.

Similarly, the court may hear a constitutional argument when an individual or corporation is involved in litigation; it is not uncommon for such parties to challenge the constitutionality of a law in order to avoid its application.

(ii) *Legal Disputes*

The same arguments as to whether a statute is *intra vires*, or within the legislative capacity of the enacting government, or is *ultra vires*, are often raised in the context of legal disputes relating to the interpretation of legislation, or as to whether a federal or provincial statute is applicable to the dispute at trial.

These legal disputes arise within the context of a factual situation, but the facts are not in question. Only the law is in issue. Governments, individuals and corporations may argue that certain legislation is *ultra vires*, or on the other hand, that it is *intra vires* only if interpreted in a certain way. The parties may be either seeking to avoid the application of the legislation or may be trying to bring their situation within the legislation's ambit.

(iii) *Reference Cases: Asking the Court's Opinion*

While the methods above involve ruling on the validity of laws within the context of disputes, the courts may often be called upon to give a legal opinion where it is likely that legislation will lead to disputes.

By virtue of the *Supreme Court Act*,[36] the federal government may refer to the courts' questions concerning the validity of either federal or

---

[34] P.W. Hogg, *Constitutional Law of Canada*, 2d ed. (Carswell, 1985) at 310.

[35] This Latin phrase means "outside the powers"; *intra vires* means "within the powers".

[36] *Supra*, note 1, s. 53.

provincial Acts,[37] or constitutional issues for determination. While it is rare for other areas of law to be referred, the Act does not confine this to only constitutional issues.[38] Provincial statutes have also been enacted permitting provincial governments to bring reference cases and, to date, the constitutionality of these reference procedures has never been challenged.[39]

The Constitution does not explicitly state that courts have the jurisdiction to review legislation. While ordinary federal and provincial legislation authorizes judicial review, it would still be possible for the courts to hear these references even without specific legislative enactments. In 1912, the Judicial Committee of the Privy Council ruled that although this ability of the courts was not explicit in the *British North America Act, 1867* (now the *Constitution Act, 1867*), such an ability was incidental to the complete self-government of Canada.[40] These legislative schemes and the willingness of the courts to hear constitutional questions have allowed judges to express opinions on abstract constitutional issues.

The opinions handed down by the courts in reference cases are technically non-binding on governments. However, governments usually treat them as binding, therefore they have become an effective tool in shaping the interpretation and functioning of the Constitution. In *Re Resolution to Amend the Constitution*,[41] the federal government sought a judicial opinion on the rules relating to amending the Constitution. This political aspect did not deter the courts. At the time of this case, this was a highly charged political issue. In practice, the courts have shown a willingness to answer the legal elements,[42] even if a reference case has a large political aspect. In this respect, the courts only require that the issue be "justiciable" (*i.e.*, appropriate for a court of law to rule upon) and have at least a legal aspect.[43] A court may refuse to answer a question if it is too vague.[44]

This type of judicial intervention, however, is not without its prob-

---

[37] Either federal or provincial statutes may be referred to the court under this Act. See *Alberta (Attorney General) v. Canada (Attorney General)*, [1939] A.C. 117 and *Reference re Minimum Wage Act (Saskatchewan)*, [1948] S.C.R. 248, 91 C.C.C. 366.

[38] Hogg, *supra*, note 34, at 177.

[39] *Ibid.* at 179.

[40] *Ontario (Attorney General) v. Canada (Attorney General)*, [1912] A.C. 571 (P.C.) [referred to as "*Reference Appeal*"].

[41] *Manitoba (Attorney General) v. Canada (Attorney General)*, [1981] 1 S.C.R. 753.

[42] *Reference re Canada Assistance Plan (Canada)*, [1991] 2 S.C.R. 525.

[43] *Ibid.*; *Reference re Objection By Quebec to Resolution to Amend the Constitution*, [1982] 2 S.C.R. 793.

[44] Hogg, *supra*, note 34, at 180. See also *Re Court of Unified Criminal Jurisdiction*, (*sub nom. McEvoy v. New Brunswick (Attorney General)*) [1983] 1 S.C.R. 704, 4 C.C.C. (3d) 289.

lems. Some criticism has arisen as to the quality of decisions that emerge from abstract or hypothetical situations.[45]

The role of the judiciary in shaping the constitutional law of Canada, be it under the *Charter of Rights and Freedoms* or in respect to the division of powers in the *Constitution Act, 1982*, is growing. This can have a significant impact on the political agenda of governments. The issue then becomes whether or not this is the proper role for the courts. It is well-established at this time that it is proper for the courts to interpret the Constitution as they see fit.

(b) Standing — Who May Raise Issues of Constitutionality Before the Courts

The courts regulate who is able to challenge the constitutionality of the laws by requiring that an individual have *standing* before a court will entertain his/her arguments. This threshold is easily met in obvious cases where the individual or group is directly and immediately affected by an impugned statute. The courts have devised a test to determine if standing exists for cases where the connection is not so clear. Recently, the courts have liberalized this test for standing, providing the judiciary with wider discretion to allow interested individuals or groups to intervene in cases where they are not actual parties to the dispute.

First, a court asks if there is a serious issue to be tried. Second, it considers if the plaintiff is directly affected by the issue, or if the plaintiff has a genuine interest in the issue. Third, it weighs these arguments and asks if there is another reasonable or effective way to get the issue before the court in a way that may be preferable to the approach argued for by the person seeking standing.[46] If these criteria are met, then a person will be granted standing before the court. This is an extension of the tests formerly applied in *Borowski v. Canada (Minister of Justice)*,[47] *Thorson v. Canada (Attorney General) (No. 2)*[48] and *MacNeil v. Nova Scotia Board of Censors*,[49] allowing the courts more discretion. As a result, the role of the courts in hearing constitutional issues has widened.

---

[45] Hogg argues that these types of rulings provide an unsatisfactory rule (*ibid.*).

[46] *Canadian Council of Churches v. R.*, [1992] 1 S.C.R. 236.

[47] [1981] 2 S.C.R. 575, 24 C.R. (3d) 352, 64 C.C.C. (2d) 97.

[48] [1975] 1 S.C.R. 13.

[49] [1976] 2 S.C.R. 265, 32 C.R.N.S. 376.

4. Courts and the Charter

(a) Court of Competent Jurisdiction

The effect of s. 52(1) of the *Constitution Act, 1982,* the supremacy clause, is to preserve all pre-existing remedies for unconstitutional action and to extend those remedies to the Charter.[50] In addition, the Charter has its own remedy clause in s. 24. This section authorizes a court of competent jurisdiction to award a remedy for breach of the Charter. Section 24(2) authorizes a court of competent jurisdiction to exclude evidence obtained in breach of the Charter. A court of competent jurisdiction must be a court possessing jurisdiction over both the subject-matter and the parties to the application. A superior court is always a court of competent jurisdiction and an application for a remedy under s. 24(1), which is discretionary, can always be made to this court.[51] In addition, a trial court, even if it is not a superior court, is also a court of competent jurisdiction and can hear an application for a remedy that relates to the conduct of a trial, for example, the exclusion of evidence that has been obtained in violation of the Charter.

The Supreme Court of Canada has not yet decided whether an administrative tribunal can be a court of competent jurisdiction. However, having denied that a preliminary inquiry judge could be a court of competent jurisdiction, it is fair to say the Supreme Court will also exclude an administrative tribunal from this definition.[52]

(b) Burden of Proof

When a court decides whether a Charter right has been infringed, it is subject to the normal rules as to burden of proof, which means that the burden of proving all elements of the breach of a Charter right rests on the person asserting the breach.[53] If a breach is proven, the onus shifts to the government (or other party) to prove, pursuant to s. 1, that the challenged law is a "reasonable limit" and that it "can be demonstrably justified in a free and democratic society."[54] The standard of proof under s. 1 is the civil standard, proof by a preponderance of probability.

---

[50] P.W. Hogg, *Constitutional Law of Canada*, 3d ed. (Supp.) (Carswell, 1992), vol. 2 at 37-2.

[51] *Ibid.* at 37-16.

[52] *Ibid.* at 37-17.

[53] *Ibid.* at 35-7.

[54] *R. v. Oakes*, [1986] 1 S.C.R. 103, 50 C.R. (3d) 1, 24 C.C.C. (3d) 321.

5. The Main Doctrines of Constitutional Interpretation Used by the Courts

(a) General

One of the primary constitutional functions of the courts is to determine if legislation is within the constitutional jurisdiction of the enacting government. Sections 91 and 92 of the *Constitution Act, 1867* assign to the federal and provincial governments, respectively, the classes of subject in respect of which the governments may legislate.[55] If the federal government enacts legislation which allegedly encroaches on a subject or matter under provincial jurisdiction, the law may be challenged before the courts. This applies also to a provincial law alleged to infringe on a federal subject or matter. As discussed above, such a challenge can be initiated by a government or, more typically, by an individual or corporation affected by the impugned statute.[56]

The judiciary determines whether the statute is beyond the enacting government's power. The court will review the legislation in what is essentially a two-step process. The court must first characterize the challenged law, and through a series of considerations,[57] determine the "matter" of the legislation. Once this is done, the second broad step is to interpret the division of powers in the *Constitution Act, 1867* to determine which level of government has authority to enact legislation in relation to that matter.[58] The statute may be judged to be *intra vires*, or within the power of the government, and the challenge would fail. Alternatively, the court may declare the statute to be unconstitutional and, therefore, *ultra vires*, or outside the jurisdiction of the government, and the challenge would succeed.

(b) Sources of Authority for the Courts

(i) *Common Law and the Inherent Supremacy of the Constitution*

The Constitution is inherently the supreme law of the land, and any law inconsistent with it may be struck down by the courts. If it were otherwise, one level of government would be able, for example, to amend

---

[55] See Chapters 4, 5 and 6, *infra*.

[56] Hogg, *supra*, note 34, at 310-312.

[57] See Chapter 4 for further discussion.

[58] Hogg, *supra*, note 34 at 313.

unilaterally the division of powers in the Constitution.[59] Traditionally, this argument also rested on the fact that the Constitution was an Imperial statute and the statutes of the Dominion government could not be in conflict with it.[60]

(ii) *Sections 24 and 52 of the Constitution Act, 1982*

Sections 24 and 52 of the *Constitution Act, 1982* reflect the principle that the courts can strike down laws or legislation that are inconsistent with the Constitution. It is interesting to note, however, that the courts have indicated that the source of their ability to strike down laws is not found in either s. 24 or 52.[61] The courts had this power prior to 1982. Section 52(1) explicitly states that the Constitution is the "supreme law of Canada"; therefore, federal, provincial and territorial legislation is inoperative to the extent that it conflicts with the Constitution.[62] In addition, the *Constitution Act, 1982* includes s. 24 of the *Charter of Rights and Freedoms*. This section permits the courts to assess laws that may infringe a guaranteed right or freedom. Section 24 allows the court to impose many remedies, including rendering the legislation inoperative.

(c) Specific Doctrines Relating to the Division of Powers

When a division of powers conflict arises and the constitutionality of a statute is challenged, there is a series of tests used by the courts to determine if the enacting government has the constitutional authority to legislate in relation to that matter. These tests are discussed below.

(i) *The "Object and Purpose" of the Legislation*

Legislation before a court is analyzed to determine its "object and purpose" or its "pith and substance".[63] The court then refers to the enumerated classes of subjects within ss. 91 and 92, and determines if the "matter" of the statute falls within one of these classes.

---

[59] *Ibid.* at 93.

[60] *Ibid.* at 94-95.

[61] *Ibid.* at 93.

[62] See *Reference re Language Rights under S. 23 of Manitoba Act, 1870 and S. 133 of Constitution Act, 1867*, [1985] 1 S.C.R. 721 [referred to as "*Reference re Manitoba Language Rights*"].

[63] J.D. Whyte & W.R. Lederman, *Canadian Constitutional Law*, 2d ed. (Butterworths, 1977) at 4-14.

In doing this, the court examines the whole scheme of the legislation, not just the section involved in a dispute. If, for example, the matter in federal legislation is clearly found to come within the federal classes of subjects in s. 91, then the legislation will be valid or *intra vires*. If, however, it comes within the power of the provincial legislature set out in s. 92, then it would be declared invalid or *ultra vires*.

(ii) *The "Colourability" Doctrine*

Often, an enacting government may attempt to "preserve the appearance of constitutionality in order to conceal an unconstitutional objective."[64] This is referred to as a "colourable" attempt to cloak the real purpose of the legislation and "a colourable device will not avail."[65] The colourability doctrine seeks to protect the integrity of the division of powers by preventing legislatures from doing indirectly what they cannot do directly.[66]

(iii) *The "Effects" Test and "Ancillary" Doctrine*

If the court's analysis is inconclusive after the first step above, it proceeds to a second step which is to look at the effect of the legislation. In this analysis, consideration is still given to the stated object and purpose and the actual "pith and substance" of the Act.

However, the court distinguishes between a law that incidentally affects matters under the jurisdiction of another government, and one that singles out these matters. The former is acceptable, while the latter clearly is not.[67] As a result, there is a difference between being "in relation to a subject" and being merely "ancillary" to that subject-matter.[68] A federal law, for example, may have an incidental effect on a matter under provincial jurisdiction, provided that the law is truly in relation to a federal matter.

To a certain degree, therefore, the peripheral features of legislation may be challenged, without arguing that the legislation itself is unconstitutional. The court has held that the federal government, for example, may encroach on the provinces' jurisdiction in an incidental way, but that

---

[64] L. Davis, *Canadian Constitutional Law Handbook* (Canada Law Book, 1985) at 459.

[65] *Churchill Falls (Labrador) Corp. v. Newfoundland (Attorney General)*, [1984] 1 S.C.R. 297 at 332. See also Davis, *ibid.* at 459.

[66] Davis, *ibid.* at 460-461. See also *Amax Potash Ltd. v. Saskatchewan (Government)*, [1977] 2 S.C.R. 576 at 590-591.

[67] Whyte & Lederman, *supra*, note 63 at 63.

[68] *Munro v. Canada (National Capital Commission)*, [1966] S.C.R. 663.

at a certain point an encroachment may exceed what is necessary to implement the federal law.[69] If the effect is "necessarily incidental to" an otherwise constitutional law, and the purpose of the challenged provision has a "rational, functional connection" to such legislation, then the court will uphold the provision despite the fact that the provision, if standing alone, would be *ultra vires*.[70] The court will, in this analysis, consider the degree to which the law intrudes on another government's powers. Marginal encroachment will more likely be tolerated than one which is highly intrusive, but this will be determined on the facts of each case.[71]

(iv) *Fields of Concurrent Jurisdiction and the Doctrine of Paramountcy*

Federal and provincial statutes may both be deemed constitutional despite the existence of some overlap into the jurisdiction of the other level of government. Courts have recognized that there may be a double aspect to a particular matter, and some duplication is seen as constitutionally valid. In this way, the courts have been responsible for the development of concurrent fields of jurisdiction in which both levels of government can legislate.

Usually where the provincial or federal aspect of the subject is overriding and clear, the courts will try to find exclusive jurisdiction. However, where the federal and provincial indicators are equivalent, and there is no clear factor favouring exclusivity, then the courts may find a double aspect to the matter in question.[72]

If the courts find that a federal and a provincial law on the same matter are both valid, but contain conflicting provisions, then the paramountcy doctrine applies and the federal law prevails to the extent of the inconsistency. However, the courts interpret conflict narrowly in order to ensure that the federal paramountcy doctrine does not diminish the powers of the provincial governments. Once the courts find an exclusive jurisdiction for a level of government, then there is no room for the other; only if a court finds a real multiplicity of aspects will the double aspect doctrine be applied. Always there is an underlying respect for the exclusive fields of jurisdiction.[73]

As a result of concurrent fields of jurisdiction, there may be duplication of federal and provincial laws. Unlike the case of conflict where a

---

[69] *Peel (Regional Municipality) v. MacKenzie*, [1982] S.C.R. 9, 68 C.C.C. (2d) 289.

[70] *Papp v. Papp*, [1970] 1 O.R. 331 (C.A.).

[71] *City National Leasing Ltd. v. General Motors of Canada Ltd.*, [1989] 1 S.C.R. 641.

[72] *Hodge v. R.* (1883), 9 App. Cas. 117 (P.C.).

[73] *Bell Canada v. Québec (Commission de la santé et de la sécurité du travail du Québec)*, [1988] 1 S.C.R. 749.

federal law prevails, duplication does not invoke the laws of federal paramountcy but allows all legislation to operate validly.[74] Only if the provincial law weakens or inhibits the enforcement of the federal legislation will
the doctrine of paramountcy stipulate that the federal law prevails, even
though there is no actual conflict between the laws.[75]

In the case of contradiction between orders made under valid, duplica-
tive federal and provincial legislation, the federal Act or order prevails.
In the case of mere duplication, for greater certainty, the federal order
prevails.[76] Conflict, however, is read narrowly by the courts to mean that
compliance with one law necessarily results in a breach of the other.[77] If
there is no conflict, the theory of operating compatibility applies and effect
is given to both laws.[78] This restrictive approach to finding conflict is
endorsed by the Supreme Court of Canada today.[79] If it is possible to
comply with both laws by following the stricter standards of one, then
there can be concurrent operation of the statutes.[80] Furthermore, there
must be actual operating inconsistency on the facts of the case, not just
possible inconsistency, before a court will find a conflict and declare a
provincial law invalid.[81]

Under the doctrine of paramountcy, when the federal law overrides
provincial legislation the provincial statute will be "inoperative" to the
extent of the conflict. However, should the federal paramount law be
repealed, the provincial law will automatically be "revived". The federal
Parliament cannot, however, directly repeal a provincial Act regardless
of how far out of its jurisdiction it may be. A conflict in legislation can
only be settled by the courts.[82]

(v) *The Doctrine of "Severability"*

If a provision in an Act does not meet the tests of constitutionality
imposed by the court, the whole Act need not be declared unconstitutional.

---

[74] *Multiple Access Ltd. v. McCutcheon*, [1982] 2 S.C.R. 161, 18 B.L.R. 138.
[75] *R. v. Chaisson* (1982), 66 C.C.C. (2d) 195, 13 D.L.R. (3d) 499 (N.B. C.A.), affirmed
[1984] 1 S.C.R. 266, 11 C.C.C. (3d) 385.
[76] *Gillespie v. Gillespie* (1973), 6 N.B.R. (2d) 227 (C.A.).
[77] *Construction Montcalm v. Minimum Wage Commission*, [1979] 1 S.C.R. 754.
[78] *Smith v. R.*, [1960] S.C.R. 776, 33 C.R. 318, 128 C.C.C. 145.
[79] *Deloitte, Haskins & Sells Ltd. v. Alberta (Workers' Compensation Board)*, [1985] 1 S.C.R.
785.
[80] *Reference re S. 92(4) of the Vehicles Act, 1957 (Saskatchewan)*, [1958] S.C.R. 608, 121
C.C.C. 321; *O'Grady v. Sparling*, [1960] S.C.R. 804, 33 C.R. 293, 128 C.C.C. 1; *Mann
v. R.*, [1966] S.C.R. 238, 47 C.R. 400, [1966] 2 C.C.C. 273.
[81] *Bell v. Prince Edward Island (Attorney General)*, [1975] 1 S.C.R. 25, 24 C.R.N.S. 232,
14 C.C.C. (2d) 336.
[82] B. Laskin, *Canadian Constitutional Law*, 4th ed. (Carswell, 1973).

If the offending provision may be removed without defeating the enforceability and purpose of the entire Act, then that clause alone may be declared unconstitutional. This doctrine of "severability" will be applied unless the provisions of an Act are too interwoven and interdependent to be severed.[83]

(vi) *Principles of Statutory Interpretation*

The courts are generally not anxious to find a breach of jurisdiction and may be willing to invoke principles of statutory interpretation to *read down* provisions of an Act to some extent to preserve the constitutionality of the statute. The court may also take an active role in expanding the scope of benefit-conferring legislation, in order to make it constitutional. This is a controversial issue in relation to the role of the court, because to some extent the court begins to act like a legislature, rather than like an interpreter of laws.[84]

In addition, it has been suggested that if two levels of government have sought to jointly regulate an area of activity through agreement, the courts should adopt a reasonable interpretation of the legislation so as to not frustrate these goals.[85]

(d) Use of *Stare Decisis* and Precedent by the Courts

The Canadian judiciary adopts the doctrine of precedent (or *stare decisis*) under which the decision of a higher court within the same jurisdiction acts as binding authority on a lower court within that same jurisdiction.[86] A court's decision in another jurisdiction on the same issue acts as persuasive authority. Judges can, however, distinguish cases in order to avoid the binding or persuasive nature of *stare decisis*. With regard to Charter litigation, few Canadian cases decided prior to 1982 will be applicable when applying the doctrine of precedent. However, those cases arising out of the *Canadian Bill of Rights*[87] will be more relevant but not compelling.[88] The distribution of legislative powers provided in the *Constitution Act, 1867* has, since the Act came into force, been subjected to a vast array of case law. Although the Supreme Court of Canada is now

---

[83] *Reference re Alberta Bill of Rights Act*, [1947] A.C. 503 (P.C.). See also, for further discussion, Davis, *supra*, note 64 at 509-514.

[84] Davis, *ibid.* at 501-502.

[85] *Ibid.* at 411. See also Chapter 6.

[86] Gall, *supra*, note 23 at 220.

[87] S.C. 1960, c. 44 [R.S.C. 1985, App. III].

[88] Hogg, *supra*, note 50, vol. 1 at 8-19.

the highest court in the country, it still refers to the decisions of the Judicial Committee of the Privy Council in the United Kingdom which was the highest body of appeal for Canadian cases until 1949. However, the decisions of the Privy Council have no more and no less binding force than the Supreme Court's own decisions.

(e) Conclusion

For practical reasons, the drafters of our Constitution described the respective powers and responsibilities under ss. 91 and 92 in very general language. Our complex society does not neatly break down into these same compartments. It is important to remember that society has evolved and technology has developed beyond those matters contemplated in the division of powers at the time the Constitution was written. As a result, there is often an overlap, and sometimes a conflict, between federal and provincial jurisdictions.[89]

The interpretative doctrines that the courts have developed reflect the need to allow the Constitution to grow and develop to fit the changing needs of our society. When approaching such a dispute in the federation between governments, it is important to remember that the facts of the case and the fundamental principles of federalism are of key importance.

---

[89] Whyte & Lederman, *supra*, note 63 at 4-7.

PART II

DIVISION OF POWERS

4

The Federal Level of Government

1. Some General Concepts Relating to Powers

(a) A Federal Union with Two Levels of Government

The Preamble to the *Constitution Act, 1867* says that the provinces are "federally united" to form Canada. Our federal system is one in which each province has exclusive authority over most of the local affairs of the province and its residents. The national government, usually referred to as the "federal" government, is responsible for the country as a whole and for matters that cross provincial boundaries.[1]

(b) Three Branches of Government

In Canada, both the federal and provincial levels of government have three basic components or "branches" of government. The roles played by these branches are "essential features of our constitution."[2] The three branches are the legislature, the executive and the judiciary, and each is intended to fulfill a particular function of government. The "separation of powers" doctrine is concerned with how each of these three branches *within a single level* of government relate to each other. It is not to be confused with the "division of powers" which is concerned with how powers are distributed *between the federal and provincial levels* of government. The separation of powers doctrine is succinctly summarized by Chief Justice Dickson in the *Fraser* case:

> There is in Canada a separation of powers among the three branches of government — the legislature, the executive and the judiciary. In broad terms, the role of the judiciary is, of course, to interpret and apply the law; the role

---

[1] See Chapter 8 for a discussion of aboriginal self-government.
[2] *Canada v. Operation Dismantle Inc.*, [1985] 1 S.C.R. 441 at 491.

of the legislature is to decide upon and enunciate policy; the role of the executive is to administer and implement that policy.[3]

Generally, the doctrine is understood to mean that each branch has certain powers and must not interfere with the powers of the other branches. The doctrine is essentially inapplicable in Canadian constitutional law[4] in respect of the relationship between the executive and legislative branches.[5]

(c) The Division of Powers

There is no standard method of deciding which powers in a federally united country should be given to provinces and which should lie with the national government. Canada's political and constitutional history is strewn with disagreements on this very point.

One of the pillars of the Canadian federal system is the explicit distribution of law-making or "legislative powers" between Parliament and each of the provincial legislatures. Part VI of the *Constitution Act, 1867* (which includes ss. 91 to 95) fulfills this purpose largely by assigning responsibility over "matters" coming within different "classes of subjects" to the Parliament and the provincial legislatures.

The courts have interpreted the Constitution Acts as having distributed all possible legislative powers between the federal and provincial levels of government.[6] However, the provincial list of powers is considered to be finite so that if a matter is not covered within a class of subject expressly given to the provinces, that matter will fall within the jurisdiction of Parliament.[7] Certain specific federal powers are identified in the Act "for greater certainty" as the opening words of s. 91 acknowledge.[8]

Section 91 of the *Constitution Act, 1867* is the most often referred to source of federal legislative powers. The corresponding source of provincial legislative powers is s. 92. It is important to remember that ss. 91 and 92 are not the only sections in the 1867 Act which assign legislative powers

---

[3] *Fraser v. Canada (Treasury Board), (sub nom. Fraser v. P.S.S.R.B.)* [1985] 2 S.C.R. 455 at 469-470.

[4] J.E. Magnet, *Constitutional Law of Canada*, 4th ed. (Yvon Blais, 1989), vol. 1 at 88.

[5] P.W. Hogg, *Constitutional Law of Canada*, 2d ed. (Carswell, 1985) at 189. Note that Hogg argues that in order to be consistent with the theory of responsible government, there is no separation of powers between the legislature and the executive.

[6] See Chapter 8 in relation to aboriginal self-government.

[7] See *Bank of Toronto v. Lambe* (1887), 12 App. Cas. 575 at 588 (P.C.); *Murphy v. Canadian Pacific Railway*, [1958] S.C.R. 626.

[8] See *Interprovincial Co-operative Ltd. v. R.*, [1976] 1 S.C.R. 477 at 514.

to one or both levels of government.[9] Nor is the *Constitution Act, 1867* the only constitutional Act which assigns legislative powers.[10]

Federal legislative and executive powers are discussed in this Chapter. Provincial powers are discussed in Chapter 5. Powers shared by both levels of government are covered in Chapter 6. The powers of territorial governments, which are set out in ordinary federal legislation rather than in the *Constitution Act, 1867*, are examined separately in Chapter 7. Chapter 8 examines aboriginal self-government and some of the issues this emerging field creates in relation to federal and provincial powers.

(d) Theory Behind Distribution of Powers[11]

It has been argued that there is a clearly discernable theory underlying the distribution of powers when viewed in the context of the 1860s when the *Constitution Act, 1867* was written:

> What clearly emerges is a bestowal on the Dominion of responsibilities which have as their characterizing trait the management of the economy. . . . Epithets aside, it was the patterns, values and institutions of everyday community contact that were indicated as the legitimate domain of the provinces.[12]

However, such an orderly approach was never really followed by the courts:

> [A]lmost at the outset, the Act's scheme was scrapped. Once fences between the classes of subjects were down, it was anybody's guess how to brand the creatures [*i.e.*, matters] anywhere on the range.[13]

(e) Nature and Scope of Powers

When considering a legislative power described in the Constitution, it is necessary to think about its function: what are its political, economic

---

[9] See, for example, ss. 93-95, 101, and 132, which are discussed later in this Chapter and in Chapter 5.

[10] See, for example, the *Constitution Act, 1871* which assigns Parliament legislative authority over territories, and the *Constitution Act, 1886* which empowers Parliament to provide for the representation of territories in Parliament.

[11] For a more detailed discussion of this topic, see A.S. Abel, ed., *Laskin's Canadian Constitutional Law*, 4th. rev. ed. (Carswell, 1975); or A.S. Abel, "The Neglected Logic of 91 and 92" (1969) 19 U.T.L.J. 487: excerpts from this article are also found in J.D. Whyte, D. Bur & W.R. Lederman, *Canadian Constitutional Law*, 3d ed. (Butterworths, 1992) at 4.8-4.32.

[12] Abel, *Laskin's Canadian Constitutional Law, ibid.* at106-107.

[13] *Ibid.* at 115.

or social dimensions? Legislative powers can be categorized in relation to: (a) scope, (b) nature, and (c) whether Parliament or the provinces, or both, can exercise them.

The process of categorizing the scope and nature of legislative powers provides a framework for analysis of the theoretical and practical dimensions of government, but it certainly will not always point the way to a clear answer to a constitutional problem involving jurisdictional issues.

(i) *Scope*

The Constitution Acts were not intended to, and do not, give detailed descriptions of all the matters that can be the subject of legislation by Parliament and the provincial legislatures. Sections 91 and 92 of the *Constitution Act, 1867* are worded very generally.

Aside from the generality of the wording of the enumerated heads of power, both s. 91 and s. 92 also contain "catch all" clauses. The opening words of s. 91 serve this purpose by stating that Parliament can make laws for the "peace, order and good government of Canada, in relation to all matters not coming within the classes of subjects . . . assigned exclusively to the legislatures of the provinces."

In the case of the provincial legislatures, s. 92(16) serves as the catch-all by assigning to provinces "[g]enerally all Matters of a merely local or private Nature in the Province."

Clearly there are some classes of subjects which are very narrow in scope. For example, "currency and coinage" (s. 91(14)) or "beacons, buoys, lighthouses, and Sable Island" (s. 91(9)) obviously cover fewer matters and are more limited in scope than "the regulation of trade and commerce" (s. 91(2)) or the "criminal law" (s. 91(27)).

In general, legislation dealing with matters within the broader classes of subjects gives rise to a greater number of court challenges because phrases like "trade and commerce" (s. 91(2)) are not at all easy to interpret, particularly when viewed in competition with a provincial power over "property and civil rights" (s. 92(13)) or "matters of a merely local or private nature in the province" (s. 92(16)).

(ii) *Nature*

As related above, the nature of powers assigned to the national Parliament has been described as essentially economic in nature, while those assigned to provinces were generally in relation to the affairs of citizens and their communities.[14] In practice, this distinction has all but disappeared.

---

[14] *Ibid.* at 106-107.

Federal and provincial powers could also be classified as either "institutional" or "governmental".[15] This may be a useful way to think about the enumerated powers which otherwise look like a grab bag of unrelated subjects. Again, however, such tidy distinctions have not been maintained in practice or by the courts.

"Institutional" powers are those that allow Parliament or a legislature to structure and operate the institutions of government itself. For example, among the classes of subjects assigned to Parliament are salaries and allowances of civil and other officers of the government of Canada (s. 91(8)) and a general Court of Appeal for Canada and courts for the administration of the federal laws (s. 101). Provincial legislatures are assigned the "establishment and tenure of Provincial offices and the appointment and payment of provincial officials" (s. 92(4)), municipal institutions (s. 92(8)), and courts for the province (s. 92(14)).

"Governmental" powers on the other hand relate more directly to the business of governing the affairs of Canadians. In this category, classes of subjects assigned to Parliament include the regulation of trade and commerce (s. 91(2)), taxation (s. 91(3)), Indians and lands reserved for Indians (s. 91(24)), marriage and divorce (s. 91(26)), and the criminal law (s. 91(27)).

(iii) *Most Powers are Exclusive*

An important point to remember is that in our federal system most of the powers assigned to the federal government and to the provincial governments are exclusive to that level of government. "Exclusive" in this sense simply means that if a province has authority under the Constitution for certain matters, Parliament as a rule cannot legislate for those matters, and vice versa.

There are, however, exceptions. For example, the courts have upheld federal Acts where matters covered by the legislation are within the exclusive legislative jurisdiction of a province provided the matters are "necessarily incidental" to effective federal legislation authorized by a federal power under the Constitution Acts.[16] The principle applies equally where provincial legislation may touch upon a federal matter in a necessarily incidental way.

Some powers are also "concurrent", meaning that both levels of government can legislate in respect of the same matters. If both levels of

---

[15] *Ibid.* at 106.

[16] See *Canada (Attorney General) v. British Columbia (Attorney General)*, [1930] A.C. 111 (P.C.) [the "*Fish Canneries* case"]; *Multiple Access Ltd. v. McCutcheon*, [1982] 2 S.C.R. 161, 18 B.L.R. 138.

government do pass legislation respecting the same matter, and the legislation conflicts, one statute will be paramount over the other. The overridden statute is still valid but it will not operate as long as the paramount statute remains in force. An example of a concurrent power where a federal statute will be paramount is found in s. 92A(3) of the *Constitution Act, 1867* which deals with export of non-renewable resources, forestry resources and electrical energy from a province. An example of a concurrent power with provincial paramountcy is s. 94A which deals with old age pensions and supplementary benefits. Concurrent powers are discussed in Chapter 6.

Another important point to remember is that there are some fundamental limitations on the exercise of powers by the executive and legislative branches. The most obvious limitations are found in the *Canadian Charter of Rights and Freedoms*.[17] The *Canadian Bill of Rights*,[18] which is an ordinary federal statute enacted by Parliament, also contains self-imposed limitations on federal legislation.

(f) *Legislative and Executive Powers*

Mr. Justice Dickson observed in *Re Resolution to Amend the Constitution*[19] that: "The federal distribution of powers embraces not only *legislative* but also *executive* powers." [Emphasis added.] This observation is important for two reasons. First, it says that the federal government and each provincial government have two separate but related sets of powers: legislative powers and executive powers. Second, it suggests that legislative and executive powers are exercised by different bodies, which is in fact the case.

Most constitutional law textbooks concentrate primarily on the division of *legislative* powers. The legislative branch of government is a law-making branch. The main law-making body at the federal level is Parliament which is composed of three distinct institutions: the Queen, the House of Commons and the Senate.[20] At the provincial level, the main law-making body is the "legislature" which is composed of the federally appointed Lieutenant Governor and the elected "legislative assembly".[21]

---

[17] See Chapter 9.
[18] R.S.C. 1985, App. III.
[19] *Manitoba (Attorney General) v. Canada (Attorney General)*, [1981] 1 S.C.R. 753 at 820.
[20] See s. 17 of the *Constitution Act, 1867*. It is common to use the terms "Parliament", "the House of Commons" and "the federal government" as though they are synonymous. When used in a constitutional law context, however, the distinction between them must be kept in mind. "The federal government" or executive is a subset of the House of Commons, which in turn is a subset of Parliament.
[21] See, for example, s. 69 of the *Constitution Act, 1867*.

Parliament passes Acts or statutes which prohibit, regulate, authorize, delegate or ratify a very broad range of activities. Legislation enacted by Parliament, and by the provincial legislatures, is the major source of the legal rules that govern our society.

But how does Parliament decide which laws to enact? For the most part the executive branch controls the timing and nature of the legislative agenda based on its political interpretation of the wants or needs of Canadians. It is the executive branch which is at the centre of government in Canada today. In practice, the executive is the controlling mind of the legislative branch.

2. The Federal Legislative Institutions

(a) How Parliament is Established and Organized

Sections 17 and 18 of the *Constitution Act, 1867* establish the Canadian Parliament and outline the limits of its privileges, immunities and powers. Parliament is made up of three institutions: the Queen, the appointed Senate, and the elected House of Commons. All three are required for the legislative process. Statutes must be passed by the House of Commons and Senate, and assented to by the Queen through Her representative, the Governor General.[22]

Section 5 of the *Canadian Charter of Rights and Freedoms* requires that Parliament sit at least once every 12 months, and s. 4 says that no House of Commons can continue for longer than five years from the date fixed for return of the writs of a federal general election. An exception to this five-year rule is provided for in cases of real or apprehended war, invasion or insurrection, provided that not more than one-third of the members in the House of Commons vote against a continuation beyond five years.

(b) The Senate

The Senate, which is an appointed body, is often called the institution of sober second thought. Although its formal powers under the *Constitution Act, 1867* are considerable, in practice the Senate takes a secondary role to the House of Commons.

Sections 21 to 36 of the *Constitution Act, 1867* provide for the structure of the Senate. Section 24 provides that the Governor General shall

---

[22] See *ibid.*, s. 55.

"summon" qualified persons to the Senate and thus emphasizes that the Senate is an appointed rather than an elected body. Originally senators were appointed for life, but s. 29 now sets the retirement age at 75 years. In 1867, the Act called for 72 senators with 24 to be summoned from each of three "Divisions", namely Ontario, Quebec and the Maritime provinces. The idea behind equally represented Divisions was to make the Senate a body of regional representation. The two larger provinces, Quebec and Ontario, were each considered to be regions unto themselves. Under the original version of the 1867 Act, the Governor General was permitted to call a maximum of two additional senators from each Division, to bring the total to 78.

Over the years these provisions have been modified by the admission of new provinces and territories. Today there are 104 senators summoned from four Divisions.[23] The fourth Division includes Manitoba, Saskatchewan, Alberta and British Columbia. Newfoundland and the two territories do not fall within any Division.

The Governor General can still summon a maximum of two additional senators for each of the four Divisions.[24] This makes an upper limit of 112 senators. The Act does not provide for the Governor General to summon additional senators from Newfoundland or the territories. At the request of then Prime Minister Mulroney, the Governor General exercised this exceptional power in 1990 to appoint eight additional senators. This ensured the governing Conservatives a majority in the Senate at a time when they anticipated Senate opposition to the legislation establishing the goods and services tax ("GST").

Matters in the Senate are decided by majority vote.[25] The Speaker has a vote in all cases and if there is a tie, the measure is deemed to be defeated.

(c) The House of Commons

The House of Commons is the primary legislative institution at the federal level. Sections 37 to 57 of the *Constitution Act, 1867* establish, among other things, the number of members in the House of Commons and some rules governing how seats are to be distributed among the provinces and territories. Section 52 says that the number of members in the House of Commons is to be based on the proportionate representation of the provinces. Originally this rule was expressed by assigning Quebec 65 seats. All other provinces were then assigned a number of seats

---

[23] See *ibid.*, ss. 21 and 22.
[24] See *ibid.*, ss. 26 and 28.
[25] See *ibid.*, s. 36.

which would bear "the same Proportion to the Number of its Population . . . as the Number Sixty-Five bears to the Number of the Population of Quebec."[26] The new rules do not expressly fix a number of seats for Quebec but their numerical operation preserves the original rationale for the rule. Changing the principle of proportionate representation can only be done under the amending formula prescribed by s. 42(1)(*a*) of the *Constitution Act, 1982.*[27]

Originally there were 181 members in the House of Commons. Today there are 295. The rules for allocating the number of members elected from each province and territory have changed over the years. Under the current rules,[28] 99 are elected for Ontario, 75 for Quebec, 11 for Nova Scotia, 10 for New Brunswick, 14 for Manitoba, 32 for British Columbia, 4 for Prince Edward Island, 26 for Alberta, 14 for Saskatchewan, 7 for Newfoundland, 2 for the Northwest Territories and 1 for the Yukon. Senators cannot also be elected to the House of Commons.[29] The original version of s. 40 of the *Constitution Act, 1867* set the initial electoral districts for the election of members but it also said that this was only "until the Parliament of Canada otherwise provides." Electoral districts for federal elections are now set pursuant to the *Electoral Boundaries Readjustment Act.*[30] The qualifications of candidates for election are now governed by the *Parliament of Canada Act.*[31] Section 3 of the *Canadian Charter of Rights and Freedoms* guarantees citizens the right to vote in elections and to be qualified for membership in the House of Commons, subject to any reasonable limitations that might be "demonstrably justified in a free and democratic society." Other election procedures are governed by the provisions of the *Canada Elections Act*[32] and the *Dominion Controverted Elections Act.*[33]

Section 51A of the *Constitution Act, 1867* sets a rule that a province shall always be entitled to have at least as many members in the House of Commons as it has in the Senate. This is often referred to as the "Senate floor rule".

Like the Senate, matters are decided in the House of Commons by a majority vote (s. 49). But unlike in the Senate, the Speaker of the House of Commons only votes in the case of a tie, and can vote to support or defeat the measure.

---

[26] This was previously in s. 51(2) of the *Constitution Act, 1867* but the section has now been amended.
[27] See Chapter 10, "Amending the Constitution".
[28] The current rules are found in s. 51(1) of the *Constitution Act, 1867.*
[29] See *ibid.*, s. 39.
[30] R.S.C. 1985, c. E-3.
[31] R.S.C. 1985, c. P-1.
[32] R.S.C. 1985, c. E-2.
[33] R.S.C. 1985, c. C-39.

As the section on conventions in Chapter 2 explains, the operational aspects of Parliament are largely governed by conventions rather than by legal rules in the Constitution Acts.

(d) The Federal Legislative Process

At a very basic level, legislative power is simply the ability to make laws.[34] "Laws" can take various forms ranging from Acts or statutes to regulations. The *Constitution Act, 1867* only gives an indication of the broad elements of the legislative process.

A very brief description of the legislative process[35] would be as follows: The political party which forms a government has a program or agenda which they will want to achieve, for example, in relation to criminal law. Elements of this agenda may require new laws to be passed. A Minister will call for officials in his/her department to begin the work of researching the matters, developing the policy dimensions, undertaking consultations with interested or affected parties, and drafting the Bill which will eventually be introduced in Parliament for debate and passage. In practice the bureaucracy will have a very significant impact on the means a Bill uses to carry out the policy objectives of the politicians. The sponsoring Minister may have to convince his/her Cabinet colleagues and the Prime Minister about the urgency or importance of putting a particular Bill on the legislative agenda, but once that is done, barring enormous public or political pressure, the legislation will usually be passed if the party in power controls a majority of seats in the House of Commons. Amendments to a Bill may be made as a result of debates in the Commons to improve or make the Bill more acceptable to the opposition parties although rarely will the changes significantly alter the overall objectives of the legislation.

Parliament and legislatures have control over their internal procedures and processes relating to the scheduling, introduction, debating and passage of legislation. On its way to becoming law, a federal Bill passes through the elected House of Commons and the appointed Senate. Most Bills can be introduced in either the Senate or the House of Commons, although s. 53 of the *Constitution Act, 1867* requires that "money bills", which appropriate or authorize the spending of public funds or impose "any Tax or Impost", must originate in the House of Commons. The principle behind this is that spending public funds and taxing should only be done by the peoples' elected representatives and the Senate is not an

---

[34] See *P.S.A.C. v. House of Commons*, [1986] 2 F.C. 372, 27 D.L.R. (4th) 481 at 485 (C.A.).

[35] For further detail on the legislative process, see G. Tardi, *The Legal Framework of Government, A Canadian Guide* (Canada Law Book, 1992) at 122-130.

elected institution. As a result of some cases involving the *Canadian Charter of Rights and Freedoms*, such as *Singh v. Canada (Minister of Employment & Immigration)*,[36] *R. v. Askov*,[37] and *Schachter v. Canada*,[38] the question now being asked by some is whether the same principle should apply to place limitations on the type of relief the courts can grant, on the basis that these cases have required additional government spending of significant funds in situations where the court, instead of striking down legislation after finding it discriminatory, has expanded the group of beneficiaries under legislation to cure the defect.[39]

(e) Financing Federal Legislative Measures

A perennial issue in the Canadian federation is money: where does it come from, who gets to spend it, and on what should it be spent? A fundamental question for any organization is how to pay for its activities. It is no different for governments. The financing of public institutions like Parliament and the courts, bureaucratic operations, programs and services, and law enforcement is very expensive. It is also complex. The strict letter of every law may not be enforced but they are nonetheless enforceable. The costs in time, effort and expense to enforce the letter of all statutes would be staggering.

During the many past debates on constitutional reform, and as recently as the national referendum on the Charlottetown Accord on October 26, 1992, the difficult questions of public finance have tended to lurk in the shadows at the periphery of public awareness. Behind the scenes, however, politicians and government officials usually start and finish with money issues.

(i) *Raising Revenues and Spending Public Funds*

Governments, in particular the federal government, have significant powers to raise money, and influence the operation of money in the economy, including how much is borrowed, rates of inflation, rates of interest, and so on. As every working person knows, individuals and corporations pay for governments. They do this through numerous tax payments, fees and charges. Without this revenue governments could not operate and

---

[36] [1985] 1 S.C.R. 177.

[37] [1990] 2 S.C.R. 1199, 79 C.R. (3d) 273.

[38] [1992] 2 S.C.R. 679.

[39] See, for a discussion of this point, P. Monahan & N. Finkelstein, "The Charter of Rights and Public Policy in Canada" (1992) 30 Osgoode Hall L.J. 505.

programs and services we have come to expect would not exist.

The operation of the economy and the operation of government are no longer separate questions in many parts of Canada. Governments unquestionably influence economic activity in most sectors. Federal and provincial governments have not always pervaded so thoroughly the lives of Canadians, nor have Canadians always shouldered such heavy tax burdens. In 1867, governments did not, for example, play such a significant role in health care, education, welfare and social assistance. As a result, the amounts governments spent on these functions in 1867 was low by today's standards.[40]

Part VIII of the *Constitution Act, 1867* is entitled "Revenues; Debts; Assets; Taxation". In this part of the Act several important money issues were dealt with. It must be remembered that by 1867 the uniting colonies and provinces had been carrying on business for about 200 years.[41]

Pursuant to s. 102, a consolidated revenue fund or treasury was set up for the new central government and certain duties and revenues that had previously flowed to the provinces now came under the control of Parliament. Parliament was empowered by s. 106 to "appropriate" or spend this fund. Section 126 established a consolidated revenue fund for each province under the control of its legislature.

(ii) *Government Property and Assets*

In Canada's form of constitutional monarchy all public property is owned by "the Crown". The Crown is the name usually given to the legal entity that constitutes the state. Under our federal Constitution, the Crown uses and administers its property through the federal and provincial levels of government. This gives rise to the terminology "Crown in right of Canada" or "Crown in right of a province", depending on which level of government has the use and benefit of the Crown property in question.

In practice, the federal and provincial governments, and their respective legislatures, control distinct bundles of the Crown's property. For example, revenues from selling or renting public property flow to the level of government which has been assigned control of that particular public property under the Constitution. Professor Hogg has put it succinctly:

> Governments sell liquor, electricity, insurance, books, wheat, eggs and other natural products. They own railways, airlines, pipelines, telephone systems and radio and television networks. Nor do a government's commercial activi-

---

[40] P.W. Hogg, *Constitutional Law of Canada*, 3d ed. (Carswell, 1992) at 135.

[41] The situation was different for some of the provinces which joined after 1867. One must look to the terms and conditions set out in the Acts and orders-in-council admitting these provinces for the details.

ties have to coincide with the legislative power of that level of government. The activities are premised on powers which flow from the ownership and control of property, not on the catalogue of legislative powers which are independent of property ownership.[42]

As related above, in general provincial or colonial governments that owned property prior to Confederation retained it after 1867. There were a few exceptions. The federal government was a new legal entity that assumed many functions which had been exercised by the British government in relation to the colonies and naturally required some property in each of the provinces for national purposes. Section 108 provided for this. The Third Schedule to the 1867 Act enumerated 10 categories of provincial property that were transferred to the federal government. Included in the Schedule are such categories as canals, public harbours, lighthouses, piers, steamboats, dredges, public vessels, rivers and lake improvements, railways, customs houses, post offices, armouries, and various public buildings.

Early on the courts were asked to interpret what the Third Schedule was intended to transfer. In the case of *Canada (Attorney General) v. Ontario (Attorney General)* [*Fisheries*],[43] the Judicial Committee of the Privy Council examined phrases like "rivers and lake improvements" to determine if this transferred to the federal government all beds of rivers and lakes. They decided it did not. However, the transfer to Canada of "public harbours" did include the beds, although the Committee avoided giving an exhaustive definition as to what was included under this item, leaving it instead to be decided on a case-by-case basis.

Pursuant to s. 109, the provinces got to keep "all lands, mines, minerals and royalties" within their respective borders which belonged to them at the time of union. However, under s. 117 of the *Constitution Act, 1867*, Canada was empowered to keep some provincial lands or property for fortifications or for purposes of national defence. A few years after Confederation, Canada came to own vastly larger tracts of land when the territories of the Hudson's Bay Company (Rupert's Land and the North-Western Territory) were transferred to the federal government by Britain in 1870. The terms of the transfer specified, however, that Canada had to protect Indian interests and treat with the Indians for any lands taken for settlement in these regions.[44]

In 1880, the transfer to Canada of all remaining British land holdings in northern North America increased the federal government's public domain. So by 1880, the federal government had exclusive legislative

---

[42] Hogg, *supra*, note 40 at 701.
[43] [1898] A.C. 700 (P.C.).
[44] See the *Rupert's Land and North-Western Territory Order* dated June 23, 1870.

and executive control over most of Canada's present land mass. The provinces of Ontario, Quebec, and Manitoba were far smaller than they are today, Alberta and Saskatchewan did not yet exist and Newfoundland would not join the Canadian union until 1949.

Although Manitoba became a province in 1870 and Alberta and Saskatchewan were carved from the Northwest Territories in 1905, the federal government continued to own and control public lands in these provinces until 1930 so as to control immigration and settlement. Annual amounts were paid to these particular provinces up to 1930 to compensate them for the loss of revenues resulting from federal ownership. In 1930, the control of public lands in Manitoba, Saskatchewan and Alberta was transferred to these provinces by constitutional amendment.[45] British Columbia and Prince Edward Island had been put on the same footing as the original four provinces when they joined the union in 1871 and 1873 respectively. The federal government continues to own the vast majority of land in the Northwest Territories and Yukon today.[46]

(iii) *Offshore Areas*

Provincial boundaries do not as a general rule include offshore areas; some small bays and inlets have been held to be within the boundaries of some coastal provinces. Therefore, the federal Crown also controls the vast majority of offshore lands and waters that are within the territorial limits of Canada. International law governs the amount of offshore land and water to which Canada can realistically lay claim in relation to other nations. Challenges to Canadian sovereignty by United States vessels in Arctic waters in 1970 and 1985 caused Parliament to pass the *Canadian Laws Offshore Application Act*[47] which, *inter alia*, asserts ownership to offshore areas adjacent to Canada.[48]

---

[45] See the *Constitution Act, 1930* (U.K.), 20-21 Geo. 5, c. 26.

[46] Aboriginal land claims agreements with the Inuvialuit, Gwich'in, Inuit, Sahtu Dene and Métis in the Northwest Territories have provided for collective aboriginal ownership of large tracts of land. Land claims negotiations are still in progress with other aboriginal peoples in both the Yukon and Northwest Territories.

[47] S.C. 1990, c. 44; Regulations promulgated in 1986 under the *Territorial Sea and Fishing Zones Act*, R.S.C. 1985, c. T-8 also provided for the drawing of baselines around much of the Arctic archipelago. Canada claims ownership of the lands and waters within the baselines. The territorial sea of Canada extends 12 miles out from the baselines.

[48] Two cases that involved provincial claims to offshore areas were *Reference re Offshore Mineral Rights (British Columbia)* [*B.C. Offshore Reference*], [1967] S.C.R. 792 and *Reference re Newfoundland Continental Shelf*, [1984] 1 S.C.R. 86.

(iv) *Provincial Subsidies*

Section 118 set out yearly grants based on population growth which the federal government was to pay to each province "for the Support of their Governments and Legislatures." This provision was eventually repealed by the *Statute Law Revision Act, 1950*.[49] In 1907, the system of grants was further refined and laid out in the *Constitution Act, 1907*.[50] Today the *Provincial Subsidies Act*[51] and the *Federal-Provincial Fiscal Arrangements and Federal Post-Secondary Education and Health Contributions Act*[52] provide for such grants.

(v) *Equalization*

The commitment of governments to the principle of "equalization" is now set out in s. 36(2) of the *Constitution Act, 1982*. Equalization is to "ensure that provincial governments have sufficient revenues to provide reasonably comparable levels of public services at reasonably comparable levels of taxation." These equalization payments are an attempt to make sufficient revenues available to provinces which may have disparate capacities for raising revenues due to population differences and varying levels of economic activity. In other words, the objective is for the federal government to redistribute wealth to ensure that Canadians receive a minimum standard of services wherever they live in Canada.

Recently, only three provinces have not qualified for equalization payments from the federal government because of high "fiscal capacities": Ontario, Alberta and British Columbia. The Yukon and Northwest Territories do not come within the equalization system for various reasons, but they do receive substantial grants from the federal government under special five-year Formula Financing Agreements.

(vi) *Other*

Pursuant to s. 111, Canada assumed the debts and liabilities of each province existing at the time of union. Section 121 established that the political union of British North America was also supposed to be an economic union in which "[a]ll Articles of the Growth, Produce, or Manufacture of any one of the Provinces shall . . . be admitted free into each of

---

[49] (U.K.), 14 Geo. 6, c. 6.

[50] (U.K.), 7 Edw. 7, c. 11.

[51] R.S.C. 1985, c. P-26.

[52] R.S.C. 1985, c. F-8, Part I; Hogg, *supra*, note 40 at 142, n. 14; for a more detailed description, see Hogg, *id.* at 141-144.

the other Provinces." In the 1990s, internal trade barriers between the provinces are still a controversial issue.

Customs and excise taxes, a lucrative source of revenue in 1867, were brought under the power of Parliament by s. 122.[53] Section 125 prohibited the federal government from taxing the "lands or property" of provincial governments and vice versa.

3. The Federal Legislative Powers

(a) A List of Federal Legislative Powers

As the list of federal powers set out below shows, s. 91 does not list all the federal legislative powers. For example, in the *Constitution Act, 1867*, s. 93 (education), s. 94 (uniformity of laws), s. 94A (old age pensions), s. 95 (agriculture and immigration), s. 101 (courts), and s. 132 (Empire treaty obligations) also assign significant powers, as do other provisions in the *Constitution Act, 1871* (administration of territories and creation of new provinces). Sections 44 and 45 of the *Constitution Act, 1982* assign to Parliament and provincial legislatures very important powers in relation to amending the Constitution itself.

The main legislative powers of Parliament[54] found in the *Constitution Act, 1867*, the *Constitution Act, 1871*, and the *Constitution Act, 1982*[55] are as follows:

Constitution Act, 1867

- *Section 91:*[56] peace, order and good government in all matters except those assigned exclusively to the provinces, and in particular:

    1A. The Public Debt and Property.
     2. The Regulation of Trade and Commerce.
    2A. Unemployment insurance.
     3. The raising of Money by any Mode or System of Taxation.
     4. The borrowing of Money on the Public Credit.
     5. Postal Service.
     6. The Census and Statistics.
     7. Militia, Military and Naval Service, and Defence.
     8. The fixing of and providing for the Salaries and Allowances of Civil and other Officers of the Government of Canada.

---

[53] See Hogg, *ibid.* at 136.
[54] See Chapter 5 for a discussion of provincial legislative powers.
[55] See also the *Constitution Act, 1886*, which governs Parliament's powers in relation to making provision for the representation of territories in the House of Commons and Senate.
[56] See Appendices for the precise wording of the heads of power.

9. Beacons, Buoys, Lighthouses, and Sable Island.
10. Navigation and Shipping.
11. Quarantine and the Establishment and Maintenance of Marine Hospitals.
12. Sea Coast and Inland Fisheries.
13. Ferries between a Province and any British or Foreign Country or between Two Provinces.
14. Currency and Coinage.
15. Banking, Incorporation of Banks, and the Issue of Paper Money.
16. Savings Banks.
17. Weights and Measures.
18. Bills of Exchange and Promissory Notes.
19. Interest.
20. Legal Tender.
21. Bankruptcy and Insolvency.
22. Patents of Invention and Discovery.
23. Copyrights.
24. Indians, and Lands reserved for the Indians.
25. Naturalization and Aliens.
26. Marriage and Divorce.
27. The Criminal Law, except the Constitution of Courts of Criminal Jurisdiction, but including the Procedure in Criminal Matters.
28. The Establishment, Maintenance and Management of Penitentiaries.
29. [Specific exceptions to provincial powers, such as those in s. 92(10), namely:
    - shipping lines, railways, canals, telegraphs, and other works or undertakings connecting provinces
    - shipping lines between a province and another country
    - works within a province declared by Parliament to be for the advantage of Canada or two or more provinces.].

- *Section 93*: Remedial laws in relation to education where provincial laws do not comply with the terms of s. 93.
- *Section 94A*: Subject to provincial laws, old age pensions and supplementary benefits, including survivors' and disability benefits irrespective of age.
- *Section 95*: Agriculture and immigration.
- *Section 101*: Constitution, maintenance and organization of a general court of appeal for Canada and for establishment of any additional courts for the better administration of federal laws.
- *Section 106*: Federal spending from the Consolidated Revenue Fund.
- *Section 132*: Performing obligations of Canada under any treaty entered into by Britain and a foreign country (*e.g.*, the migratory birds treaty of 1916 between Britain and the United States).

Constitution Act, 1871[57]

- *Section 2*: Establishing new provinces in the territories.
- *Section 3*: With the consent of a province, altering provincial boundaries.
- *Section 4*: Providing for the peace, order, and good government of the territories.

Constitution Act, 1982

- *Section 44*: Subject to other amending procedures (ss. 41 and 42), Parliament can make laws to amend the Constitution of Canada in relation to the executive, Senate, or House of Commons.

(b) Interpretation of Federal Powers: An Overview[58]

The courts have repeatedly stated that the federal and provincial powers "must be read together, and the language of one interpreted, and, where necessary, modified by that of the other."[59]

It is the courts which ultimately interpret whether an Act or some provision of an Act is within the legislative jurisdiction of Parliament or of a provincial or territorial legislature. However, the courts only intervene when a case is brought before them or when a government asks for a court's opinion in a procedure known as a reference. In a reference, specific questions are directed to the court and other governments may intervene to provide their views of the proper interpretation of the law on a given set of facts.

The interpretative task before the courts is often not an easy one. Determining the "matter" or "pith and substance" covered by an Act or one of its provisions may not be obvious. The "classes of subjects" set out in the Constitution Acts into which a "matter" must be determined to fall or not fall are themselves usually brief, vague and general. For example, it is not immediately apparent what matters fall within the provincial class of "property and civil rights in the province" or the federal class "regulation of trade and commerce".

---

[57] These provisions must be considered together with the amending procedures contained in Part V of the *Constitution Act, 1982*. See Chapter 10, "Amending the Constitution".

[58] Much of the information in this section is taken from Abel, *Laskin's Canadian Constitutional Law, supra,* note 11.

[59] *Saumur v. Quebec (City)*, [1953] 2 S.C.R. 299 at 360, 106 C.C.C. 289, quoting *Russell v. R.* (1882), 7 App. Cas. 829 (P.C.).

The exercise of determining the "matter" of an Act has been described this way:

> So one must in every case (1) identify the "matter" to which a statute relates, (2) define the scope of each "class of subjects" which might [be] thought to be relevant, (3) assign the "matter" as identified to the most appropriate "class of subjects" as defined. . . . In having its distinctive "matter", its own pith and substance, a statute is just like any other written text. . . . [F]or determining the "matter", not that specific feature but its generic character is relevant. Like any written text, its "matter" depends on what it says read in the context in which it speaks. . . . The alternatives are to view the statute as an integrated whole or to disaggregate it into components of any desired size. Is one inspecting the forest or the trees? Whether the gaze is to be fixed intently on [for example] a section banning the manufacture, selling, keeping or offering for sale, or importing of margarine or whether the field of vision shall instead take in a great sprawling statute concerned with many phases and operations in the processing for market and marketing of dairy products may be decisively important. No discernible general logical compulsion favours either the broad or the narrow approach.[60]

However, after having assertained the matter, the court would then have to determine within which class of subject the matter falls. The conclusion is not reassuring for those that expect constitutional law to be more science than art: "There is no equation by which to distribute matters among classes of subjects."[61]

The history of the Constitution shows that the scope of particular classes of subject set out in ss. 91 and 92 have been expanded or restricted depending on the philosophies which the judges have brought to the bench. There have been both "federalist" judges and "provincial rights" judges. This is clearly an area where judicial interpretation in the context of the times has been a decisive factor. Since Confederation, the courts have done little to define in explicit terms the content of the various classes of subjects set out in ss. 91 and 92. Instead, the scope has been defined "in terms of whether the federal or provincial power over what you will — trade and commerce, criminal law, property and civil rights, for instance — does or does not sanction such and such an exercise of legislation."[62]

---

[60] Abel, *Laskin's Canadian Constitutional Law, supra*, note 11 at 97-99.
[61] *Ibid.* at 118
[62] *Ibid.* at 105.

(c) How Courts Have Interpreted Federal Legislative Powers[63]

We now turn to an examination of how the courts have interpreted some of the main federal powers. This section will illustrate that the literal words of any given "head of power" in the Constitution Acts will not provide a clear picture of the courts' current interpretation of the law surrounding it. It will also illustrate the changing nature of constitutional interpretation. The only way to obtain a clear picture of vital areas of our constitutional law is to examine the decisions that have been handed down, and that are being handed down almost daily by the courts.

The opening words of s. 91 of the *Constitution Act, 1867* give Parliament a general grant of legislative power:

> 91.   It shall be lawful for the Queen, by and with the Advice and Consent of the Senate and House of Commons, to make Laws for the Peace, Order, and good Government of Canada, in relation to all Matters not coming within the Classes of Subjects by this Act assigned exclusively to the Legislatures of the Provinces; and for greater Certainty, but not so as to restrict the Generality of the foregoing Terms of this Section, it is hereby declared that (notwithstanding anything in this Act) the exclusive Legislative Authority of the Parliament of Canada extends to all Matters coming within the Classes of Subjects next herein-after enumerated; [a list of 29 heads of power follows].

Parliament's legislative powers are said to be residual: Parliament can legislate for all matters except those matters within the heads of power assigned exclusively to provinces.[64] However, "for greater certainty" the drafters listed 29 classes of subjects under s. 91 to provide some definition to the general grant of authority to Parliament. In practice, the courts have looked more to these enumerated heads of federal power to determine federal jurisdiction and less to the general grant of power in the opening words.

(i) *Peace, Order, and Good Government: Opening Words of Section 91*

In numerous cases the courts have interpreted the general grant of legislative power, usually referred to as the "peace, order, and good government" ("POGG") power found in the opening words of s. 91 of

---

[63] Three invaluable sources were instrumental in the preparation of this section: Hogg, *supra*, note 40; Whyte, Bur & Lederman, *supra*, note 11; and L. Davis, *Canadian Constitutional Law Handbook* (Canada Law Book, 1985). Any errors or omissions are our own.

[64] Both federal and provincial powers are now limited to some degree by the *Canadian Charter of Rights and Freedoms* and by the recognition and affirmation of the rights of aboriginal peoples. See *infra*, Chapters 8 and 9.

the *Constitution Act, 1867*. The phrase "peace, order, and good government" dates back to the original grants of prerogative powers to the colonial Governors. The courts have not given a broad meaning to the POGG power. It has been used to cover three principal situations:[65]

1. where a matter appears to fall into a "gap" not covered by the enumerated federal or provincial heads of power;
2. where the matter is of national concern but is not covered by an enumerated federal power; or
3. where the matter is a national emergency and is not covered by an enumerated head.

Under the "gap" branch of the POGG power, the courts have upheld, for example, federal legislation in relation to incorporation of companies with federal objects,[66] official language matters in relation to Parliament and the federal civil service,[67] and offshore mineral resources.[68]

The national concern branch of the power was first enunciated in the *Local Prohibition* case[69] which involved the regulation and prohibition of alcohol sales under competing federal and provincial legislation directed at the same purpose.[70] It was held that Parliament could enact legislation under the POGG power to address a matter of national concern, even though the matter fell within a provincial head of power, for example, "property and civil rights" or "matters of a merely local or private nature", under s. 92.

The national concern branch of the power was in abeyance until after the Second World War. The courts then upheld federal legislation in relation to aeronautics,[71] the National Capital Commission,[72] and marine pollution.[73] Curiously, the federal *Narcotic Control Act*[74] has also been upheld under this branch.[75]

When applying the national concern test, the courts ask whether the federal legislation goes beyond local or private concerns or interests to

---

[65] Hogg, *supra*, note 40 at 439.
[66] See *Citizens Insurance Co. v. Parsons* (1881), 7 App. Cas. 96 (P.C.).
[67] *Jones v. Canada (Attorney General), (sub nom. Jones v. New Brunswick (Attorney General))* [1975] 2 S.C.R. 182, 16 C.C.C. (2d) 297.
[68] See *B.C. Offshore Reference, supra*, note 48; and *Reference re Newfoundland Continental Shelf, supra*, note 48.
[69] *Ontario (Attorney General) v. Canada (Attorney General)*, [1896] A.C. 348 (P.C.).
[70] See Hogg, *supra*, note 40 at 442-443.
[71] *Johannesson v. West St. Paul (Rural Municipality)*, [1952] 1 S.C.R. 292.
[72] *Munro v. Canada (National Capital Commission)*, [1966] S.C.R. 663.
[73] *R. v. Crown Zellerbach Canada Ltd.*, [1988] 1 S.C.R. 401, 40 C.C.C. (3d) 289.
[74] R.S.C. 1985, c. N-1.
[75] See *R. v. Hauser*, [1979] 1 S.C.R. 984, 8 C.R. (3d) 89, 46 C.C.C. (2d) 481.

address a matter which, from its inherent nature, is of concern to the country as a whole. This test is clearly difficult to apply,[76] however, it is also clear that the courts are not prepared to interpret the national concern branch in a way that would neutralize provincial powers.

In some cases, the courts have said the POGG power should only be exercised by Parliament in a national emergency.[77] This was the trend during the 1920s and 1930s,[78] but is no longer the case.[79] The cases of *Reference re Board of Commerce Act, 1919 (Alberta)*[80] in 1922 and *Toronto Electric Commissioners v. Snider*[81] in 1925 established the trend.[82] The emergency branch allows Parliament to enact laws that would normally be within the exclusive jurisdiction of provinces. Emergencies, by nature, are temporary, so the federal legislation under this branch would also be temporary.[83] Limiting the power to cases of national emergency drastically reduced the number of situations in which Parliament could legislate on the basis of POGG. *Re Anti-Inflation Act, 1975 (Canada)*[84] in 1976 is a more recent case which upheld federal legislation imposing wage and price controls on the basis of the emergency branch of POGG.

(ii) *The Public Debt and Property: Section 91(1A)*[85]

Section 91(1A) gives Parliament legislative power over "the public debt and property". There is a big difference between owning property and making laws in relation to property. Governments in Canada do both. Unlike individuals, when the federal or a provincial government owns property, in addition to using the property like an owner, it normally also has legislative jurisdiction in respect of that property.[86] Legislative jurisdiction by itself does not, however, give governments any proprietary rights. Federal property in a province is not immune from all provincial laws.[87]

---

[76] For a detailed examination of the national concern test, see Hogg, *supra*, note 40 at 446-452.

[77] See *Manitoba Free Press Co. v. Fort Frances Pulp & Paper Co.*, [1923] A.C. 695 (P.C.).

[78] See Hogg, *supra*, note 40 at 452.

[79] See *Crown Zellerbach Canada Ltd., supra*, note 73; also see Hogg, *ibid.* at 462 for a discussion of the relationship between the national concern branch and the emergency branch of the POGG power.

[80] [1922] 1 A.C. 191 (P.C.).

[81] [1925] A.C. 396 (P.C.).

[82] Hogg, *supra*, note 40 at 453.

[83] [1976] 2 S.C.R. 373; see also Hogg, *ibid.* at 461-462 for a discussion of the temporary nature of such legislation.

[84] *Ibid.*; see also Hogg, *ibid.* at 459-461.

[85] See Hogg, *ibid.* at 697-709.

[86] *Ibid.* at 701 for examples where this is not the case.

[87] See *Coughlin v. Ontario (Highway Transport Board)*, [1968] S.C.R. 569.

Under s. 91(1A), Parliament may legislate in respect of the property of the federal Crown. "Property" in this context is any property owned by the federal government whether it is land or any other form of tangible or intangible property. Governments can own property and can sell, rent, lease or otherwise use that property in all the ways an individual would use it, usually subject to the same ordinary laws that affect individuals in the use of their property.

Section 91(1A) also gives Parliament legislative authority over "the public debt". A related power is found in s. 91(4) which authorizes legislation in relation to "the borrowing of money on the public credit." The scope of the federal power in relation to public debt has not been defined by the courts but it may take on new meaning in the 1990s. Would it, for example, empower federal legislation directed at limiting the level of provincial debt arising from foreign borrowings? This power in all likelihood is limited to the national public debt of the federal government and would not support such a measure. Other provisions of the *Constitution Act, 1867*, such as s. 92(3), "the borrowing of money on the sole credit of the province", make it clear that provinces have exclusive authority over their own fiscal policies, including management of provincial public debt.

(iii) *Regulation of Trade and Commerce: Section 91(2)*[88]

Section 91(2) says Parliament can make laws for "the regulation of trade and commerce". Very early on the courts had to confront the difficult questions raised by the potentially enormous scope of the words "regulation of trade and commerce". "Trade and commerce" are usually carried on by agreements for the purchase and sale of goods and services, but the courts have not tried to define all matters that are covered by those words.[89]

In 1881, in the leading case of *Citizens Insurance Co. v. Parsons*,[90] the Judicial Committee of the Privy Council gave s. 91(2) a narrow interpretation so as not to neutralize the powers assigned to the provinces by the Constitution. There were (and still are) transactions covered by the provincial powers over "property and civil rights" (s. 92(13)) and "matters of a merely local or private nature in the province" (s. 92(16)) that had to be accounted for. Had the courts given a literal meaning to s. 91(2), these provincial powers would have been rendered meaningless.

---

[88] See Hogg, *supra*, note 40 at 521-536.
[89] *Manitoba (Attorney General) v. Manitoba Egg & Poultry Assn.*, [1971] S.C.R. 689 at 708 (Laskin J.).
[90] *Supra*, note 66.

The *Parsons* case identified two dimensions or branches in relation to the federal power: (1) interprovincial and international trade and commerce, and (2) general regulation of trade affecting the whole country. However, Mr. Justice Dickson said in *Canada (Attorney General) v. Canadian National Transportation Ltd.*[91] that the limits of the trade and commerce power are not fixed, and questions of "constitutional balance" play a crucial role in determining the extent of the power in any given case.

To apply the principles laid down in the *Parsons* case, the courts generally have to determine whether an activity or transaction is international, *inter*provincial or *intra*provincial in nature.

Early cases did not readily characterize and uphold federal statutes as being interprovincial if there were any elements in the legislation that appeared to intrude on transactions occurring wholly within a province.

When the Supreme Court of Canada became the last resort for appeals in 1949 by replacing the Judicial Committee in London, England, the trend of decisions moved towards a greater scope for the trade and commerce power. Two cases in the 1950s signalled this change: *Murphy v. Canadian Pacific Railway*[92] and *R. v. Klassen*.[93] Eventually, under the new line of cases some wholly *intra*provincial transactions were caught by federal statutes where such transactions were "incidental effects" of a larger scheme designed to regulate *inter*provincial trade and commerce.[94] However, as Mr. Justice Estey said in the 1980 case of *R. v. Dominion Stores Ltd.*:[95] "The Parliament of Canada may not, in the guise of regulating trade and commerce, reach into the fields allocated to the provinces by ss. 92(13) and 92(16) and regulate trading transactions occurring entirely within the provinces."

Although the *Parsons* case stated that the trade and commerce power also allowed Parliament to legislate in relation to matters of trade and commerce of "general interest throughout the Dominion", subsequent court decisions hesitated to uphold federal statutes on this basis. However, in the case of *Canada (Attorney General) v. Canadian National Transportation Ltd.*,[96] Mr. Justice Dickson said: "[T]he long disuse of this second branch does not impugn its constitutional validity." But he went on to say that a restrictive approach had to be taken when determining what should fall within the "general interest". The sort of legislation that would be upheld would have to be "general legislation aimed at the economy as a single integrated national unit rather than as a collection

---

[91] [1983] 2 S.C.R. 206, 38 C.R. (3d) 97, 7 C.C.C. (3d) 449, 3 D.L.R. (4th) 16 at 56.
[92] [1958] S.C.R. 626.
[93] (1959), 31 C.R. 275, 20 D.L.R. (2d) 406 (Man. C.A.), leave to appeal to S.C.C. denied (November 30, 1959).
[94] *Caloil Inc. v. Canada (Attorney General) (No. 2)*, [1971] S.C.R. 543.
[95] [1980] 1 S.C.R. 844 at 855, 50 C.C.C. (2d) 277.
[96] *Supra*, note 91 at 59 (D.L.R.).

of separate local enterprises.''[97] In practice it is not entirely clear how this test should be applied. Mr. Justice Dickson suggested the courts would be looking for something "qualitatively different from anything that could practically or constitutionally be enacted by the individual provinces either separately or in combination." Obviously, as Dickson J. acknowledged, the courts faced a "difficult problem of characterization" in such cases.[98] Five characteristics would likely mark a federal Act under this branch of the trade and commerce power:

1. the presence of a national regulatory scheme;
2. administration of the regulatory scheme by a federal agency;
3. a concern with trade in general rather than with an aspect of a particular business;
4. provinces alone or jointly would be constitutionally incapable of passing such an enactment; and
5. failure to include one or more provinces or localities in the scheme would jeopardize its successful operation in other parts of the country.

This list should not be seen as exhaustive. Unfortunately, the Supreme Court has also said the presence of some or all of these characteristics might not be sufficient to uphold a federal Act.[99]

A recurring issue of considerable importance surrounding the trade and commerce power is the extent to which it might empower Parliament to pass legislation designed to remove the effects of provincial statutes which have directly or indirectly established barriers to interprovincial trade. Parliament would undoubtedly pass legislation only in circumstances it considered very exceptional because any such action would almost certainly meet with strong opposition from provincial governments.

(iv) *Unemployment Insurance: Section 91(2A)*

The federal power over unemployment insurance was added as s. 91(2A) in 1940 by the *Constitution Act, 1940* (U.K.)[100] following the *Unemployment Insurance Reference*.[101] In this case, the Judicial Committee of the Privy Council determined that Parliament alone could not enact the sort of unemployment and old age pension scheme it intended. The power

---

[97] *Ibid.* at 61-63.
[98] *Ibid.* at 63.
[99] *Ibid.*
[100] 3-4 Geo. 6, c. 36.
[101] *Canada (Attorney General) v. Ontario (Attorney General)*, [1937] A.C. 355.

does not cover all matters relating to unemployment. Legislation under this power must have an insurance aspect.

(v) *Taxation Powers: Section 91(3)*

Parliament has power to raise money "by any mode or system of taxation" by virtue of s. 91(3) of the *Constitution Act, 1867*. By comparison, ss. 92(2) and (9) give provinces the power to raise provincial revenues through "direct taxation within the province" and licencing fees, respectively. Not until 1982 did provinces get a limited power for so-called "indirect" taxation of non-renewable natural resources, forestry and electrical energy.[102] Section 125 of the *Constitution Act, 1867* says the federal government cannot tax provincial governments and vice versa.

Parliament's power includes both direct and indirect taxation and therefore has almost limitless scope.[103] Consequently, most of the case law in relation to taxation tends to involve the validity of provincial rather than federal statutes. Direct taxes are those that the taxpayer pays from his/her own pocket and which cannot be passed on or recovered from another party. Provincial income tax and provincial sales taxes fall into this category. An indirect tax on the other hand, such as a tax on a manufacturer, will usually be built into the cost of the product and passed on and paid for by the consumer.

It is often said that there is only one taxpayer. This highlights the fact that although taxing powers are distributed between federal and provincial governments, each level of government does not have its own exclusive group of taxpayers. Each taxpayer is subject to taxation from both levels of government. To relieve some of the pressures on taxpayers federal and provincial governments have agreed on sharing arrangements whereby each level of government in effect gets a percentage of the total tax paid from certain categories such as personal income tax and corporate income tax.

In the 1940s and 1950s, following the *Report of the Royal Commission on Dominion-Provincial Relations* (Rowell-Sirois Commission, 1940), the federal government and most provincial governments entered agreements whereby the provinces retreated from certain tax fields in exchange for payments from the federal government to make up for the revenues passed up by the provinces.[104] The federal government, because of its broad taxing power, was able to set the rates and collect the taxes in these fields vacated by provinces. These so-called "tax rental agreements" were modi-

---

[102] See s. 92A(4) of the *Constitution Act, 1867*.
[103] See *Re Anti-Inflation Act, 1975 (Canada), supra*, note 83 at 390.
[104] Hogg, *supra*, note 40 at 137.

fied over the years. Quebec did not participate in this arrangement and levied its own personal income tax, corporate taxes and succession duties.[105] Other provinces such as Ontario relinquished some but not all the major tax fields to the federal government.

From 1962 on, tax collection agreements replaced the tax rental agreements. Under this scheme the federal government left some room for the provinces to set the tax rates, however, the federal government continued to collect the provincial taxes and to pay amounts to the provinces according to the terms of the agreements, thus taxpayers file a single tax return.[106] Again, Quebec did not participate and therefore collected their own taxes. Alberta and Ontario collected their own corporate income taxes, but participated in the collection agreements for other tax fields.

Governments also supplement tax revenues by borrowing amounts in Canada or abroad through vehicles such as government bond issues. Investors buy these bonds on the promise of a repayment of principal plus interest at some future date. In effect, this allows governments to spend more than they receive in revenues, but thereby create significant debt.

(vi) *Militia, Military and Naval Service, and Defence: Section 91(7)*

This federal power includes authority to enact legislation for the regulation and control of behavior and discipline of members of the services and in turn includes the making of laws for the establishment of courts to enforce such legislation.[107] The establishment of courts of original civil and criminal jurisdiction normally falls under the exclusive jurisdiction of provinces under s. 92(14), administration of justice. Section 101 empowers Parliament to "establish any additional court for the better administration of the laws of Canada", but the *MacKay* case found that military courts derived from s. 91(7).

(vii) *Navigation, Shipping and Maritime Law: Sections 91(10) & 92(10)*

Section 91(10) confers on Parliament exclusive legislative jurisdiction over "navigation and shipping". Other modern forms of transportation

---

[105] *Ibid.* at 138.
[106] *Ibid.* at 139.
[107] See *MacKay v. R.*, [1980] 2 S.C.R. 370, 54 C.C.C. (2d) 129.

and communication which were invented after 1867 are not referred to in the Constitution Acts such as bus and truck lines, railways, aeronautics, and telephone, radio and television.[108] Thus, the courts have had to deal with these modern matters in the context of wording set out in 1867.[109]

Section 91(29) further provides that Parliament has authority over "classes of subjects as are expressly excepted in the enumeration of the Classes of subjects . . . assigned exclusively to the legislatures of the provinces." In other words, one has to examine the list of provincial powers in s. 92 to identify some powers assigned to Parliament. Section 92(10) is relevant here. It provides Parliament with, among other things, jurisdiction over

> *a.* Lines of Steam or other Ships, Railways, Canals, Telegraphs, and other Works and Undertakings connecting the Province with any other or others of the Provinces, or extending beyond the Limits of the Province;
> *b.* Lines of Steam Ships between the Province and any British or Foreign Country.

As a matter of drafting, these powers could probably have been included in s. 91 itself. Section 91(13) covers similar matters: it assigns Parliament authority over ferries between a province and a foreign country, or between two provinces.

Parliament's powers permit legislation in relation to maritime law including such matters as maritime insurance and the relationship between carriers of goods by ship, and the shippers, owners or consignees of these goods.[110] However, the courts have interpreted the wording of ss. 91(10) and 92(10) together as empowering Parliament only in respect of interprovincial and international shipping. Some maritime law such as shipping operations carried on entirely within the boundaries of a single province are within provincial legislative authority under s. 92(13), the property and civil rights power.[111]

(viii) *Sea Coast and Inland Fisheries: Section 91(12)*

Section 91(12) does not just grant legislative authority over "fish". The word "fisheries" has been broadly interpreted to include all manner

---

[108] Other heads of power in s. 91 related to transport and communication are subs. (9), "beacons, buoys, lighthouses and Sable Island" and subs. (13), "ferries between a province and any British or foreign country or between two provinces."

[109] For a detailed discussion of modern transportation and communication cases, see Hogg, *supra*, note 40 at 565-601; and Whyte, Bur & Lederman, *supra*, note 11 at 11-1 to 11-130.

[110] See cases cited in Davis, *supra*, note 63 at 132, paras. 28.01-28.03.

[111] See cases cited in Davis, *ibid.* at 132, para. 28.02.

of marine animals that make up a fishery resource.[112] Parliament's power over fisheries includes generally all matters of regulation, protection and preservation, as well as matters of national concern and importance in relation to fisheries. Seasonal restrictions on harvesting, equipment and methods of harvesting, water quality and pollution matters in marine and interprovincial waters all come within this power.[113]

An example of provincially owned property which, contrary to the general rule, is subject to federal legislative jurisdiction is "fisheries". Parliament, under head 91(12), is assigned jurisdiction over "sea coast and inland fisheries", but in *R. v. Fowler*,[114] it was stated that this head of power did not give the federal Crown any proprietary rights to inland fisheries. Whatever property rights were held by individuals, corporations or provinces in 1867 were undisturbed by this assignment of legislative power to Parliament. The Judicial Committee of the Privy Council recognized that provinces as owners of fisheries could sell or grant licences or other rights to fisheries and legislate on this narrow range of matters associated with disposing of provincial property in a fishery under s. 92(5). Provincial legislatures could also legislate under their "property and civil rights" power to prescribe, for example, how a private fishery could be disposed of or passed on through a will.[115] However, it was Parliament that could regulate the broad range of matters such as how and when the fisheries were exploited. Parliament could even use the taxing power to impose "a tax by way of licence as a condition of the right to fish."[116]

(ix) *Banking, Incorporation of Banks, and the Issue of Paper Money: Section 91(15)*

Section 91(15) empowers Parliament to legislate in relation to "banking, incorporation of banks, and the issue of paper money." As is indicated by the plain wording of this head of power, it includes regulating the banking business as well as incorporating banks as businesses. A separate power, s. 91(16), also gives Parliament legislative powers over "savings banks".

What is a "bank", and how is a bank distinct from provincially incorporated businesses such as trust companies, credit unions, caisses populaires or treasury branches which seem to offer similar services?

---

[112] See *R. v. Northwest Falling Contractors Ltd.*, [1980] 2 S.C.R. 292 at 298, 53 C.C.C. (2d) 353, cited in Davis, *ibid.* at 135, para. 29.04.
[113] See *Interprovincial Co-operative Ltd., supra*, note 8 at 520.
[114] [1980] 2 S.C.R. 213 at 222, 53 C.C.C. (2d) 97.
[115] See Whyte, Bur & Lederman, *supra*, note 11 at 16-6.
[116] See *Canada (Attorney General) v. Ontario (Attorney General), supra*, note 43.

Unfortunately, the case law on this subject does not seem to provide a clear and consistent distinction. To some degree it appears that we identify a business as a "bank" because it is called a bank. The cases do not reveal a clear functional test as to what constitutes a bank based on what a business does or does not do.[117]

In the leading case of *Tennant v. Union Bank of Canada*,[118] Lord Watson of the Judicial Committee of the Privy Council described banking as "an expression which is wide enough to embrace every transaction coming within the legitimate business of a banker." Even so, the courts have not applied this conclusion in a way that would neutralize provincial control of financial institutions. Provinces can regulate trust companies, credit unions, and other provincially incorporated institutions which provide many services also available in federally regulated banks.

While s. 91(15) allows Parliament to control paper money, for some reason the drafters created separate heads of power, ss. 91(14) and 91(20), to confer powers over "currency and coinage" and "legal tender", respectively.

Through s. 91(15), Parliament obtains powers to control monetary policy. The Bank of Canada, which is an independent institution established under federal legislation, is the primary instrument for setting and carrying out monetary policies.[119]

Other powers related to money, credit and banking which are assigned to Parliament are s. 91(18), "bills of exchange and promissory notes", and s. 91(19), interest.

(x) *Bankruptcy and Insolvency: Section 91(21)*[120]

Section 91(21) assigns Parliament exclusive authority over "bankruptcy and insolvency". This power also provides legislation designed to govern the administration or distribution of a debtor's property for the benefit of his/her creditors.[121] Bankruptcy involves a process whereby a person or company unable to pay debts has their property placed under the control of another who then administers it for the benefit of

---

[117] See, for example, *Canadian Pioneer Management v. Saskatchewan (Labour Relations Board)*, [1980] 1 S.C.R. 433; for a discussion of this issue, also see Hogg, *supra*, note 40 at 625-626.

[118] [1894] A.C. 31 at 46 (P.C.).

[119] See, for a discussion of the Bank of Canada, D. Laidler, *How Shall We Govern the Governor: A critique of the Governance of the Bank of Canada* (C.D. Howe Institute, 1991).

[120] For a more detailed discussion of this power, see Hogg, *supra*, note 40 at 631-643; see also Davis, *supra*, note 63 at 144-147 for quotations from the cases referred to in this section.

[121] See *Robinson v. Countrywide Factors Ltd.*, [1978] 1 S.C.R. 753 at 794.

creditors.[122] Insolvency is a broader term that embraces debtors who have not yet reached the stage of bankruptcy, but cannot pay their debts when due. A broader range of measures are applied under the legislation to allow the debtor or creditor to intervene, with the courts assistance, to stop individual action by creditors and to administer the debtor's property to protect the general interest of creditors.[123] Parliament can pass laws to set the relative priorities of creditors.[124]

Provinces also have some jurisdiction in these areas, for example, where municipal institutions are involved.[125]

(xi) *Indians and Lands Reserved for the Indians: Section 91(24)*

Section 91(24) says Parliament has exclusive authority over "Indians, and lands reserved for the Indians." In 1939, the Supreme Court of Canada said in the case of *Reference re Head 24, S. 91 of the British North America Act, 1867*[126] that the word "Indian" in s. 91(24) included Eskimos (Inuit). Although s. 35(2) of the *Constitution Act, 1982* now defines the "aboriginal peoples of Canada" as including "Indians, Inuit and Métis", the courts have not yet ruled decisively on whether the term "Indian" in s. 91(24) includes Métis.

The scope of this head of power is still in some doubt regarding the types of laws Parliament can enact in relation to Indian people and Indian lands.[127] The main federal Act under s. 91(24) is the *Indian Act*.[128] It has a limited application and excludes Metis, Inuit and certain other categories of aboriginal people who, for one reason or another, do not fall within the definition of Indians set out in the Act.

Although Parliament has exclusive authority over "Indians and lands reserved for the Indians,"[129] it has long been held by the courts that provincial laws apply to Indians and on Indian reserves, provided the laws apply generally within the province, do not single out Indians, and are not inconsistent with federal laws. Provincial traffic laws are one such example.[130]

---

[122] See, for a definition of bankruptcy and insolvency, *Canadian Bankers' Assn. v. Saskatchewan (Attorney General)*, [1956] S.C.R. 31 at 46.

[123] See *British Columbia (Attorney General) v. Canada (Attorney General)*, [1937] A.C. 391 (P.C.).

[124] *Ontario (Attorney General) v. Wentworth Insurance Co.*, [1969] S.C.R. 779 at 807.

[125] *Mississauga (City) v. Peel (Regional Municipality)*, [1979] 2 S.C.R. 244.

[126] [1939] S.C.R. 104.

[127] See, for a discussion of this power, Hogg, *supra*, note 40 at 663*ff.*

[128] R.S.C. 1985, c. I-5.

[129] See Chapter 8 for a discussion of the inherent right of aboriginal peoples to self-government.

[130] See *R. v. Francis*, [1988] 1 S.C.R. 1025, 41 C.C.C. (3d) 217.

Indian reserves are not enclaves where only federal laws apply.[131]

The nature of aboriginal title to lands in Canada is a difficult and evolving question of property law and constitutional law. Under s. 91(24), it is clear that Parliament has been assigned jurisdiction over "lands reserved for the Indians." Since the *St. Catherine's Milling & Lumber* case,[132] it has been recognized that if the aboriginal interest in lands within a particular province is surrendered to the Crown, the use and benefit of that land reverts to the province, not the federal Crown. Furthermore, the land would no longer be under federal legislative jurisdiction once it ceases to be "lands reserved for the Indians."

Issues of aboriginal law spring mainly from the interplay between federal and provincial legislation[133] and aboriginal and treaty rights in relation to land, hunting, trapping, fishing, religious and cultural practices, adoption, and many other aspects of aboriginal life. It is now clear that legislation cannot validly extinguish or diminish aboriginal or treaty rights unless it can meet a strict test of justification and proportionality.[134]

(xii) *Marriage and Divorce: Section 91(26)*

Section 91(26) says Parliament has exclusive jurisdiction over "marriage and divorce". By contrast, s. 92(12) assigns provinces exclusive legislative power over "the solemnization of marriage in the province". At first glance one might have expected marriage and divorce to be an exclusive provincial power because it seems more consistent with s. 92(12) and the "property and civil rights" power assigned to provinces by s. 92(13). Parliament was probably given power over marriage to allow federal legislation to set down uniform rules for marriage recognition.[135] Divorce was probably placed under Parliament's jurisdiction to make it more difficult for individuals to obtain.[136]

There are few cases[137] involving federal marriage legislation and as a result the scope of the federal power in relation to marriage has not been

---

[131] See Hogg, *supra*, note 40 at 672.

[132] *St. Catherine's Milling & Lumber Co. v. R.* (1888), 14 App. Cas. 46 (P.C.).

[133] Provincial legislation cannot validly alter treaty rights: *R. v. Moosehunter*, [1981] 1 S.C.R. 282 at 293, 59 C.C.C. (2d) 193 (Dickson J.); see also *R. v. Sparrow*, [1990] 1 S.C.R. 1075, 56 C.C.C. (3d) 263, discussed in Chapter 8, on the effects of s. 35 of the *Constitution Act, 1982* as protection from provincial legislation.

[134] See *R. v. Sparrow, ibid.*, which is discussed in detail in Chapter 8.

[135] Abel, *Laskin's Canadian Constitutional Law, supra*, note 11 at 107; see also Hogg, *supra*, note 40 at 645-662.

[136] Abel, *ibid.* at 107.

[137] See *Re Marriage Legislation in Canada*, [1912] A.C. 880 (P.C.).

clearly defined by the courts.[138] Under the divorce branch of the power, Parliament enacted a *Divorce Act*[139] in 1968 which contains provisions relating to maintenance, custody, care and upbringing of children of the marriage, and various orders the courts may give in relation to these matters. Courts have upheld these provisions of the *Divorce Act* as being necessary incidents to the power over divorce.[140] However, many of these matters have also been the subject of provincial legislation and numerous cases have challenged the federal provisions.[141] To date, the corollary relief provisions in the *Divorce Act* have withstood all attacks.[142]

(xiii) *Powers in Relation to Criminal Law: Section 91(27)*[143]

The criminal law power, like the trade and commerce power, is difficult to confine to a tidy and predictable scope of operation. The main head of power, found in s. 91(27), states that Parliament has exclusive authority over

[t]he Criminal Law, except the Constitution of Courts of Criminal Jurisdiction, but including the Procedure in Criminal Matters.

A related federal power is found in s. 91(28) which gives Parliament jurisdiction over the establishment, maintenance and management of penitentiaries. Provinces by contrast are assigned jurisdiction under s. 92(6) for the establishment, maintenance and management of public and reformatory prisons in and for the province.[144]

Parliament has exclusive authority to create criminal offences and provide for such procedural matters as evidence requirements. Section 91(27) implies that provinces have jurisdiction over the system of courts that try criminal offences, and in fact s. 92(14) says that provinces have exclusive authority over

[t]he Administration of Justice in the Province, including the Constitution, Maintenance, and Organization of Provincial Courts, both of Civil and of Criminal Jurisdiction, and including Procedure in Civil Matters in those Courts.

---

[138] Hogg, *supra*, note 40 at 647. Hogg states that most laws concerning marriage have been passed by the provinces under the "property and civil rights" power (s. 92(13)) and the "solemnization of marriage" power (s. 92(12)).

[139] See now R.S.C. 1985, c. 3 (2nd Supp.).

[140] See *Zacks v. Zacks*, [1973] S.C.R. 891.

[141] See *Papp v. Papp*, [1970] 1 O.R. 331 (C.A.).

[142] Hogg, *supra*, note 40 at 649.

[143] This section draws most of its information from Hogg, *ibid.* at 467-495.

[144] *Ibid.* at 517.

However, provinces are also given a further power in s. 92(15) which makes it very difficult in practice to know where the federal criminal law jurisdiction ends and where provincial jurisdiction begins. Section 92(15) says provinces have exclusive jurisdiction over

> [t]he Imposition of Punishment by Fine, Penalty, or Imprisonment for enforcing any Law of the Province made in relation to any Matter coming within any of the Classes of Subjects enumerated in this Section.

How does one determine which government can do what? The initial question is how can we tell a criminal law from any other law? In a contest between a federal and a provincial statute this can be a very difficult question to answer.

The scope of the criminal law has not been defined. New criminal laws can be created by Parliament as it sees fit. Criminal laws were loosely described as any prohibited action that carried a penal sanction.[145] Provinces are also allowed to impose penal sanctions under s. 92(15) for the enforcement of provincial laws. Clearly a broadly interpreted criminal law power could allow Parliament to move into most areas over which provinces legislate.

The courts rejected the argument that simply because a statute forbids or prohibits something, it is criminal law.[146] The courts have to look further at what the true, but often elusive, purpose of the legislation is to determine whether it is properly characterized as criminal law.

In the *Margarine Reference*,[147] Mr. Justice Rand of the Supreme Court of Canada said public purposes such as public peace, security, health, and morality "are the ordinary though not exclusive ends served by [criminal] law." In that case, prohibitions against margarine dealt "directly with the civil rights of individuals in relation to particular trade within the provinces" and was therefore a provincial matter.

In contrast, in the case of *McNeil v. Nova Scotia (Board of Censors)*[148] a provincial scheme for the censorship of films was upheld as valid provincial law even though it seemed to be directed at a public purpose, morality, which Mr. Justice Rand had said was ordinarily served by federal criminal law. More unusual was the case of *R. v. Hauser*[149] which said

---

[145] *Proprietary Articles Trade Assn. v. Canada (Attorney General)*, [1931] A.C. 310 at 324 (P.C.); also see Hogg, *ibid.* at 470.

[146] *Reference re Validity of S. 5(a) of the Dairy Industry Act (Canada)*, [1949] S.C.R. 1, affirmed (*sub nom. Canadian Federation of Agriculture v. Quebec (Attorney General)*) [1951] A.C. 179 (P.C.) [the "*Margarine Reference*"].

[147] *Ibid.*

[148] [1978] 2 S.C.R. 662, 44 C.C.C. (2d) 316.

[149] [1979] 1 S.C.R. 984, 8 C.R. (3d) 89, 46 C.C.C. (2d) 481.

that the federal *Narcotic Control Act* was *not* criminal law but was valid federal law under the peace, order and good government power.[150]

It is often difficult to discern a difference between federal *Criminal Code* provisions on dangerous driving, for example, and provincial statutes which deal with highway traffic safety. Technically, the federal provisions are criminal law but the provincial provisions are not. The federal penal sanctions in some cases may not be noticeably different from the provincial penal sanctions enacted under s. 92(15). The difficulty in putting sturdy fences around the federal and provincial fields of legislative action has led Professor Hogg to note that "over much of the field which may loosely be thought of as criminal law legislative power is concurrent" between Parliament and provincial legislatures.[151]

(xiv) *The Federal Power to Create Courts: Section 101*[152]

The basic principle of the court system in Canada is that the superior courts established by the provinces have jurisdiction in all matters federal and provincial.[153] An exception to this is s. 101 which says that Parliament can legislate to establish a general court of appeal for Canada, and to establish any additional courts "for the better administration of the laws of Canada." Under this power Parliament has established the Supreme Court of Canada and the Federal Court of Canada.[154]

The words "laws of Canada" in s. 101 contain a limitation in that they refer only to existing federal legislation, regulations and federal common law.[155] The Federal Court only has jurisdiction over cases involving such existing laws. In practice, a person intending to take court proceedings involving federal laws or federal institutions and agencies must carefully consider whether the Federal Court or a superior court of a province is the proper forum to hear the case.

(xv) *The Federal Spending Power: Section 106*

The federal "spending power" is not an explicit head of power under s. 91. It derives from several provisions of the *Constitution Act, 1867*, such as the federal taxing power in s. 91(3) which allows the raising of

---

[150] Hogg, *supra*, note 40 at 467-468.

[151] *Ibid.* at 494.

[152] See Davis, *supra*, note 63 at 339-347 for quotations from the cases cited in this section.

[153] *Perehinic v. Northern Pipeline Agency*, [1983] 2 S.C.R. 513.

[154] See Chapter 2 for further discussion of courts established under s. 101.

[155] *McNamara Construction (Western) Ltd. v. R.*, [1977] 2 S.C.R. 654.

revenues, the power over "the public debt and property" in s. 91(1A), and s. 106 which states that Parliament can "appropriate" or spend money from the Consolidated Revenue Fund. The principle of equalization payments set out in s. 36(2) of the *Constitution Act, 1982* also provides some endorsement for the spending power. The broad scope of the spending power has been supported by decisions of the courts in cases such as *Reference re Canada Assistance Plan (Canada)*[156] and *Finlay v. Canada (Minister of Finance)*.[157]

The federal spending power is a manifestation of the old adage that "money talks". Over the years federal governments have been able to influence matters within exclusive provincial jurisdiction by offering to share the costs of certain provincial programs in important fields such as education, health care and social assistance. Some funding may be unconditional, but the more difficult situation for provinces is when federal funding is made conditional on provinces meeting certain terms and conditions dictated by the federal government. The terms and conditions may be set out in federal Acts such as the *Canada Health Act*[158] and the *Canada Assistance Plan*.[159]

The number and form of shared-cost programs has varied over the years. Initially, large cash grants were made by the federal government to fund up to 50 per cent of a program, but more common today is a combination of cash and tax room.[160] This federal spending has made some public services available in the poorer provinces where it is unlikely that the provincial government could have offered such a program. The effect of the federal offer of money in some of these areas has been to entice provinces into spending large portions of their own budgets in order to capture federal funds.

The four most important shared-cost programs today involve post-secondary education (established 1951), hospital services (1958), doctor services (1968) and the Canada Assistance Plan (1966) which covers social services and income support.[161]

It is also worth noting that provinces might, in principle, have some scope for spending provincial funds on matters that fall within the exclusive jurisdiction of Parliament or another province. Section 126 of the *Constitution Act, 1867*, similar to s. 106 in the case of Parliament, empowers a provincial legislature to spend from the province's Consolidated Revenue Fund; however, the words "for the public service of the

---

[156] [1991] 2 S.C.R. 525.
[157] [1990] 2 F.C. 790, 71 D.L.R. (4th) 422 (C.A.), reversed [1993] 1 S.C.R. 1080.
[158] R.S.C. 1985, c. C-6.
[159] R.S.C. 1985, c. C-1.
[160] Hogg, *supra*, note 40 at 150.
[161] *Ibid.* at 145.

Province'' at the end of the section would have to be taken into consideration. Section 106 does not contain similar limitations on the federal spending power. In a practical sense, it is unlikely that a province could, for example, coerce the federal government into taking particular measures in relation to federally regulated national parks in the province simply on the promise of provincial cost-sharing.

There are situations, however, where provinces spend provincial moneys for programs and services on aboriginal peoples on reserves, although Indians and lands reserved for Indians are under exclusive federal jurisdiction.[162]

It is more likely that one province could influence a program or activity in another province through a cost-sharing arrangement with that province. For example, one province might be able to justify investing in a road building program in an adjoining province that would link up with road systems in the sponsoring province and thereby facilitate some business or industry in the sponsoring province.

(xvi) *The Federal Treaty Power: Section 132*

The federal executive has the power to make treaties which are binding on Canada in international law.[163] Parliament plays no role in negotiation or signing of treaties, but plays a significant role in their implementation.[164] Parliament has power to implement treaties only to the extent that it involves matters of federal legislative jurisdiction. If the treaty interferes with provincial subject-matters then the individual provinces must ratify and implement the federally negotiated treaty before it becomes binding on that province.[165]

4. The Federal Executive Powers

(a) How the Federal Executive is Established and Organized

The rules which govern the executive and its powers spring from four main sources. First, ss. 9 to 16 of the *Constitution Act, 1867* refer to the formal executive branch of government and confer on it certain powers.

---

[162] See Chapter 8 for a discussion of aboriginal self-government.

[163] *Ibid.* at 241-242.

[164] *Ibid.* at 244-245.

[165] H.M. Kindred *et al., International Law — Chiefly as Interpreted and Applied in Canada* (Emond Montgomery, 1993) at 168-170; also see *Canada (Attorney General) v. Ontario (Attorney General)*, [1937] A.C. 326 (PC) [the *"Labour Conventions* case''].

(Notably, the Act does not actually establish the office of the Governor General.) Second, the conventions of responsible government operate to modify these written provisions in the *Constitution Act, 1867*.[166] Third, the rules of common law which the courts of England and Canada have developed over the centuries in their decisions further identify and define executive powers. Fourth, Parliament has delegated significant powers, such as regulation-making authority, to the executive by ordinary statute. We are primarily concerned here with the first three matters.

(b) Structure of the Formal Executive

Part III of the *Constitution Act, 1867* is entitled "Executive Power" and contains ss. 9 to 16 which provide as follows:

- *Section 9:* The executive government and authority for Canada is continued and vested in the Queen of England.
- *Section 10:* The Governor General carries on "the Government of Canada" on behalf of and in the name of the Queen.
- *Section 11:* An advisory body called the "Queen's Privy Council" is to aid and advise in the government of Canada and members of this body are chosen and removed by the Governor General.
- *Sections 12 and 13:* Certain powers, authorities and functions are to be exercised by the Governor General with the "advice and consent" of the Privy Council, including powers under other provisions of the Constitution Acts which refer to the "Governor in Council".
- *Section 14:* The Governor General can appoint "Deputies" in other parts of Canada to exercise powers assigned by the Governor General.
- *Section 15:* The Queen continues as the "Command-in-Chief" of Canada's militia and naval and military forces.
- *Section 16:* Until the Queen otherwise directs, the seat of government is to be Ottawa.

In reality Canada is not, of course, governed by the Queen, the Governor General or the Queen's Privy Council as suggested by ss. 9, 10 and 11. The Queen and the Governor General have largely ceremonial roles in relation to Canada's federal government, although as a legal formality their participation in the executive and legislative functions is required, if in name only. The Governor General is appointed by the Queen only on recommendation of the Prime Minister of Canada. The Queen's Privy

---

[166] See the discussion of conventions in Chapter 2.

Council is also a bit of a fiction as far as actual governing is concerned. The full membership of the Council includes the active cabinet ministers, cabinet ministers of past governments, as well as honourary members. Appointments are for life. Only those members who are incumbent ministers have any role in the government of the day.

(c) Structure of the Conventional Executive

Understanding who makes up the conventional executive, how they are chosen, and how the executive operates are more matters of politics than of constitutional law. These matters are tied, by a rather complex thread, to the right to vote.

The right to vote is a democratic right which has been constitutionally entrenched in our written Constitution since 1982 by s. 3 of the *Canadian Charter of Rights and Freedoms.*[167]

(i) *Responsible Government*

Since the "Glorious Revolution" in England in 1688, Parliamentary government has replaced the Monarch as an active ruler. Under the system of responsible government, the Queen's ministers, which we also call the Cabinet or executive, are answerable not to the Queen, but to the elected House of Commons. If the majority of members in the House of Commons support the Cabinet, they can stay in office up to five years. Section 4(1) of the *Charter of Rights and Freedoms* provides that no House of Commons shall continue for longer than five years from the date fixed for the return of the writs of a general election. Political parties and the discipline exercised by the party leader and organization are critical in most legislatures in Canada in the process of maintaining the support of the government in power.[168]

---

[167] Prior to 1982, federal and provincial legislation determined who could and could not vote, and at various times disqualified large groups of people as the legislators saw fit in the context of their times. For example, women could not vote in federal elections prior to 1918 and, until the 1960s, many aboriginal people were not able to vote in federal elections without losing their status as Indians under the *Indian Act*. Some parts of the country were not within federal electoral districts. Canadians living in the eastern Arctic of the Northwest Territories were not within any federal electoral district until the 1950s.

[168] The Northwest Territories is the only legislature which does not rely on political parties in the election of members, the formation of a cabinet or in the day-to-day functioning of the legislature. See K. O'Keefe, "Northwest Territories: Accommodating the Future" in G. Levy & G. White, eds., *Provincial and Territorial Legislatures in Canada* (University of Toronto Press, 1989) at 207-220.

(ii) *Political Parties*

A political party is an organization of persons with a set of common goals in relation to governing. The organizational and policy formulating talents of the party leadership and members are brought to bear during elections to ensure that members of the party are in place to run for office in all or as many electoral districts as possible. The objective, simply put, is to put forward the party's goals and policy objectives and to win as many seats in the House of Commons as possible. If a party wins a majority of the seats in the House of Commons it may form the government. A party, like most other organizations, has its own corporate constitution to govern its operation, but this constitution has no direct connection to, nor does it have any status under, the Constitution of Canada.

(iii) *Choosing a Party Leader*

The method by which political parties choose or remove a leader is governed by the party's own corporate constitution which is drawn up and approved only by party members. The leader of the political party which forms a government after an election becomes the Prime Minister. Members of the political party will have chosen this leader at a convention of party delegates at some time prior to the federal election. Occasionally the leader of a party resigns in circumstances where that party is already sitting as the federal government. For example, following the resignation of Brian Mulroney, Kim Campbell was elected to replace him as the leader of the Progressive Conservative Party of Canada by party delegates at a convention in June 1993 and became the Prime Minister of Canada without a federal election having been called. John Turner became Prime Minister in a similar way in the summer of 1984 when Prime Minister Pierre Trudeau resigned as leader of the federal Liberal Party.

(iv) *Running Candidates in Elections*

Through federal, provincial and territorial elections we choose representatives from the particular constitutency in which we are qualified to vote. In most, although not all, cases the person elected for that constituency is a member of a political party. The federal electoral districts were originally set out in s. 40 of the *Constitution Act, 1867* but were qualified by the words "until the Parliament of Canada otherwise provides." Over the years Parliament has modified the boundaries and number of electoral districts many times by statute, most recently the *Con-*

stitution Act, 1985 (Representation).[169] Today there are 295 electoral districts. In 1867, there were 181 comprised of 82 for Ontario, 65 for Quebec, 19 for Nova Scotia, and 15 for New Brunswick.

In theory the people, that is the voters, are ultimately in charge in a democracy. However, the right to vote gives citizens a say in choosing who will govern, but does not give citizens a say in the day-to-day decision-making of the government once it is in office. At election time a plurality of voters in each electoral district chooses, by their vote, a person who will sit in Parliament. But members of Parliament sit as "representatives" which means that between elections they have discretion as to the best way to represent the interests of the electorate. In practice that discretion is even further limited by the operation of political parties and party discipline.

(v) *Winning Elections: First Past the Post*

It is important to note that the Canadian system does not elect a government on the basis of the percentage of *votes* received in an election, but rather on the basis of the number of *members elected*. They are quite different things. A party can hold over 50 per cent of the seats with much less than 50 per cent of the total votes cast. Our electoral system operates on the basis of "pluralities". For example, if three candidates are running for election in a riding, one may receive 40 per cent of the votes cast, while the other two get 35 per cent and 25 per cent, respectively. The candidate who wins 40 per cent of the vote will be elected even though a total of 60 per cent, the majority of voters, did not vote for that candidate.

(vi) *Forming a Government*

By convention, where the members of a party are a majority in the House of Commons, the leader of that party is invited by the Governor General to form the government.

(A) *Majority Government*

A majority government is one in which a single political party controls 50 per cent plus one seats in the House of Commons. In the law-making processes of Parliament, members vote to approve or reject legis-

---

[169] S.C. 1986, c. 8, Part I.

lation and other measures. Section 49 of the *Constitution Act, 1867* requires that "[q]uestions arising in the House of Commons shall be decided by a majority of *voices*" [emphasis added]; therefore, having the support of a majority of members can be crucial to carrying out a government's legislative agenda and receiving Parliament's approval to raise and spend the money needed to carry on government operations, including programs and services.

(B) *Minority Government*

Occasionally, a political party with less than a majority of the seats will be invited to form the government. Such a government is vulnerable to being defeated in votes relating to its legislative agenda and appropriation of moneys or running the government. In such a case the government is said to have lost the "confidence" of the House and will either call a general election to attempt to win a majority of seats, or alternatively may step down and allow the Governor General to invite another party to form a government.

(C) *Coalition Government*

There are also situations where a coalition of two political parties, each with less than a majority of seats, will agree formally or informally to use their combined strength to control a majority of the members of the House and thus form a government. Such arrangements usually call for compromises between the political philosophies and agendas of the two parties, so that each has some say over the direction of the coalition government.

(vii) *The Prime Minister*

By convention, the Prime Minister is really the chief executive officer and, along with cabinet ministers, exercises the executive powers. The words in the Preamble to the Act which say that Canada is to have a Constitution similar in principle to Great Britain are taken to have implied this practice and tradition.[170] A Prime Minister in the Canadian system may wield enormous power because he/she exerts significant control not only over the executive and administrative branches of government, but

---

[170] *Manitoba (Attorney General) v. Canada (Attorney General), supra*, note 19 at 805-806.

also over the legislative functions by virtue of his/her leadership of the party with a majority in the House of Commons.

The Prime Minister chooses the Cabinet. In addition, the Prime Minister can have significant influence on the composition and actions of the Senate and controls patronage generally. For example, s. 32 of the *Constitution Act, 1867* says that the Governor General "summons", that is appoints, persons to the Senate, but in reality the Prime Minister chooses the people and the Governor General executes the formalities.[171]

The Prime Minister also names judges to fill vacancies on the Supreme Court of Canada and other superior courts, although once in office a very strong convention of judicial independence operates to safeguard judges against political influence.

In spite of the power of the Prime Minister, in Canadian federal elections the only voters who can actually cast ballots directly for a potential Prime Minister are those persons resident in the constituency where a party leader is in the running to be a member of Parliament. Therefore, to accept or reject a party leader, voters elsewhere in the country must do so indirectly by accepting or rejecting the candidate in their constituency who is a member of that leader's party.

(viii) *Choosing a Cabinet*

Once invited to form a government, the leader of the winning party, now the Prime Minister, chooses a "Cabinet", which is usually a group of about 20 to 35 members of his/her party who have been elected to the House of Commons. Party members from the Senate might also be asked to sit in the Cabinet even though they have acquired their seats in this Parliamentary body by appointment rather than by election. In other words, not all members of Cabinet, the primary executive body, are necessarily elected by Canadians.

The "rules" for choosing cabinet ministers are political rather than legal. Most often a Prime Minister seeks to establish a balance of regional

---

[171] For a short period between 1987 and 1990, the Prime Minister and the provincial Premiers agreed to be governed by the political agreement called the Meech Lake Accord which provided that the Prime Minister would fill vacancies in the Senate from a list of names submitted by the Premier of the province to which the vacancy related. A senator from Newfoundland was appointed under this procedure, but in the case of Alberta, provincial legislation was passed to provide that elections would be held to determine the name of the person who would be nominated from the province. Stan Waters, who was elected under this statutory scheme, was eventually appointed to the Senate after some considerable delay by the Prime Minister. Following the collapse of the Meech Lake Accord in June 1990, the Prime Minister announced that he was reverting back to the traditional method of appointing senators.

and provincial interests by choosing MPs from across the country. Cabinet is the body that most people mean when they refer to the "federal government". Cabinet ministers preside over the departments or agencies that make up the bureaucracy and are responsible for the direction, as well as the actions and functions, of those departments and agencies. Collectively the Cabinet sets the direction for the government in power.

(ix) *Directing Parliament and the Civil Service*

Between elections the real decision-making in relation to policies, programs, services, government spending and initiatives for new legislation lies not with the voters, but with the executive or Cabinet. As was related at the beginning of this Chapter, and in Chapter 2 in connection with conventions, Cabinet is, for the most part, the controlling mind of Parliament and the civil service.[172]

(d) The Main Executive Powers Set Out in the Constitution Acts

The federal executive powers are at least as extensive as the range of matters over which Parliament has legislative jurisdiction. Similarly the range and scope of executive powers of the provincial level of government follow the distribution of legislative powers set out in the Constitution Acts.

The Constitution Acts also contain a number of specific provisions which allow the "Governor General", the "Governor General in Council" or "the Government of Canada" to exercise executive decision-making. In most cases where the Governor General is called upon to exercise executive powers he/she has previously been advised of a course of action by the Prime Minister and is bound by convention to follow that advice.[173] Some of the executive powers contained in the Constitution Acts are as follows:

Constitution Act, 1867

In relation to the Senate:

- *Section 24*: To "summon" qualified persons to the Senate to be Senators.

---

[172] For a discussion of the conventions surrounding the Cabinet, ministers and the civil service, see A. Heard, *Canadian Constitutional Conventions, The Marriage of Law and Politics* (University of Toronto Press, 1991) at 48-75; for a discussion of the legal framework of government operations, see Tardi, *supra*, note 35.

[173] For a discussion of the conventions surrounding the office of Governor General, see Heard, *ibid.* at 16-47.

- *Section 26*: Adding either four or eight senators to the Senate (one or two from each Division) [Prime Minister Mulroney exercised this option in 1990 in order to ensure the passage of the bill establishing the Goods and Services Tax].
- *Section 32*: Summoning persons to fill vacancies in the Senate.
- *Section 34*: Appointing a Senator to act as Speaker in the Senate.

In relation to the House of Commons:

- *Section 38*: Summon and call together members of the House of Commons.
- *Section 50*: Dissolving the House of Commons.
- *Section 54*: Recommending votes, resolutions, addresses or bills that call for spending public money or imposing taxes. [Note: This is part of the federal legislative process.]
- *Section 55*: Assenting to, or withholding assent, or reserving for the Queen's "signification", bills passed by Parliament. [Note: This is part of the federal legislative process.]

In relation to the provincial executive:

- *Section 58*: Appointing a Lieutenant Governor for each province. [See further information under Division of Powers: Provincial Powers.]
- *Section 67*: Appointing an Administrator to fill the office of a Lieutenant Governor who is absent or unable to carry out his/her duties.
- *Section 90*: Assent to, or withhold assent to, a provincial bill reserved by the Lieutenant Governor.

In relation to the federal legislative process:

- *Section 91*: Acting as part of the federal legislative process on behalf of the Queen. [The Queen's powers were delegated to the Governor General by Letters Patent in 1947.]

In relation to education:

- *Section 93(3)*: Hearing appeals from any Act or decision of a provincial authority affecting rights or privileges in relation to education of Protestant or Roman Catholic minorities.
- *Section 93(4)*: Determining whether remedial federal legislation is required to give effect to the education objectives of s. 93 where provinces fail to act.

In relation to judges and courts:

- *Section 96*: Appointing judges of the superior, district and county courts of each province.
- *Section 99*: Removing judges of superior courts on address from Parliament.

In relation to oaths:

- *Section 128*: Receiving the Oath of Allegiance from persons appointed to the Senate or elected to the House of Commons and, prior to 1968 (when the upper house was abolished), from persons appointed to the upper house ("Legislative Council") in Quebec.
- *Section 132*: Performing, along with Parliament, the obligations of Canada or any province arising under treaties between Great Britain and foreign countries.

Some of the powers listed above would rarely, if ever, be used today, for example the powers of reservation and disallowance referred to in ss. 55 and 90. Others would only be used in very exceptional circumstances, for example the educational powers referred to in ss. 93(3) and (4).

Additional very important powers relating to, among other things, the amendment of the Constitution are conferred on the Governor General by the *Constitution Act, 1982*. This Act is also the only place in the written Constitution which mentions the "Prime Minister":

Constitution Act, 1982

In relation to aboriginal matters:

- *Section 35.1*: This section, which was added in 1983, commits the Prime Minister to convene a conference with Premiers and representatives of the aboriginal peoples before amending certain constitutional provisions which relate directly to aboriginal peoples.
- *Section 37*: This section, which was automatically repealed by s. 54 on April 17, 1983, required the Prime Minister to convene a conference with Premiers, representatives of the Northwest Territories and Yukon, and representatives of the aboriginal peoples, to discuss "constitutional matters that directly affect the aboriginal peoples of Canada, including the identification and definition of the rights of those peoples to be included in the Constitution of Canada." Following this Conference, an amendment was made to s. 35 of the *Constitution Act, 1982* which provided for some amendments to ss. 25 and 35 and for two additional conferences.
- *Section 37.1*: This section was added in 1983 and was automati-

cally repealed by s. 54.1 on April 18, 1987. It required the Prime Minister to convene at least two more conferences on aboriginal constitutional matters, but dropped the language about "identification and definition of rights". Instead, the section provided that holding such conferences should not be negatively interpreted in relation to whatever aboriginal rights were already protected by s. 35(1) of the *Constitution Act, 1982*. In fact, conferences were eventually held in 1984, 1986 and 1987, but did not lead to any agreed identification or definition of rights, nor to any further constitutional amendment in relation to aboriginal peoples.

In relation to amendments:

- *Section 38*: Issuing proclamations to amend the Constitution where authorized, in accordance with the details of ss. 38, 39 and 42, by Parliament and two-thirds of the provincial legislative assemblies representing "at least fifty per cent of the population of all the provinces." [Note: The population of the northern territories is not mentioned. See Chapter 10 on the Amending Formulas.]
- *Section 41*: Issuing proclamations to amend the Constitution where authorized by Parliament and each provincial legislative assembly.
- *Section 43*: Issuing proclamations to amend the Constitution where authorized by Parliament and the one or more provincial legislative assemblies to which the amendment applies.
- *Section 48*: The Queen's Privy Council advises the Governor General to issue proclamations "forthwith" once Parliament and the requisite number of provincial legislative assemblies have approved the amendment.
- *Section 49*: The Prime Minister is required to convene a conference with Premiers by April 18, 1997 to review the provisions in this "Part" of the Constitution relating to amendments. [Note: Other provisions outside of this Part also relate to amendments, such as the *Constitution Act, 1871*.]

In relation to French versions of Constitution:

- *Section 55*: Enacting by proclamation French versions of the Acts contained in the Schedule to the *Constitution Act, 1982*.

In relation to minority language educational rights:

- *Section 59*: Proclaiming in force section 23(1)(*a*) of the *Constitution Act, 1982* relating to minority language educational rights where authorized by the legislative assembly or government of Quebec.

(e) Common Law, Conventional and Statutory Rules Relating to the Executive

Other executive powers, prerogatives and privileges are not referred to in the Constitution Acts at all. Such powers are the products of our legal and political traditions as interpreted over many years by the courts of Canada and England.[174] In addition, there are numerous statutes which delegate aspects of Parliament's authority to the executive branch. It would not be possible to cover these powers, prerogatives and privileges in a book of this scope.[175]

---

[174] See section on conventions in Chapter 2.

[175] See Davis, *supra*, note 63 at 691-747; Heard, *supra*, note 172; Hogg, *supra*, note 40 at 257-277; Tardi, *supra*, note 35 at 59-63 and 82-90.

5

Provincial Level of Government

1. The Provincial Legislative Powers

While s. 91 of the *Constitution Act, 1867* outlines the main legislative powers of the federal Parliament, s. 92 sets out the main legislative powers of the provincial legislatures.

(a) Federalism

The *Constitution Act, 1867* distributes powers exclusively to either the federal Parliament or provincial legislatures, and thus effectively divides the legislative power into two. This distribution reflects our system of federalism. Through the assignments of power under ss. 91 and 92, this Act grants and denies these legislative bodies the power to legislate on certain subject-matters.[1]

(b) How Provinces' Legislative Powers are Organized

The provincial legislatures, like Parliament, have both exclusive and concurrent powers of legislation. The provinces have the constitutional power to legislate exclusively in areas specified in s. 92.

Sixteen specific heads of power are exclusively assigned to the provinces under s. 92 and include such matters as direct taxation within the province, finance, local works and undertakings, property and civil rights, justice and the court system, and matters of a local and private nature.

The provinces have the power to legislate concurrently with the federal Parliament on matters specified in the *Constitution Act, 1867* as natural resources, education, agriculture and immigration.

---

[1] P.W. Hogg, *Constitutional Law of Canada*, 2d ed. (Carswell, 1985) at 258.

(c) Any Power Left Over is Federal Because of Doctrine of Exhaustiveness

The Canadian courts have determined that the *Constitution Act, 1867* has exhausted the whole range of legislative powers to be assigned to either legislative body. As a result, only the federal Parliament or provincial legislature can exercise the constitutional power to legislate. Matters that are not specifically assigned in s. 91 or s. 92 can still be subject to legislation. However, if the matter does not fall within the province's list of powers, or if any power is "left over", the courts have held that it falls within the sphere of the federal legislative power.[2]

(d) Exclusive Provincial Legislative Powers

Sixteen specific heads of power are assigned to provinces by the *Constitution Act, 1867*. The most important of these are discussed below.

(i) *Direct Taxation Within the Province: Section 92(2)*

Section 92(2) provides that the provinces may make laws in relation to "direct taxation within the province in order to [raise revenue for a] provincial [purpose]." A provincial tax must be direct, imposed within a province and for the purpose of raising revenue for provincial endeavors.[3] As a result, a person outside the province does not have to fund a government from which he/she receives no benefits.[4]

Unlike the federal government, which can impose both direct and indirect taxation,[5] the provincial governments only have the jurisdiction to impose "direct taxation". John Stuart Mills' definition of the distinction between direct and indirect tax has been accepted as the appropriate test for constitutional purposes:

> A direct tax is one which is demanded from the very person who it is intended or desired should pay it. Indirect taxes are those which are demanded from one person in the expectation and intention that he shall indemnify himself at the expense of another, such as the excise or customs.[6]

---

[2] L. Davis, *Canadian Constitutional Law Handbook* (Canada Law Book, 1985) at 489.

[3] V. Krishna, *The Fundamentals of Canadian Income Tax*, 4th ed. (Carswell, 1993) at 5.

[4] P.W. Hogg, *Constitutional Law of Canada*, 3d ed. (Supp.) (Carswell, 1992), vol. 1 at 30-7.

[5] Section 91(3). Note, however, that in 1982 provinces were given limited indirect taxation powers in relation to non-renewable and forestry resources, and electrical energy, by the *Constitution Act, 1982*, s. 92A(4).

[6] J.S. Mills, *Principles of Political Economy* (D. Appleton & Co., 1907).

This definition was applied in *Bank of Toronto v. Lambe*[7] and is generally relied on in all subsequent cases.[8] Furthermore, for the taxation to be "within the province", the person or corporation being taxed must have more than a nominal presence in the province. For example, a plane flying through provincial airspace is not located in a *situs* that supports a provincial plan of taxation on an aircraft's entry into the province.[9] As a result, the federal and provincial powers overlap when they apply direct tax.[10]

(ii) *Management and Sale of Public Lands: Section 92(5)*

The provincial legislature has full authority to pass laws in relation to any provincially owned property, including its natural resources. Public lands may be disposed of in any way the government sees fit since the provincial government is the owner of the property. Therefore, as a source of revenue, provincial public lands may be sold, licensed or rented.[11] This provides the province with a broad power to dispose of provincial property.[12]

(iii) *Municipal Institutions: Section 92(8)*

Under s. 92(8), the provinces have the power to create legal entities known as municipalities to manage municipal affairs. Municipal powers are limited to those delegated by the province and the province can only delegate to the municipalities those powers which fall within the s. 92 provincial heads of power.[13] For example, the province can delegate authority to a municipality to issue licences only if their issuance is within the provincial scope of authority under s. 92(9). The municipality can then only exercise its powers within the boundaries of that delegation.[14]

---

[7] (1887), 12 App. Cas. 575 (P.C.).

[8] Hogg, *supra*, note 1 at 605.

[9] *R. v. Air Canada*, [1980] 2 S.C.R. 303 at 316.

[10] See also: J.E. Magnet, "The Constitutional Distribution of Taxation Powers" (1978) 10 Ottawa L. Rev. 473; *Atlantic Smoke Shops Ltd v. Conlon*, [1943] A.C. 550 (P.C.).

[11] Hogg, *supra*, note 4 at 28-5 to 28-6.

[12] Hogg, *supra*, note 1 at 570.

[13] *Yellowknife (City) v. Canada (Labour Relations Board)*, [1977] 2 S.C.R. 729.

[14] *Ross v. R.*, [1955] S.C.R. 430 at 435.

(iv) *Provincial Licensing: Section 92(9)*

Although s. 92(9) lists a variety of licences which the provincial governments can issue, this list is not exhaustive. The provinces may issue other licences not specifically mentioned if they pertain to matters which are local in nature and if the exercise of the legislative power is not in conflict with federal authority.

Under the s. 92(9) licensing power, conditions and penalties may be attached as necessary to regulate the licensed *field of business or conduct*.[15] Fees may be required as a condition of the licence in order to function as a general source of revenue or to offset the administrative costs of the regulation.[16]

(v) *Local Works and Undertakings: Section 92(10)*

The provinces have jurisdiction over all *intra*provincial works and undertakings, including all modes of transportation and communication.[17] Shiplines, if they operate completely within the province, are also included under this head of provincial power in spite of the federal power over navigation and shipping.[18]

However, a work or undertaking falls outside of provincial authority when it extends beyond provincial boundaries because it is then an *inter*provincial undertaking.[19]

(vi) *Solemnization of Marriage: Section 92(12)*

Although the federal government has power over marriage and divorce,[20] s. 92(12) gives the provinces jurisdiction over the solemnization or performance of the marriage ceremony. The provincial exercise of this power has typically involved legislation determining the *nature* of the marriage ceremony, such as the issuance of the licence[21] and legislation defining who is competent to perform the ceremony.[22]

---

[15] *Lieberman v. R.*, [1963] S.C.R. 643 at 650, 41 C.R. 325, [1964] 1 C.C.C. 82.

[16] *Prince Edward Island (Potato Marketing Board) v. H.B. Willis Inc.*, [1952] 2 S.C.R. 392 at 429-430.

[17] *Construction Montcalm Inc. v. Minimum Wage Commission*, [1979] 1 S.C.R. 754 at 774.

[18] *Canada (Conseil des relations ouvrières) v. Agence Maritime Inc.*, [1969] S.C.R. 851 at 859.

[19] In *Toronto (City) v. Bell Telephone Co.*, [1905] A.C. 52 (P.C.), a telephone company authorized to operate outside of a province was deemed to be under federal jurisdiction.

[20] See also s. 91(26).

[21] *Alspector v. Alspector*, [1957] O.R. 454 at 464 (C.A.).

[22] *Gilham v. Steele*, [1953] 2 D.L.R. 89 (Alta. S.C.).

(vii) *Property and Civil Rights Within the Province: Section 92(13)*

Section 92(13) is probably the most important head of provincial power. It is frequently relied upon by the provinces in arguing for the validity of provincial legislation.[23]

The wording of this section is so broad that almost any statute, with the possible exception of pure criminal law, could potentially fall within this area of provincial jurisdiction. Because of this section's wide scope, it has been frequently referred to as the provincial equivalent of the federal residual power found in the "peace, order and good government clause" ("POGG clause").[24]

Jurisdiction over "property" allows the provinces to legislate with regards to anything capable of ownership, including real property, personal property and intellectual property.[25] "Civil rights" includes those rights arising out of contract,[26] torts and debtor/creditor situations.[27] "Civil rights", in this context, is used to refer to proprietary civil rights and not to civil liberties such as freedom of expression.[28] It should also be noted that the power under s. 92(13) extends only to property and rights "within the province"; provincial attempts to legislate in a manner affecting extraprovincial property and civil rights would be *ultra vires* the province.[29]

Section 92(13) has a wide ambit, and it is not surprising that federal legislation may often have an effect on property and civil rights even though the main goal of the federal legislation may be a legitimate area of federal jurisdiction.[30]

Some areas that would normally fall within s. 92(13) have been carved out in s. 91 as federal powers by specific enumerated heads, such as banking (s. 91(15)) or trade and commerce (s. 91(2)). On the other hand, areas that would normally be within s. 92(13), and which have national dimensions, have been interpreted by the courts as being within federal jurisdiction through the POGG clause.[31] Due to the potential for overlap, the scope of s. 92(13) has been repeatedly subject to judicial consideration.

---

[23] J.E. Magnet, *Constitutional Law of Canada*, 4th ed. (Yvon Blais, 1989), vol. 1 at 427.

[24] Lysyk also argues that s. 92(13) and s. 92(16) are often read together by the Supreme Court of Canada: K. Lysyk, "Constitutional Reform and the Introductory Clause of Section 91: Residual and Emergency Law-Making Authority" (1979) 57 Can. Bar Rev. 531.

[25] See, however, ss. 91(22) and (23) which give Parliament jurisdiction over patents and copyrights.

[26] *Citizens Insurance Co. v. Parsons* (1881), 9 App. Cas. 96 (P.C.).

[27] Magnet, *supra*, note 23 at 423.

[28] Hogg, *supra*, note 1 at 455-456.

[29] Magnet, *supra*, note 23 at 423 and W.H. McConnell, *Commentary on the British North America Act* (MacMillan, 1977).

[30] *Canada (Attorney General) v. Ontario (Attorney General)*, [1937] A.C. 326 (P.C.) [the "*Labour Conventions* case"].

[31] *Munro v. Canada (National Capital Commission)*, [1966] S.C.R. 663.

(viii) *Administration of Justice in the Province: Section 92(14)*

While the provinces have authority over the administration of justice as well as civil procedure in the provinces, legislation must not impinge on the federal powers over criminal law and procedure. However, there will be a natural and acceptable overlap between the respective federal and provincial authorities.[32] The provincial Attorney General is responsible for the constitution and maintenance of the civil and criminal court system, police, criminal investigations and prosecutions and corrections.[33] This provision also authorizes the provinces to police and prosecute federal criminal offences[34] and includes the establishment of courts of criminal jurisdiction. Although the provinces may in some circumstances make general inquiries into crime, they may not go so far as to encroach on federal prosecutions.[35]

(ix) *Penal Sanctions: Section 92(15)*

The provinces can enact penal sanctions to enforce provincial laws as long as the provincial law is clearly within one of the provincial heads of jurisdiction.[36]

(x) *Matters of a Local Nature: Section 92(16)*

Together with property and civil rights in the province, this section is one of the most important heads of provincial power. It is a prerequisite to all provincial heads of power that the matter be local or private and wholly within the province.[37] However, matters not specifically falling under any other enumerated provincial powers which are of a local and private nature, will also be caught by this section. When legislation can be characterized as being of a local or private nature, those who assert that it comes under s. 91 have the burden of proving so.[38]

---

[32] *Di Iorio v. Montreal Jail*, [1978] 1 S.C.R. 152, 35 C.R.N.S. 57.

[33] *Ibid.* at 326 (S.C.R.).

[34] Hogg, *supra*, note 1 at 398.

[35] *Canada (Attorney General) v. Canadian National Transportation Ltd.*, [1983] 2 S.C.R. 206, 38 C.R. (3d) 97, 7 C.C.C. (3d) 449.

[36] Hogg, *supra*, note 1 at 395; *Prince Edward Island (Provincial Secretary) v. Egan*, [1941] S.C.R. 396, 76 C.C.C. 227.

[37] *Canada (Attorney General) v. Dupond*, (*sub nom. Canada (Attorney General) v. Montreal (City)*), [1978] 2 S.C.R. 770 at 792.

[38] *Ibid.* at 793.

Some examples of matters of a local or private nature are "people in distress" such as abused children,[39] and the control of agricultural or industrial production.[40] Products imported from another province, as long as they are consumed within the targeted province, fall within the provincial regulatory power of this section.[41] Passing legislation in an attempt to prevent conditions amenable to the development of crime, rather than punishment of criminal acts, is also regarded as a local or private matter.[42]

Section 92(16), which acts like a provincial "catch-all" power, is the final item in the enumerations under s. 92. By contrast, the federal catch-all power is contained in the opening words of s. 91.[43] Section 92(16) assumes that matters of a local or private nature which are not already enumerated in s. 92 do still fall within provincial competence, excluding subjects which may be of national concern. This permits the provinces, for example, to assume power over new technology. All other new matters fall within the jurisdiction of the federal Parliament.[44]

2. The Provincial Executive Powers

(a) How the Provincial Executive is Established and Organized

Provincial executive power is governed by the Constitution and by convention.

The provinces, in effect, are states within a state and the structure of provincial institutions is similar to that of the federal government. The respective provincial legislatures are generally controlled by their provincial executive. In ss. 58 to 68, the formal provincial executive is established. It is composed of the Lieutenant Governor and an Executive Council.

However, unlike the Governor General at the federal level, the office of Lieutenant Governor in the provinces is provided for in the *Constitution Act, 1867* in ss. 58, 59 and 60. The Lieutenant Governor has the powers of the Governor General, but at the provincial level, by virtue of s. 90. Under s. 58, the federal government has the power to appoint each province's Lieutenant Governor. This person is the representative of the Crown in the province, possessing all the prerogative powers of the

---

[39] *Ontario (Attorney General) v. Scott,* [1956] S.C.R. 137 at 147, 114 C.C.C. 224.

[40] *Reference re Agricultural Products Marketing Act (Canada),* [1978] 2 S.C.R. 1198 at 1293.

[41] *Quebec (Attorney General) v. Kellogg's Co.,* [1978] 2 S.C.R. 211 at 226.

[42] *McNeil v. Nova Scotia (Board of Censors),* [1978] 2 S.C.R. 662, 44 C.C.C. (2d) 316 at 693 (S.C.R.).

[43] Lysyk, *supra,* note 24.

[44] *Ontario (Attorney General) v. Canada (Attorney General),* [1896] A.C. 348 (P.C.) [the "*Local Prohibition case*"].

Monarch and any powers set out in the *Constitution Act, 1867*.[45]

(b) Structure of the Formal Executive

Under the heading "Provincial Constitutions" in Part V of the *Constitution Act, 1867*, the executive powers of the provinces are outlined. Sections 58 to 68 provide as follows:

- *Section 58:* The Governor General shall appoint a Lieutenant Governor for each province.
- *Section 59:* The Lieutenant Governor shall hold office at the pleasure of the Governor General but cannot be removed within five years of his/her appointment except for cause.
- *Sections 60 and 61:* The salary of the Lieutenant Governor shall be determined and provided for by Parliament and the Lieutenant Governor shall take an Oath of Allegiance before assuming the duties of his/her office.
- *Section 62:* The Act applies to the chief executive officer of a province whether or not he/she is called "Lieutenant Governor".
- *Section 63:* The Lieutenant Governor shall appoint persons to the Executive Councils of Ontario and Quebec.[46]
- *Section 64:* The executive authority in Nova Scotia and New Brunswick is continued until altered by these provinces.
- *Section 65:* Certain powers, authorities and functions are to be exercised by the Lieutenant Governors of Ontario and Quebec under the advice of their respective Executive Councils.
- *Section 66:* The Lieutenant Governor in Council is the Lieutenant Governor acting under the advice of the Executive Council.
- *Section 68:* Until the Executive Government of each province directs otherwise, the location of the seats of government in each province shall remain as they are.

(c) Structure of the Conventional Executive

The Lieutenant Governor, the Premier and the cabinet ministers compose the executive of the provincial government. The Lieutenant Governor is an appointed and largely figurehead position, similar to that of the

---

[45] *Maritime Bank (Liquidators of) v. New Brunswick (Receiver General)*, [1892] A.C. 437 (P.C.). See R.I. Cheffins & P.A. Johnson, *The Revised Canadian Constitution — Politics as Law* (McGraw-Hill Ryerson, 1986) at 83-84.

[46] See the Acts or terms of admitting other provinces for relevant provisions.

Governor General in the federal government. Although there are numerous powers accorded to him/her, the Canadian system of "responsible government" ensures that the Lieutenant Governor's powers are exercised under the direction of elected representatives. For example, the Lieutenant Governor has the power to appoint cabinet ministers but, by "convention" or common practice, he/she follows the advice of the Premier as to who shall be appointed.[47] Section 90 of the *Constitution Act, 1867* allows the Lieutenant Governor to withhold his/her assent from a provincial legislative bill.[48] However, this withholding of assent is not practised and, by convention, the Lieutenant Governor will assent to all government bills.[49]

The Premier is the effective head of the provincial government.[50] Generally, the provincial government is formed by the political party which has the majority of representatives elected to the legislative assembly. The leader of this majority party traditionally becomes the Premier of the province.[51]

The Premier generally wields full power over the Cabinet. Although the ministers are formally appointed by the Lieutenant Governor, the Premier has complete discretion in deciding who shall compose the Cabinet, which ministry they will lead and, if necessary, their dismissal.[52] These ministers are responsible for giving advice and for the administration of the provincial government.

The Cabinet, with the Premier at the helm, determines the parliamentary agenda for each session. The Cabinet is also responsible for the administration of departments of the bureaucracy and the ministers formulate and introduce their department's policies into Parliament. A vast majority of the bills passed in the legislature are "government bills" meaning that they have the Cabinet's approval and are introduced by a minister.[53]

It is important to remember that the legislative process is driven by the Cabinet and the Premier. This demonstrates the close relationship between the legislature and the executive. The Cabinet, composed of ministers who themselves are members of the legislature, is responsible to the other representatives in the provincial legislature.[54] It is required that these ministers, individually and collectively, obtain the confidence

---

[47] J.D. Whyte & W.R. Lederman, *Canadian Constitutional Law*, 2d ed. (Butterworths, 1977) at 9-3.

[48] Hogg, *supra*, note 4 at 5-17.

[49] Davis, *supra*, note 2 at 390.

[50] *Ibid.* at 389.

[51] G.G. Bell & A.D. Pascoe, *The Ontario Government, Structure and Functions* (Wall & Thompson, 1988) at 15.

[52] Whyte & Lederman, *supra*, note 47 at 9-9 to 9-10.

[53] Whyte & Lederman, *ibid.* at 9-8 to 9-9.

[54] Davis, *supra*, note 2 at 746.

of a majority of the legislature.[55] An integration of Cabinet and legislature occurs as a result.[56] There is no clear separation of powers between the executive and the legislature.

(i) *Who Governs the Governors?*

The provincial executive holds the real power of governing the province and its legislature. The executive is responsible for the formation and administration of policies.

The Lieutenant Governor appears, under the *Constitution Act, 1867*, to have control over the executive due to his/her constitutional power of appointment. However, because the Lieutenant Governor's role is largely that of a figurehead, it is the Premier who exercises governing control over the provincial government. The Premier selects the individuals to be appointed to the Cabinet and he/she is also the first minister of the Cabinet. Ultimately, provincial voters decide who will govern.

(ii) *Responsible Government*

The provincial executive is "responsible" to the elected provincial legislature. The Cabinet is composed of ministers who are elected members of the legislature and these cabinet ministers individually and collectively must have the "confidence" of a majority of the elected representatives.[57]

The concept of responsible government has prevailed in relation to the office of the Lieutenant Governor. Although granted many powers under the Constitution, the Lieutenant Governor is primarily a figurehead and is responsible to the Premier and other members of the executive. These elected representatives direct the exercise of these powers by the Lieutenant Governor.

(iii) *Political Parties*

Political parties play a valuable and vital role in provincial government just as they do at the federal level. A party may form the provincial government if it wins a majority of the seats in the provincial legislature. By tradition and custom, the leader of the winning political party becomes

---

[55] *Ibid.* at 389.
[56] *Ibid.* at 45.
[57] *Ibid.* at 389.

the Premier.[58] In the selection of cabinet ministers, the Premier will choose individuals elected to the legislative assembly who are from his/her caucus.

(iv) *Choosing a Party Leader*

Traditionally, a convention will be held by party members to elect an individual to represent the party as leader. The leader of the political party has incredible influence and power within the provincial government. If elected into the provincial legislature, each party leader will represent his/her respective party in the legislature. If this leader represents the party with the second highest number of seats elected to the legislature, the party leader assumes the role as leader of the official opposition party. If this leader represents the party which has the majority of seats, his/her party forms the government and he/she will become the Premier of the province.

(v) *The Premier*

As mentioned previously, the Premier is the leader of the governing political party in a province. The Premier's roles include first minister of the Cabinet, the primary spokesperson in the legislature and an elected representative of a particular constituency.[59] Other functions involved are the organization and the selection of cabinet ministers for appointment by the Lieutenant Governor, approval of the appointment of deputy ministers, approval of members of certain governing bodies, advice to the Lieutenant Governor and authorization of government policy.[60] Despite the Lieutenant Governor's constitutional powers, the Premier is the head of the provincial government.

(vi) *Choosing a Cabinet*

Once a political party wins the necessary election to form a government, a Cabinet or "executive council" will be chosen. The Lieutenant Governor is vested with the power to appoint individuals on the executive council. However, by convention, the Premier selects the members for Cabinet. These cabinet ministers are chosen from members of the legislature and members of the Premier's caucus.[61] Each member will be respon-

---

[58] Bell & Pascoe, *supra*, note 51 at 5.
[59] *Ibid.*
[60] *Ibid.*
[61] *Ibid.* at 15.

sible for the policies and administration of a particular department in addition to the department's functions and actions.

(d) The Main Executive Powers and Their Source

(i) *Powers Set Out in the Constitution Acts*

(A) *Constitution Act, 1867*

The power of the provincial executive government follows the distribution of the legislative powers granted to the provinces in s. 92 of the *Constitution Act, 1867.*

Under the *Constitution Act, 1867*, the Lieutenant Governor or first ministers are called upon to exercise executive functions. Some of the executive powers outlined in the *Constitution Act, 1867* include:

In relation to the provincial legislature:

- *Section 54:* The Lieutenant Governor recommends to the provincial legislature votes, resolutions, addresses or bills for the appropriation of any amount of revenue or for taxation purposes.
- *Section 55:* The Lieutenant Governor assents to or withholds assent or reserves for the Queen's "signification" bills passed by the provincial legislature. [Rarely used.]
- *Section 68:* The executive government of each province is vested with the power to direct a transfer of all the seats in their respective province to another location. [Rarely used.]

(B) *Constitution Act, 1982*

In relation to aboriginal matters:

- *Section 35.1:* The Premier has the right and duty to attend a constitutional conference to discuss any proposed amendments to Class 24 of s. 91 of the *Constitution Act, 1867* or to s. 25 of the *Constitution Act, 1982* which relate to aboriginal issues and rights.
- *Section 49:* The Premier may attend a constitutional conference to review the provisions of the amending formulae by 1997.

(ii) *Common Law Powers of the Executive*

The courts have legally recognized and expanded certain powers of the executive government in the provinces. In the landmark decision *Maritime Bank (Liquidators of) v. New Brunswick (Receiver General)*[62] (1892), the Court held that, although appointed by the federal government, the Lieutenant Governor was not an agent of the federal government. Instead, the Court declared that the Lieutenant Governor was a representative of the Queen and as a result, he/she enjoys the powers, privileges and immunities of the Crown.[63] This decision expanded the powers of the Lieutenant Governor and illustrates the independence from the federal government that the provincial executive enjoys.

The judiciary has also protected the powers and rights of the executive. Although the courts can interpret issues concerning executive jurisdiction and power, the policies and objectives of the executive are not subject to judicial review.[64] Consequently, these policies are not within the discretion of the judiciary.

(iii) *Powers Delegated by the Legislature to the Executive*

Due to the immense number of laws which are enacted in the provinces each year, the provincial legislatures have delegated powers to the executive councils.[65] The legislature can enact the outline of the legislative scheme and then delegate the power to the Lieutenant Governor in Council (*i.e.*, provincial cabinet) to make regulations on detailed matters.[66] The executive council acts as a legislative body in this context.

---

[62] *Supra*, note 45.
[63] Hogg, *supra*, note 1 at 217.
[64] Davis, *supra*, note 2 at 552.
[65] Hogg, *supra*, note 1 at 283.
[66] *Ibid.*

6

Shared Federal/ Provincial Powers

1. Concurrent Powers Specified in the Constitution

Sections 92A, 93, 94 and 95 of the *Constitution Act, 1867* explicitly confer concurrent powers on both the federal Parliament and the provincial legislatures. The rest of the powers are exclusive to either the Parliament (s. 91) or legislatures (s. 92). In Canada, exclusivity is the rule and concurrency the exception.[1] By contrast, in the United States and Australia concurrency is the rule and exclusivity the exception.

(a) Natural Resources: Section 92A

Section 92A, added by the *Constitution Act, 1982*, was designed to answer provincial concerns over their ability to effectively protect their natural resources against federal intrusion. It enables the provinces to control the export of their natural resources to the other provinces (although not to another country). This reverses the restrictions that the Supreme Court of Canada had imposed on the provinces in this regard.[2] Provincial power under s. 92A to regulate natural resources is far from unrestricted, and deals only with "primary production" as defined in the Sixth Schedule to the *Constitution Act, 1982*.[3]

Traditionally, the provinces have dealt with natural resources through other provisions.[4] For example, s. 109 of the *Constitution Act, 1867* deals with provincial ownership of some natural resources and s. 92(5) deals with the sale and management of public lands and timber. Most forestry lands are owned by the province and, as with public lands (s. 92(5)), they can be licensed, sold or otherwise managed similar to any privately

---

[1] P.W. Hogg, *Constitutional Law of Canada*, 3d ed. (Supp.) (Carswell, 1992), vol. 1 at 15-40.

[2] *Canadian Industrial Gas & Oil Ltd v. Saskatchewan*, [1978] 2 S.C.R. 545; *Central Canada Potash Co. v. Saskatchewan*, [1979] 1 S.C.R. 42.

[3] This was added by s. 51 of the *Constitution Act, 1982*. See J.D. Whyte & W.R. Lederman, *Canadian Constitutional Law*, 2d ed. (Butterworths, 1977) at 16-19.

[4] Whyte & Lederman, *ibid.* at 16-17.

owned property.[5] If forestry products are exported, the province retains its jurisdiction when legislating for conservation purposes (since this would be considered managing the resource), but price-fixing, for example, would be stretching the concept into federal jurisdiction.[6]

Section 92A confirmed and clarified provincial authority over the means of production and distribution of electrical energy (except nuclear power which remains under federal authority) that existed prior to the *Constitution Act, 1982.* Each province also has the power to enact laws in relation to the export of electrical energy to other parts of Canada, but not outside the country. This power runs concurrently with the federal authority over trade and commerce. Federal legislation has paramountcy in the case of a conflict.[7]

Section 92A has widened the scope of provincial taxation authority — it has vested within the provinces the ability to impose *indirect* taxes on certain types of non-renewable natural resources and grants them concurrent though subordinate jurisdiction with Parliament with respect to interprovincial trade in these resources.[8]

(b) Education: Section 93

Section 93 gives the provinces jurisdiction over the establishment and administration of schools and post-secondary institutions in the province,[9] with the exception of four restrictions enumerated within s. 93.

This section also protects the rights and privileges of school boards that existed at the time of Confederation. To determine whether a law in relation to school boards is valid, one must first determine the exact nature of the school board right, especially in regard to financing, grants and taxation.[10] One should note that the section protects religious and not linguistic rights.[11]

Narrow federal intervention is allowed only in relation to that which is "incidental to particular heads of federal powers" such as schools on Indian reserves (s. 91(24)) or on military bases (s. 91(7)).[12]

Section 93 imposes a number of limitations on the ability of provinces to legislate in regard to minority groups and denominational schools. One

---

[5] Hogg, *supra*, note 1 at 29-11.

[6] *Reference re Agricultural Products Marketing Act (Canada)*, [1978] 2 S.C.R. 1198.

[7] Hogg, *supra*, note 1 at 29-18.

[8] R.I. Cheffins & P.A. Johnson, *The Revised Canadian Constitution — Politics as Law* (McGraw-Hill Ryerson, 1986) at 121-122.

[9] P.W. Hogg, *Constitutional Law of Canada*, 2d ed. (Carswell, 1985) at 823.

[10] *Caldwell v. Stuart*, [1984] 2 S.C.R. 603, 15 D.L.R. (4th) 1 at 21-22.

[11] *Quebec (Attorney General) v. Blaikie*, [1981] 1 S.C.R. 312 at 324, 60 C.C.C. (2d) 524.

[12] Hogg, *supra*, note 9 at 823.

part of s. 93 states that the federal government may enact "remedial laws", but it has never been used.[13] Section 93 applies to Nova Scotia, New Brunswick, Quebec and Ontario, the four original provinces, and its application was extended to British Columbia and Prince Edward Island when they joined Confederation. However, slightly different versions of s. 93 were negotiated and enacted in statutes admitting the remaining provinces to the Confederation.[14]

(c) Pensions: Section 94A

This section provides for concurrent legislative powers with respect to old age pensions.[15] It acknowledges the jurisdiction of the provinces, but allows the federal government to make laws with regard to old age pensions and supplementary benefits.[16]

(d) Agriculture and Immigration: Section 95

Under s. 95, concurrent jurisdiction is accorded to the federal and provincial governments in dealing with agriculture and immigration. The province retains its authority when dealing with issues completely within the province; the federal government assumes authority when an issue concerns more than one province.[17]

An instance where provincial legislation exceeded its jurisdiction was the case of *Saskatchewan (Attorney General) v. Canada (Attorney General)*.[18] The provincial government introduced a statute concerned with interest (a federal power) that eased the mortgage burden on farmers as a crop failure loomed — the legislation was *ultra vires* the province as it dealt in "pith and substance" with the federal power of "interest". The benefits of this legislation were economic in nature and, therefore, only indirectly related to agriculture.

---

[13] *Ibid.* at 824.
[14] *Ibid.*
[15] Cheffins & Johnson, *supra*, note 8 at 122.
[16] Hogg, *supra*, note 9 at 337.
[17] F. Varcoe, *The Constitution of Canada* (Carswell, 1965) at 172.
[18] [1949] A.C. 110 (P.C.).

2. Natural Fields of Overlap

There is, in practice, a substantial area of "concurrency" in Canada, even with respect to topics covered by the two exclusive lists of powers in ss. 91 and 92. This results from two doctrines. First, under the double aspect doctrine, a matter may have a double aspect. This means that from one perspective the matter may come within the federal list, and from another perspective, within the provincial list.

The incidental effect doctrine also leads to "concurrency". If the pith and substance of a law comes within the list of the legislative body that enacted it, then the law is valid and it is no objection to the law that it also incidentally regulates a matter within the list of the other level of government.

(a) Criminal Law

Section 91(27) of the *Constitution Act, 1867* confers on the federal Parliament the power to make laws in relation to criminal law.[19] However, s. 92(14) gives the provinces the power to police and prosecute offences under the *Criminal Code*. Therefore, the criminal law is not as centralized as other fields of federal legislative power, where federal administration normally follows federal enactment.[20]

(b) Shared Cost Programs

The federal and provincial governments may share the cost of a program within a particular province.[21] These programs amount to a conditional grant whereby the federal government transfers funds to the provincial governments on the condition that the latter use the money for certain programs such as health care. It thus appears that federal conditional grants amount in substance to federal dictation of provincial spending priorities.[22] However, changes have been made towards greater provincial autonomy whereby fiscal penalties would not be imposed if a province chose not to participate in a particular program.[23]

---

[19] Hogg, *supra*, note 1 at 18-2.

[20] *Ibid.*

[21] Hogg, *supra*, note 9 at 120.

[22] *Ibid.* at 121.

[23] An example is the federal contribution to post-secondary education, hospital insurance and medicare which changed from cash to a combination of cash and tax points in 1977. This eliminated the federal leverage over the provinces to withhold cash, a federal sanction traditionally used against provinces that would not comply.

(c) Courts

Pursuant to s. 92(14), the provinces have the power to make laws in relation to "the administration of justice in the province." This power includes courts of criminal and civil jurisdiction, and naturally the provinces overlap into the federal criminal law area under s. 91(27). However, the provincial power does not include criminal procedure since this is provided for under s. 91(27).[24]

(d) Property

Section 92(13) of the *Constitution Act, 1867* gives power over property and civil rights to the provinces. However, the POGG clause in the preamble to s. 91 could encompass matters which would otherwise come within s. 92(13) if the matter attained a national dimension so as to bring it within the federal sphere.[25]

(e) Navigation and Shipping

Section 91(10) of the *Constitution Act, 1867* confers on the federal Parliament jurisdiction over "navigation and shipping" while s. 92(10)(*a*) gives the provinces power over "lines of steam or other ships" and to "canals".[26] If the court is dealing with an interprovincial or international undertaking, it is under federal control. If the undertaking is intraprovincial, then it will be under provincial jurisdiction.[27]

3. Common Law Doctrines

(a) Doctrine of Paramountcy

Where two governments enact inconsistent or conflicting statutes, the later statute is deemed to have repealed the earlier one to the extent of the inconsistency.[28] Where there is a conflict between the statutes of the federal Parliament and a provincial legislature, the courts have adopted the rule of "federal paramountcy" which states that the federal law prevails.[29]

---

[24] Hogg, *supra*, note 9 at 133.
[25] *Ibid*. at 455.
[26] *Ibid*. at 494.
[27] *Ibid*.
[28] *Ibid*. at 353.
[29] *Ibid*. at 354.

(b) Pith and Substance

Many statutes have one feature or aspect which comes within a provincial head of power and another which comes within a federal head of power.[30] For example, a law prohibiting careless driving has a criminal aspect, which is federal, and a highway regulation aspect, which is provincial. The courts make a judgment as to which is the most important feature of the law and characterize the law by that primary feature.[31] The dominant feature is referred to as the "pith and substance" of the law.

(c) Effect

Since the "pith and substance" doctrine enables one level of government to enact laws which may incidentally affect matters outside its jurisdiction, the courts will also consider the effect of the statute, namely, how it changes the rights and liabilities of those who are subject to it.[32] For example, in the *Alberta Bank Taxation Reference*,[33] the Privy Council concluded that the statute should be characterized as banking rather than taxation after determining the proposed Alberta tax would have a severe impact on banks.

4. Delegation of Powers

The federal Parliament and any provincial legislature has the power to delegate to a subordinate body the power to make laws which are called "subordinate" or "delegated" legislation. The subordinate body could, for example, be a minister, a court, an administrative agency, a municipality, a university or a public corporation.[34] The amount of law created by delegated bodies greatly exceeds that enacted by the primary legislative bodies.

Federal inter-delegation allows the delegation of federal power to the provinces or of provincial power to the Dominion. Consequently, disputes will arise concerning the resulting disruption of the constitutional distribution of powers. The Supreme Court of Canada in the *Nova Scotia Inter-delegation* case[35] held that *legislative* inter-delegation was unconstitutional

---

[30] *Ibid.* at 314.
[31] *Ibid.*
[32] *Ibid.* at 320.
[33] *Reference re Alberta Legislation*, [1939] A.C. 117 (P.C.).
[34] Hogg, *supra*, note 9 at 284.
[35] *Nova Scotia (Attorney General) v. Canada (Attorney General)*, [1951] S.C.R. 31.

and can only be done by constitutional amendment. Professor Hogg believes the Supreme Court of Canada's decision may have been incorrect because a delegation of power does not divest the delegator of its power nor does it confer permanent power on the delegated body.[36]

The case of *Prince Edward Island (Potato Marketing Board) v. H.B. Willis Inc.*[37] provided a slightly different form of inter-delegation which was upheld by the Supreme Court of Canada. Here the court held that *administrative* inter-delegation was acceptable because the delegated body was not the provincial legislature but an administrative agency created by the provincial legislature. Therefore, although the federal Parliament cannot delegate power directly to the provincial legislature, the federal Parliament could, if it chose, "adopt as its own" a provincial agency and authorize it to exercise federal powers.[38]

---

[36] Hogg, *supra*, note 9 at 297.

[37] [1952] 2 S.C.R. 392.

[38] Hogg, *supra*, note 9 at 299.

7

Territorial Government in the Northwest Territories and Yukon

1. Introduction

Territorial government has been an important stage in the growth and development of government throughout Canada's history. The Constitution Acts, however, say almost nothing about territorial government. Until recently, the literature on the Constitution has largely ignored the territories. The territorial level of government is an oddity in a federal state that divides exclusive powers between the federal government and the provinces. Territorial legislatures do not have exclusive powers. As a matter of constitutional law, Parliament has ultimate authority over all matters in the territories. Parliament has simply delegated governmental responsibilities to institutions in the territories which have been established directly by, or under the authority of, federal statutes.

2. Terminology

At present, there are two distinct territories in Canada: the Yukon and the Northwest Territories. Despite its plural form, the Northwest "Territories" is a single jurisdiction. On April 1, 1999, the Northwest Territories will be divided by a roughly north/south boundary to form two separate territories. The eastern territory will be called Nunavut.[1] The western territory will continue to be called the Northwest Territories until such time as Parliament amends the current *Northwest Territories Act*[2] ("NWT Act").

---

[1] See the *Nunavut Act*, S.C. 1993, c. 28 [to come into force April 1, 1999 or earlier by order of the Governor in Council].

[2] R.S.C. 1985, c. N-27. As of the date of printing of this volume, a body called the Constitutional Development Steering Committee, comprising representatives of the diverse political interests in the western region, has been studying options for a new territorial Constitution for the western territory to replace the current *NWT Act*. Recommendations will be made to the federal government on a new territorial Constitution, including a name for the new western territory.

Terminology in the *NWT Act* and *Yukon Act*[3] differs in some respects from that used in relation to provinces in the *Constitution Act, 1867*. The major differences are as follows:

1. The chief executive officer of a province is a Lieutenant Governor, but in a territory the term is "Commissioner".[4]
2. The "legislature" of a province consists of the appointed Lieutenant Governor and the elected "legislative assembly". It is the legislature which is assigned authority to make "laws" under s. 92. By contrast, the elected body in the territorial Acts is called a "council" rather than a legislative assembly. The Commissioner and council acting together are called the "Commissioner in Council" rather than a legislature, and this body is assigned authority to make "ordinances" rather than laws.

The difference in terminology is attributable to the difference in constitutional status between provinces and territories, and to the delegated nature of territorial government. In practice, the words "Council", "Commissioner in Council" and "ordinance" have all but disappeared from use.[5] The *Nunavut Act*[6] is a modernized version of the *NWT Act* and *Yukon Act*. While it continues to use the word "Commissioner", it has adopted the terminology of "legislative assembly", "legislature", and "laws". For the most part, this Chapter examines the *NWT Act* and *Yukon Act*.

---

[3] R.S.C. 1985, c. Y-2.

[4] The *NWT Act* and *Yukon Act* give the Commissioner all the executive powers of the Lieutenant Governor which presided over the territories prior to 1905: see s. 6 of the Acts. There are differences in the method of appointment, however, and it is doubtful the Commissioners are Lieutenant Governors for purposes of ss. 58-68 of the *Constitution Act, 1867*, although the federal *Interpretation Act*, R.S.C. 1985, I-21, does define "Lieutenant Governor", for the purposes of federal legislation, to include the Commissioners of the territories unless a contrary intention appears in the legislation in question.

[5] Enactments of the territorial legislative bodies use the terms "legislative assembly" in place of "council" and "laws" or "Acts" in place of "ordinances".

[6] Above, note 1.

NUNAVUT TERRITORY

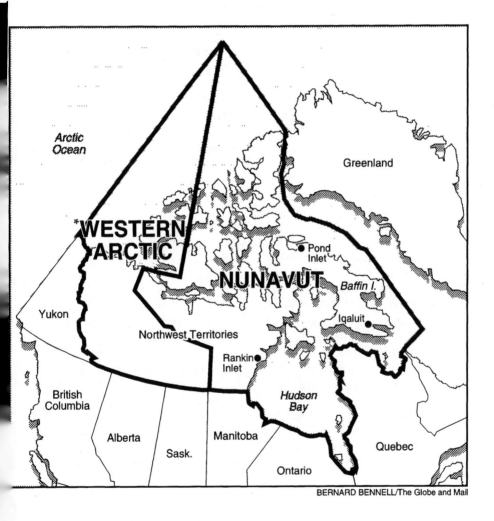

BERNARD BENNELL/The Globe and Mail

---

* This western area will continue to be called "Northwest Territories" as provided for in the *Northwest Territories Act*, R.S.C. 1985, c. N-27, until such time as that Act is amended or replaced.

3. Federal Jurisdiction Over the Territories

In 1864 and 1866, when the Fathers of Confederation were drafting resolutions that would lead to a union of British North American colonies, they included in Article 2 of the resolutions a provision for the eventual admission to the union of British Columbia, Prince Edward Island and the North-Western Territories. There is some geographical uncertainty as to exactly what tracts of land this entailed at the time. Section 146 of the *Constitution Act, 1867* was the legal rendering of Article 2 when the resolutions were drafted up in statute form for passage by the United Kingdom Parliament in 1867. It provided, among other things, that at the request of the Canadian Parliament, the Queen could "admit Rupert's Land and the North-Western Territory, or either of them, into the Union by Order in Council." Rupert's Land was a vast trading area comprising the drainage basin of Hudson Bay and James Bay which had been granted by Royal Charter to the Hudson Bay Company in 1670. Under this Royal Charter, the Company had held control and governance of these lands until they were sold back to the British Crown in 1869 for purposes of transfer to Canada.

In 1870, the *Rupert's Land and North-Western Territory Order*, which is now part of the Constitution of Canada,[7] transferred these lands from Britain to Canada. In 1880, the remainder of British possessions and territories adjacent to Canada were transferred to Canada by a second Order in Council. The lands covered by this transfer included the Arctic islands and parts of the Yukon.[8] Therefore, by 1880 the Northwest Territories comprised all of the present-day Northwest Territories, Yukon, Alberta, and Saskatchewan, and most of the lands in what are now Manitoba, Ontario and Quebec.[9]

In 1869, before the territories were transferred to Canada, the Canadian Parliament enacted the *Temporary Government of Rupert's Land Act* to provide for a rudimentary form of government in this vast region. In 1870, immediately after the transfer, the Canadian Parliament created Manitoba, at that time a tiny province centered on the present-day city of Winnipeg.[10] The motivation for creating Manitoba had come from the efforts of the Métis leader, Louis Riel; however, this enactment raised doubts as to the Canadian Parliament's constitutional authority for creating new provinces. To dispel any further doubts, the British Parliament passed the *Constitution Act, 1871* to make it clear that the Canadian Parlia-

---

[7] See Item 3 of the Schedule to the *Constitution Act, 1982*.

[8] See the *Adjacent Territories Order*, July 31, 1880 [Item 8 of the Schedule to the *Constitution Act, 1982*].

[9] See N. Nicholson, *The Boundaries of the Canadian Confederation* (MacMillan, 1979).

[10] See the *Manitoba Act, 1870* (Can.), 33 Vict., c. 3.

ment could create new provinces in the territories and had exclusive authority to provide for the "administration, peace, order, and good government of any territory not for the time being included in any province."[11]

The *Constitution Act, 1871* is the constitutional source of authority for the Acts which Parliament has passed to provide for government in the territories. The three main Acts are the *NWT Act, Yukon Act* and the *Nunavut Act*.[12] These Acts establish legislative bodies for the territories and delegate to them a range of powers which closely follows provincial legislative powers assigned by s. 92 of the *Constitution Act, 1867*.

4. Territorial Constitutions

The *NWT Act, Yukon Act*[13] and *Nunavut Act* are the principal documents of the territorial constitutions. However, they are not part of the "Constitution of Canada" as that phrase is defined by s. 52(2) of the *Constitution Act, 1982*; that is, the territorial constitutions are not entrenched and can be amended directly or indirectly by ordinary Acts of Parliament without invoking any of the formal amending formulae contained in the *Constitution Act, 1982*.

In form and content, the *NWT Act* and *Yukon Act* are virtually identical. The *Nunavut Act* is a modernized version of these Acts which eliminates some provisions which are unusual to find in a constitution, such as the provisions dealing with reindeer, intoxicants, mentally disordered persons and neglected children.[14] Also eliminated from the *Nunavut Act* are the provisions found in both the *NWT Act* and *Yukon Act* which say that every person who contravenes the Act is guilty of an offence and liable to fine or imprisonment.[15]

Parliament's power to amend or even repeal the territorial constitutions appears at first glance to be unfettered; however, s. 3 of the *Charter of Rights and Freedoms* guarantees certain democratic rights to Canadian citizens. Section 3 says that every citizen has a right to vote in an election of members of a "legislative assembly" and to be qualified for membership therein. Section 30 of the Charter makes it clear that the expression

---

[11] See ss. 2 and 4, respectively, of the *Constitution Act, 1871* (U.K.), 34-35 Vict., c. 28.

[12] Most provisions of this Act are not yet in force. The new territory of Nunavut is intended to come into being on April 1, 1999.

[13] See *The Yukon's Constitutional Foundations* (Northern Directories, 1991) a two volume set: S. Smyth, *The Yukon Chronology*, vol. 1; K. Cameron & G. Gomme, *A Compendium of Documents Relating to the Constitutional Development of the Yukon Territory*, vol. 2.

[14] See, for example, ss. 45-56.

[15] Section 60 of the *NWT Act*.

"legislative assembly" includes "the appropriate legislative authority" of the Yukon Territory and Northwest Territories. Also, s. 32(1)(*a*) of the Charter indicates that Parliament and the government of Canada are bound to apply Charter principles in respect of all their dealings in relation to the Yukon Territory and Northwest Territories.[16]

Modern aboriginal land claims agreements can now be seen as an integral part of the territorial constitutions. The agreements recognize and affirm a wide range of rights in relation to lands and resources, including management of these matters. The agreements create "institutions of public government" and various administrative bodies which have protection under the Constitution of Canada as a result of s. 35 of the *Constitution Act, 1982*. The provisions of these modern day treaties in many cases are paramount in situations where a federal or territorial law is in conflict with the aboriginal land claim agreement. The more recent agreements, some of which are still under negotiation, contain provisions that contemplate the establishment of aboriginal self-government arrangements.

5. Territorial Representation in Parliament

Like the provinces, territories can return representatives to the House of Commons and Senate. The *Constitution Act, 1886* (U.K.)[17] clarified the Canadian Parliament's power to provide for representation of territories in the House of Commons and Senate. However, given the sparse population of the territories, the constitutional rules which allocate seats to territories are distinct from the rules prescribing representation for the provinces. The most recent provisions are contained in the *Constitution Act (No. 1), 1975*[18] which amends s. 51(2) of the *Constitution Act, 1867* to provide for a fixed number of seats for each territory. The Yukon is allocated one member in the House of Commons and the Northwest Territories is allocated two members. Therefore, territories are not subject to the distribution rules set out for provinces in s. 51(1). In addition, territories are not subject to the "proportionate representation rule" in s. 52 which says that the number of members in the House of Commons may be increased from time to time provided the proportionate representation of the provinces is not disturbed. The *Constitution Act (No. 2), 1975*[19] provides for one senator from each of the two existing territories.[20]

---

[16] Note that no amendments have yet been made to the Constitution Acts to account for the creation of Nunavut Territory in 1999. For example, there are direct references to the Yukon Territory and Northwest Territories, but not to Nunavut Territory, in ss. 30 and 32 of the Charter, and elsewhere in the Constitution Acts.

[17] 49-50 Vict., c. 35.

[18] S.C. 1974-75-76, c. 28.

[19] S.C. 1974-75-76, c. 53.

[20] No provision has yet been made for the representation of Nunavut Territory in the Senate. See, *supra*, notes 16 and 17.

6. Powers of Territories

(a) Territorial Legislative Powers

While the *Constitution Act, 1871* gives Parliament exclusive authority over the administration, peace, order, and good government of the territories, Parliament has delegated the responsibility for governing the territories to the two existing territorial governments under the *NWT Act* and *Yukon Act*. As related above, on April 1, 1999, the Northwest Territories will become two separate jurisdictions each with its own territorial legislative assembly and government. In effect, Parliament is revoking its delegation of authority to the Legislative Assembly of the Northwest Territories in respect of the eastern Northwest Territories and delegating it instead to a newly created Nunavut legislature.

Section 16 of the *NWT Act*[21] says:

> The Commissioner in Council may, subject to this Act and any other Act of Parliament, make ordinances for the government of the Territories in relation to the following classes of subjects: [22 enumerated heads of power follow].

The classes of subjects delegated to the territories are patterned on s. 92 of the *Constitution Act, 1867*. Four omissions from the territorial list of powers are noteworthy:

1. Provinces have power to amend their own constitutions;[22] territorial legislative assemblies have no such power.
2. Sections 109 and 92(5) give provinces ownership and legislative authority, respectively, in relation to provincial public lands and the natural resources associated with them. By comparison, most public lands in the territories are owned by the federal Crown[23] and are under exclusive federal legislative authority. A small percentage of the surface of public lands are under the administration and legislative con-

---

[21] The corresponding provision in the *Yukon Act* is s. 17.

[22] This provincial power was originally in s. 92(1) of the *Constitution Act, 1867*, but is now found in s. 45 of the *Constitution Act, 1982*.

[23] See, for example: s. 44(1) of the *NWT Act*. Aboriginal treaties and modern land claims agreements have recognized aboriginal ownership of large tracts of land in the territories. See, for example: Treaty 8 (1899); Treaty 11 (1921); Western Arctic Claims Agreement with the Inuvialuit (1984); Gwich'in Land Claim Agreement (1992); Tungavik Federation of Nunavut Comprehensive Claim Agreement (1993); Sahtu Dene and Métis Comprehensive Claim Agreement (1993); Teslin Tlingit Council Claim Agreement (1993); First Nation of Nacho Nyak Dun Claim Agreement (1993); Champagne and Aishinik First Nations Claims Agreement (1993); and Vuntut Gwich'in First Nation Claim Agreement (1993).

trol of the territorial governments, and they have the beneficial use and revenues from these lands.[24]

3. Provincial jurisdiction in respect of natural resources in the provinces, including electricity, non-renewable and forest resources, was clarified and added to in 1982 by a constitutional amendment.[25] No similar powers were given to territories.[26]

4. Under s. 92(3) of the *Constitution Act, 1867*, provinces can legislate for "the borrowing of money on the sole credit of the province." The comparable provisions in the territorial Constitutions[27] only empower the territories to legislate for borrowing or lending or investing surplus territorial moneys and stipulate that no money may be borrowed without the approval of the federal Cabinet.

One notable addition to the territorial constitutions not found in provincial constitutions, with the exception of New Brunswick,[28] are provisions which "entrench" in the federal Acts territorial legislation providing for official languages in the territory. While the language legislation was originally passed by the territorial legislature, amendments to the *Yukon Act*[29] and *NWT Act* prevent these legislatures from amending these statutes without the concurrence of Parliament. The exception is territorial amendments which enhance the rights or services relating to official territorial languages. In the case of the Northwest Territories, for example, English and French and six aboriginal languages are the official languages of the territory.

The powers enumerated in s. 16 of the *NWT Act* and s. 17 of the *Yukon Act* are in some cases more specific than the powers assigned to the provinces by s. 92 of the *Constitution Act, 1867*. Some powers mentioned in the territorial list of powers in the *NWT Act* (and the *Yukon Act*) which are *not* specifically mentioned in the provincial list are:

1. elections of members of the council (legislative assembly) and controverted elections (s. 16(*c*));

2. issuing of licences or permits to scientists and explorers and the prescription of conditions for these licences (s. 16(*k*));

---

[24] See, for example, ss. 16(*n*.1), 44(1) and 44.1 in the *NWT Act*.

[25] See s. 92A of the *Constitution Act, 1867*.

[26] In 1986, the Northwest Territories was devolved legislative authority over forest resources and fire suppression by orders in council under s. 16(*v*) of the *NWT Act* which allows the Governor in Council to "designate" other matters as being under the legislative authority of the territories. Some provisions in these orders in council were based on s. 92A.

[27] See *NWT Act*, s. 20 and *Yukon Act*, s. 21.

[28] See s. 16(2) of the *Canadian Charter of Rights and Freedoms*.

[29] See, for example, the *Yukon Act*, Part II.1, ss. 46.1 and 46.2, enacted R.S.C. 1985 (4th Supp.), c. 31, s. 99.

3. levying tax on furs to be taken from the territories (s. 16(*l*));
4. preservation of game in the territories (s. 16(*m*));
5. closing up, varying, opening, establishing, building or management and control of roads, streets, lanes or trails on public lands (s. 16(*o*)); and
6. the expenditure of money for territorial purposes (s. 16(*s*); see by comparison s. 126 of the *Constitution Act, 1867*) [section references are to the *NWT Act*].

Some territorial powers are similar but not identical to the wording of provincial powers in s. 92. In this category are powers over:

1. direct taxation for territorial, municipal or local purposes (s. 16(*a*));
2. licensing of any business, trade, calling, industry, employment or occupation in order to raise a revenue for territorial, municipal or local purposes (s. 16(*e*));
3. incorporation of companies with territorial objects, including tramways and street railway companies but excluding railway, steamship, air transport, canal, telegraph, telephone or irrigation companies (s. 16(*f*));
4. establishing prisons, jails and lockups, the matters affecting employees, and all matters relating to prisoners including their employment outside as well as within a prison (s. 16(*j*));
5. education (s. 16(*n*)); and
6. hospitals (s. 16(*q*)) [section references are to the *NWT Act*].

The *NWT Act* and *Yukon Act* permit the federal Cabinet to disallow any provision or Act of a territory at any time within one year after its passage.[30] As with disallowance provisions in relation to provinces,[31] conventions have emerged which limit this power in practice.

Section 21(1) of the *NWT Act* and a corresponding provision in the *Yukon Act* require all territorial legislation to be transmitted to the Governor in Council, within 30 days of passage, and to be laid before Parliament. This provision is a vestige from a period when laws enacted by the territories had to be sent to Ottawa in order for the federal government to declare them in force. In the case of *Pokiak v. Steen*,[32] the Northwest Territories Supreme Court decided that this provision was directory, not mandatory, and did not affect the validity of a territorial statute which had not been laid before Parliament in the required time.

---

[30] See *NWT Act*, s. 21(2) and *Yukon Act*, s. 22(2).
[31] See ss. 56 and 90 of the *Constitution Act, 1867*.
[32] [1988] N.W.T.R. 272 (S.C.).

(b) Interpretation of Powers

An important interpretative provision is contained in s. 17 of the *NWT Act* and s. 18 of the *Yukon Act*. It says that none of the territorial heads of power shall be construed as giving the territories greater powers than a province with respect to any class of subjects assigned to the provinces by the *Constitution Act, 1867*.

In addition, the provisions granting legislative powers to the territories are qualified by the opening words of ss. 16 (*NWT Act*) and 17 (*Yukon Act*) which say that territorial enactments are "subject to this Act and any other Act of Parliament." In other words, unlike provinces, territories cannot exclusively make laws in relation to classes of subjects assigned to them.

There is not as much case law interpreting territorial heads of power as there is interpreting provincial and federal heads of power. In the case of *Yellowknife (City) v. Canada (Labour Relations Board)*,[33] the Supreme Court of Canada said that the scope of Parliament's authority in respect of a territory is not restricted by a territory's legislative authority in the same way as federal powers are restricted by a province's legislative powers.

Parliament can delegate to the territories legislative powers which provinces do not possess. In the case of *R. v. Davies*,[34] the Yukon Supreme Court said that the traditional concept of division of powers between federal and provincial legislatures has no relevance in determining whether or not legislation is within the legislative competence of a territory. Parliament's ability to delegate powers to a territory is neither dependent upon nor limited by the traditional division of powers found in ss. 91 and 92 of the *Constitution Act, 1867*.[35]

(c) Territorial Executive Powers

The original *Northwest Territories Act, 1875* provided for a Lieutenant Governor as the chief executive officer of the territory. Under the current *NWT Act*, *Yukon Act* and *Nunavut Act*, however, the chief executive officer is called the Commissioner. There is no mention of an executive council in the *NWT Act* or *Yukon Act*; however, s. 11 of the *Nunavut Act* does provide for an executive council.

While the title "Commissioner" is not necessarily determinative of the powers and role of the office, the Acts indicate important distinctions between territorial Commissioners and provincial Lieutenant Governors.

---

[33] [1977] 2 S.C.R. 729.
[34] [1990] N.W.T.R. 394 (Y.T. S.C.).
[35] See also *Manitoba (Attorney General) v. Canadian Pacific Railway*, [1958] S.C.R. 744 at 767-768.

Section 4 of the *NWT Act*, for example, says that the Commissioner shall administer the government under instructions given from time to time by the Governor in Council or the Minister of Indian Affairs and Northern Development.[36] The fact that a federal minister alone can instruct the Commissioner is somewhat unusual in a modern democracy, but since the late 1970s, conventions have emerged which have rendered this reporting relationship less important. However, instructions which have operational relevance for territories do occasionally still issue to the Commissioners.

For example, in the case of the Northwest Territories, a formal executive council was not instituted until 1975. This was also the first year that all members of the legislative assembly were elected.[37] By contrast, the Yukon legislative assembly has been chosen by election since 1909.[38] The establishment of territorial executive councils, or "executive committees" as they were originally called, was done by the federal Minister of Indian Affairs and Northern Development simply writing a letter to each of the Commissioners. These letters of instruction advised each Commissioner to appoint executive members nominated by the legislative assembly, and to chair executive council sessions. The Commissioner stepped down as chairman of the executive council in the Yukon in 1978, and in 1985 in the Northwest Territories, again on instructions contained in letters from the federal minister.

In the case of *St. Jean v. R.*,[39] the Yukon Supreme Court said that in some ways the Commissioner acts like a federal civil servant and, in his/her administrative capacity, takes instructions from the Governor in Council or the Minister of Indian Affairs and Northern Development. However, this administrative function must be distinguished from his/her legislative function.

The manner of selecting members to the executive council in the Yukon differs from the Northwest Territories. In the Yukon, candidates for election to the legislative assembly run as members of political parties. As a result, the leader of the party which forms the government selects his/her cabinet from among elected party members. However, in the Northwest Territories, all candidates for election run as independents. The members of the legislative assembly, at the first session after an election, elect from among themselves a leader and seven members to act as ministers on the

---

[36] The corresponding section in the *Yukon Act* is s. 4. Unlike in the *NWT Act* and *Yukon Act*, s. 6 of the *Nunavut Act* requires that the instructions be in writing and that they be made available to the executive council and laid before the legislative assembly.

[37] Prior to 1975, the federal government still appointed members to sit in the legislative assembly of the Northwest Territories.

[38] See, for a description of the Yukon legislative assembly, P.L. Michael, "The Yukon, Parliamentary Tradition in a Small Legislature" in G. Levy & G. White, eds., *Provincial and Territorial Legislatures in Canada* (University of Toronto Press, 1989) at 189-206.

[39] [1987] N.W.T.R. 118, 2 Y.R. 116 (Y.T. S.C.).

executive council. The leader of the executive council does not, therefore, choose the cabinet, but does assign the portfolios of the individual ministers.[40]

7. Aboriginal Claims and Self-Government

One cannot examine territorial government in Canada without taking into account the aboriginal and treaty rights protected by s. 35 of the *Constitution Act, 1982*. Most of the geographical area of the two territories is or has been under claim by aboriginal peoples. Constitutionally protected land claims agreements within the meaning of s. 35(3) of the *Constitution Act, 1982* have been concluded with the Inuit, Inuvialuit, Gwich'in, Sahtu Dene and Métis, and are in progress with other aboriginal peoples in the western Northwest Territories and Yukon First Nations. In addition, some treaty peoples are negotiating the fulfillment of Treaties 8 and 11 which were signed in 1899 and 1921, respectively.

The expression "land claims agreements" is a misnomer because these agreements transcend simple land issues. The details of each claim are too complex to examine here; however, it is clear that these modern treaties will have significant implications for the institutional, administrative, political and constitutional future of the territories. Already claims agreements have created "institutions of public government" which appear to be independent of either federal or territorial governments, and which appear to have a higher constitutional status than the institutions created by the *NWT Act* or *Yukon Act*. These institutions of public government are noteworthy because they guarantee the participation of aboriginal representatives in decision-making on a wide range of resource management and environmental bodies.

Some claims agreements also make provision for the negotiation of aboriginal self-government agreements. Aboriginal self-government is examined in the next Chapter.

In summary, territorial government has recently been undergoing rapid and fundamental change, particularly since the late 1970s. Significant changes are still to be expected. Implementing the division of the Northwest Territories alone will result in new approaches to government. The new Nunavut territorial government will commence its work in the midst of implementation of the Inuit aboriginal claims agreement which was ratified by Parliament in the summer of 1993. In the western region of the Northwest Territories, efforts are underway among aboriginal and non-aboriginal interest groups to negotiate and draft the terms of a new Con-

---

[40] See K. O'Keefe, "Northwest Territories, Accommodating the Future" in Levy & White, *supra*, note 38 at 207-220.

stitution for the western territory prior to 1999. If agreement can be reached on a new Constitution in the western region, and if the federal government accepts the model, Parliament would presumably repeal the existing *Northwest Territories Act* and replace it with the new arrangement.

In the Yukon, a comprehensive aboriginal claim agreement is very close with 14 Yukon First Nations, including provisions for aboriginal self-government arrangements. In the Yukon, and in the Northwest Territories, the aboriginal self-government issue will probably be the most challenging aspect of territorial constitution writing in the years ahead, particularly if current efforts to merge "public" government and aboriginal self-government continue.

8

Rights of Aboriginal Peoples of Canada

1. Introduction

A Royal Commission on Aboriginal Peoples described aboriginal rights this way:

> The doctrine of Aboriginal rights is not a modern innovation, invented by courts to remedy injustices perpetrated in the past. It is one of the most ancient and enduring doctrines of Canadian law. It is reflected in the numerous treaties of peace and friendship concluded in the seventeenth and eighteenth centuries between Aboriginal peoples and the French and British Crowns, in the Royal Proclamation of 1763 and other instruments of the same period, in the treaties signed in Ontario, the West, and the North-West during the late nineteenth and early twentieth centuries, in the many statutes dealing with Aboriginal matters from the earliest times, and not least in a series of judicial decisions extending over nearly two centuries.[1]

2. Definition

It is commonly acknowledged that "there is . . . no generally accepted definition of aboriginal rights."[2] The history of legal relations between various aboriginal groups and the British and Canadian governments must be analyzed on a case-by-case basis. Similarly, the legal rights of aboriginal peoples vary from jurisdiction to jurisdiction, and even within a single jurisdiction. Many aboriginal peoples live on reserves; others live in urban settings. Some signed pre-Confederation treaties. Others signed the numbered post-Confederation treaties. Some have now signed modern treaties called "comprehensive land claims agreements". Others never entered treaties at all. Some treaties were not fulfilled by governments according to their terms. Some are of questionable validity. Treaties on the prairies were altered by the Natural Resource Transfer Agreements

---

[1] Royal Commission on Aboriginal Peoples, *Partners in Confederation, Aboriginal Peoples, Self-Government, and the Constitution* (Canada Communication Group, 1993) at 9-10.

[2] P.W. Hogg, *Constitutional Law of Canada*, 3d ed. (Carswell, 1992) at 680.

and their accompanying constitutional amendments in 1930. Some modern treaties establish new boards and agencies called "institutions of public government" which ensure significant aboriginal participation in the decision-making processes connected with management of natural resources. Some modern treaties also make provision for negotiation of aboriginal self-government agreements.

3. Three Sets of Constitutional Provisions

There are three main sets of provisions in the Constitution which pertain directly to aboriginal peoples. Each set has a different function:

1. Section 91(24) of the *Constitution Act, 1867* assigns to Parliament exclusive legislation authority over "Indians, and Lands reserved for the Indians."[3]
2. Section 25 of the *Canadian Charter of Rights and Freedoms* shields "aboriginal, treaty or other rights or freedoms" of aboriginal peoples from erosion by the general guarantees of other individual or collective rights contained in the Charter.
3. Sections 35 and 35.1 of the *Constitution Act, 1982*, which recognize and affirm "existing" aboriginal and treaty rights, define who the aboriginal peoples are, guarantee these rights to male and female aboriginal persons equally, and provide government commitments not to change the three parts of the Constitution dealing directly with aboriginal peoples unless there has first been a constitutional conference to discuss the proposed amendments.

Constitutional issues relating to aboriginal peoples reached a turning point in 1982 with the inclusion in the *Constitution Act, 1982* of the set of provisions entitled "Rights of the Aboriginal Peoples of Canada". These provisions are contained in Part II of the Act and are distinct from the *Charter of Rights and Freedoms*. The main provision is s. 35 which recognizes and affirms the existing aboriginal and treaty rights of the aboriginal peoples.[4] Section 35(2) defines aboriginal peoples as including Indians, Inuit and Métis.

---

[3] See Chapter 4 for a discussion of this provision.
[4] For the story of the patriation process that led to the *Constitution Act, 1982*, see D. Milne, *The Canadian Constitution* (James Lorimer & Co., 1993).

4. Constitutional Conferences on Aboriginal Issues

There were uncertainties about the proper interpretation to be given to these provisions from the outset. This was indicated by s. 37 of the *Constitution Act, 1982*, which required a constitutional conference to be held within one year of Part II coming into force, namely by April 17, 1983. The purpose of the conference was "the identification and definition of the rights of those peoples to be included in the Constitution of Canada." This conference was held on March 15 to 16, 1983, and led to some relatively minor constitutional amendments on June 21, 1984.[5] These were the first amendments made under the new amending formulae.

The first constitutional conference revealed the complexity of aboriginal constitutional issues, and one of the amendments made in 1984 provided for two additional conferences.[6] In addition, a third conference was agreed to in a political accord signed in 1983. Representatives of four national aboriginal organizations and the two territorial governments participated in discussions with the Prime Minister and Premiers at these three constitutional conferences. By 1987, the central theme for debate had become recognition in the Constitution of an inherent aboriginal right of self-government. Some parties to the discussions argued that the wording of s. 35 already recognized a right of self-government. No agreement was reached by the end of the third conference as to whether such a right already existed in s. 35(1), or whether the Constitution should be amended to clarify any such right and provide for its fulfillment.[7]

Aboriginal self-government received national attention again in 1992 during the constitutional reform talks which gave rise to the agreement commonly known as the "Charlottetown Accord". The Charlottetown Accord contained the most sweeping and ambitious set of constitutional reforms since the Federation began in 1867, among them significant matters relating to rights of aboriginal peoples. In this agreement, four national aboriginal organizations and the federal, provincial and teritorial governments all agreed to amend the Constitution to include a straight forward recognition of the inherent aboriginal right of self-government. Also agreed to was a more complex series of amendments related to putting self-government and treaty rights into practice. Accompanying these proposed amendments were political accords containing political commitments relating to financing self-government among other things. On October 26,

---

[5] See the *1983 Constitutional Accord on Aboriginal Rights* and the *Constitution Amendment Proclamation, 1983*, SI/84-102, reproduced in Appendix 2 in D. Milne, *ibid.*

[6] This requirement appeared as s. 37.1 in the *Constitution Act, 1982*, but was repealed on April 18, 1987 by the operation of s. 54.1 of that Act.

[7] For a detailed account of the constitutional conferences on aboriginal issues, see B. Schwartz, *First Principles, Second Thoughts: Aboriginal Peoples, Constitutional Reform and Canadian Statecraft* (Institute for Research on Public Policy, 1986).

1992, two referenda were held, one in Quebec and the other covering the rest of Canada, to determine the attitude of Canadians to this reform package. The package failed to receive approval in several provinces and therefore was abandoned.

5. Existing Rights

An immediate issue which arises from the wording of s. 35 is whether or not a right existed as of 1982 when the protection clause was entrenched in the Constitution. Over the years, aboriginal and treaty rights were restricted by the accumulated effects of federal or provincial legislation. The Supreme Court of Canada has now clearly stated that s. 35 did not entrench these restrictions to the detriment of the rights mentioned in the section.[8] As long as some vestige of the right was in existence in 1982, it received constitutional protection.

The intention of Parliament to restrict aboriginal or treaty rights must be clearly expressed and justified. With aboriginal and treaty rights now protected by the Constitution, it is doubtful that Parliament would be able to extinguish these rights through ordinary legislation, although it could have done so prior to 1982. The *Sparrow* case[9] sets out the tests which any such federal legislation must meet when it seeks to restrict aboriginal rights or treaty rights. The *Sioui* case[10] says that the consent of the aboriginal peoples affected is required before a treaty can be altered. The *Horseman* case[11] says that a constitutional amendment is effective to alter treaty rights.[12]

6. A Closer Look at Section 35 and the *Sparrow* Case

(a) Background

R. v. Sparrow is the leading case on the interpretation of s. 35. The Supreme Court of Canada emphasized the importance of context and the need for a case-by-case approach to s. 35(1). The case involved a member of the Musqueam band charged with using a drift net which violated the

---

[8] See *R. v. Guerin*, [1984] 2 S.C.R. 335; *R. v. Sparrow*, [1990] 1 S.C.R. 1075, 56 C.C.C. (3d) 263.

[9] *Sparrow, ibid.*

[10] *Sioui v. Quebec (Attorney General), (sub nom. R. v. Sioui)* [1990] 1 S.C.R. 1025, 56 C.C.C. (3d) 225.

[11] *R. v. Horseman*, [1990] 1 S.C.R. 901, 55 C.C.C. (3d) 353.

[12] For a more in depth discussion of these matters, see Hogg, *supra*, note 2 at 663-695.

band's Indian food fishing licence under regulations of the *Fisheries Act*. The right to fish in this case was not connected with a reserve or waters adjacent to a reserve. There was evidence to show that the general area had been fished by the ancestors of the Musqueam people for at least 1500 years, and even though the evidence for the period 1867 to 1961 was scanty, the Supreme Court of Canada upheld the British Columbia Court of Appeal conclusion that the existence of an aboriginal right was not really "in serious dispute". The Crown argued that the aboriginal right to fish had been extinguished by the accumulated effect of regulations since 1867. Progressively greater restrictions had been placed on Indian fishing after 1871.[13]

(b) Court's Analysis of Aboriginal and Treaty Rights

Aboriginal rights stem from the traditional use and occupancy of lands by aboriginal peoples. Long before the arrival of Europeans, aboriginal peoples were living in organized societies with laws and traditions. Aboriginal rights in relation to certain activities have been recognized since earliest contact and have continued up to the present day.

"Treaty rights" are those described in treaties or modern land claims agreements with aboriginal peoples. Treaties in many cases recognized only a limited set of rights, or extinguished aboriginal rights in exchange for those rights described in the treaty documents. The *Nowegijick* case[14] said that treaties should be liberally construed by the courts and doubtful expressions resolved in favour of the aboriginal peoples.[15]

(c) Meaning of the Word "Existing"

The Supreme Court of Canada said that s. 35(1) applied to rights that were in existence in 1982 but did not revive rights extinguished prior to 1982. The phrase "existing aboriginal rights" must be interpreted flexibly so as to permit their evolution over time. The rights protected are not simply the rights in the form they existed in the distant past. Nor is an existing right under s. 35(1) read so as to incorporate the specific manner in which it was regulated before 1982. In other words, the right is not merely what is left over after all regulations are taken into account. The

---

[13] As it turned out, the Supreme Court did not rule on the charge against Mr. Sparrow, but sent it back to trial. The charge was subsequently dropped by the Crown.

[14] *Nowegijick v. R.*, [1983] 1 S.C.R. 29 at 36.

[15] Some modern treaties have included express provisions to remove any presumptions in favour of the aboriginal party.

Crown's intention to extinguish an aboriginal right has to be "clear and plain".

(d) Meaning of "Recognized and Affirmed"

The affirmation of aboriginal rights contained in s. 35(1) requires a "generous, liberal interpretation of the words in the constitutional provision." Although the Crown argued that any obligation to Indians, Métis and Inuit was merely political in nature, the court said that s. 35(1), at the least, provides a solid constitutional base upon which subsequent negotiations can take place. The Government of Canada has the responsibility to act in a fiduciary capacity with respect to aboriginal peoples.[16] Section 35(1) is a solemn commitment that must be given meaningful content. Aboriginal and treaty rights that are recognized and affirmed are not absolute. Federal legislative powers in respect of aboriginal peoples continue. However, in the exercise of these powers the federal government must honour its duty to aboriginal peoples. Therefore, laws that infringe aboriginal rights must be justified by government. Government will be held to a high standard of honourable dealing.

Federal legislation that affects the exercise of aboriginal rights will be valid if it satisfies the test for justifying interference with a right as set out in the *Sparrow* case. Regulation of rights must be according to a valid governmental objective. The extent of legislative or regulatory impacts will be scrutinized to ensure that they are consistent with recognition and affirmation of a right.

(e) The Legal Tests in *Sparrow*

There are three steps involved in analyzing a case under s. 35(1):

- *Step 1:* Is there an existing aboriginal or treaty right involved? The aboriginal party must establish that a particular aboriginal or treaty right claimed by he/she actually exists.
- *Step 2:* Has the aboriginal or treaty right been infringed? The aboriginal party must show, *prima facie*, that the legislation in question places an adverse restriction on the right. At this stage, the Court will examine questions such as:

---

[16] For a discussion of the fiduciary relationship see M.J. Bryant, "Crown-Aboriginal Relationships in Canada: The Phantom of Fiduciary Law" (1993) 27 U.B.C. L. Rev. 19; also see B. Slattery, "First Nations and the Constitution: A Question of Trust" (1992) 71 Can. Bar Rev. 261.

(a) What are the characteristics or incidents of the right? (The courts must be sensitive to the aboriginal perspective on the meaning of the right.)
(b) Is the limitation reasonable?
(c) Does the legislation impose undue hardship?
(d) Does the legislation deny the holders of the right their preferred means of exercising the right?

- *Step 3:* Is the legislation justified? The federal government has the onus of justifying its legislation where an adverse impact on a right is created. At this stage the courts will examine questions such as:

  (a) Is there a valid legislative objective such as conservation or public safety? There must be something more to the objective than mere "public interest".
  (b) The special trust relationship and responsibility of the federal government for aboriginal peoples must be the first consideration in determining whether the legislation is justified.
  (c) Has there been as little infringement as possible in order to effect the desired result of the legislation?
  (d) If expropriation occurs, has fair compensation been paid?
  (e) Has the aboriginal group been consulted?
  (f) In assessing justification, are there any other factors to be considered in the circumstances of the case?

These steps may not be easy to apply in any given case.

7. Provincial Powers in Relation to Aboriginal Peoples

The courts have established that, as a general rule, provincial laws apply to "Indians and lands reserved for the Indians".[17] There are, however, significant exceptions to this general principle.[18] In addition, the *Sparrow* case says that s. 35 affords aboriginal and treaty rights constitutional protection against provincial legislative power.

8. Aboriginal Self-Government

Aboriginal peoples were the original inhabitants of the lands that now comprise Canada. The numerous nations of aboriginal peoples governed

---

[17] Hogg, *supra*, note 2 at 671.
[18] See Hogg, *ibid.* at 671-679 for a discussion of the situations in which provincial laws do not apply.

identifiable territory according to their laws and traditions. French and British Monarchs entered treaties and military alliances with aboriginal nations. These facts have been recognized before the courts.[19]

Aboriginal issues have been studied in depth by the Royal Commission on Aboriginal Peoples which began in August 1991. The Commission issued an Interim Report in August 1993 entitled *Partners in Confederation, Aboriginal Peoples, Self-Government and the Constitution.* This Report concluded that s. 35 of the *Constitution Act, 1982* already recognized and affirmed the inherent aboriginal right of self-government.

The Report has revolutionary implications and is likely to frame the debate on this issue for years to come. The Report does not settle the issue conclusively because the Supreme Court of Canada has not ruled on the existence or non-existence of an inherent aboriginal right of self-government. To date, the federal government and some provincial and territorial governments have expressed agreement with the Report's main conclusion that s. 35 already recognizes and affirms an inherent aboriginal right of self-government. Some provinces have been more qualified in their support.

Some of the main observations and conclusions contained in the Report of the Royal Commission on Aboriginal Peoples (August 1993) include:

- The common laws and political systems of aboriginal nations are a source of law and authority in Canada.[20]
- Canadian courts have recognized a special body of aboriginal rights based on unwritten sources such as long-standing custom and practice.[21]
- Aboriginal rights include rights to land, rights to hunt and fish, special linguistic, cultural and religious rights, and rights held under customary systems of aboriginal law.[22]
- Early relations between indigenous americans and Europeans: By 1763, aboriginal-British relations were based on two principles: (i) aboriginal peoples were generally recognized as autonomous political units capable of holding treaty relations with the Crown; and (ii) aboriginal nations were entitled to the territories in their possession unless and until they ceded them away.[23]

---

[19] See, for example: *Calder v. British Columbia (Attorney General)*, [1973] S.C.R. 313; *Sparrow, supra,* note 8; *Sioui, supra,* note 10; Report of the Royal Commission on Aboriginal Peoples, *supra,* note 1.

[20] Royal Commission on Aboriginal Peoples, *ibid.* at 7.

[21] *Ibid.* at 8.

[22] *Ibid.* at 9.

[23] *Ibid.* at 13-14.

- Royal Proclamation of 1763: The Royal Proclamation of 1763[24] has been characterized by a judge of the Supreme Court of Canada as an Indian Bill of Rights and as having the force of an Act of Parliament: "It was a law which followed the flag as England assumed jurisdicition over newly-discovered or acquired lands or territories."[25]
- Portions of the Royal Proclamation of 1763 portray Indian nations as autonomous political units living under the Crown's protection and retaining their internal political authority and their territories.[26]
- Doctrine of aboriginal rights: The doctrine of Aboriginal rights is a body of law which defines the basic constitutional links between aboriginal peoples and the Crown, regulates the interactions between general Canadian legal and governmental systems and aboriginal laws, governmental institutions and territories.
- Aboriginal title is federal common law which means it is a body of unwritten law that is common to the whole of Canada and extends in principle to all jurisdicitions.[27]
- Process of Constitution building: The pact struck between Upper and Lower Canada, Nova Scotia, and New Brunswick which created Canada in 1867 included the treaties and other processes whereby aboriginal peoples were affiliated with the Crown and entered the Federation.
- Aboriginal nations did not lose their inherent rights when they entered into a confederal relationship with the Crown and they retained their ancient Constitutions so far as they were not inconsistent with the new relationship.
- The *Constitution Act, 1982*: Section 35 confirms and entrenches the status of aboriginal peoples as original partners in Confederation and their historically defined political units may include individuals of varied racial origins.
- Self-government as a constitutional right: An inherent right of self-government exists in Canadian law and is protected by s. 35(1) of the *Constitution Act, 1982* as one of the "exisiting aboriginal and treaty rights of the aboriginal peoples of Canada."
- The effect of the *Constitution Act, 1867* was to restructure existing levels of authority so that British, federal or provincial governments and aboriginal communities all had, in varying degrees, overlapping powers over matters affecting aboriginal peoples.

---

[24] Note the reference to the Royal Proclamation of 1763 in s. 25(*a*) of the *Canadian Charter of Rights and Freedoms*.

[25] Royal Commission on Aboriginal Peoples, *supra*, note 1 at 16.

[26] *Ibid.*

[27] *Ibid.* at 20; see also *Wewayakum Indian Band v. Canada*, [1989] 1 S.C.R. 322.

- Section 129 of the *Constitution Act, 1867* provides continuity whereby laws and powers existing before 1867 remained in force in the new Federation and federal legislation since 1867 has not deprived Indian peoples of all governmental authority.
- The Constitution recognizes and affirms governmental rights for Indians, Inuit and Métis.
- Nature and scope of the right: The right is inherent and does not derive from a grant in the written Constitution, nor a delegation from another level of government.
- Aboriginal governments have circumscribed rather than unlimited powers which are exerciseable only within the framework of the Federation.
- Aboriginal governments exercising their jurisdiction are not subject to federal or provincial override unless it can be justified on the basis of the tests in the *Sparrow* case.
- How the right may be implemented: Aboriginal self-governments could exercise jurisdiction over some matters immediately and on their own initiative. Core matters involving vital concerns of their communities are more clearly within the scope of aboriginal jurisdiction. Matters which have a major impact on other jurisdictions will require agreements to clarify the roles of governments.
- Outer limits of the right and interaction with federal and provincial governments: The aboriginal sphere of authority has the same scope as the federal head of power in s. 91(24) over "Indians, and Lands reserved for the Indians." Federal and aboriginal governments have concurrent powers in this sphere, with aboriginal paramountcy, unless the federal government can meet the justification test in the *Sparrow* case.
- *Canadian Charter of Rights and Freedoms*: The aboriginal *right* of self-government is shielded from Charter review by s. 25, but the individual members of aboriginal groups enjoy Charter rights in relations with their aboriginal governments.

The Report also contains observations and suggestions on implementing aboriginal self-government.[28] These matters will have to be worked out through negotiations and arrangements between aboriginal peoples and federal, provincial, territorial and perhaps municipal governments in the years ahead.

---

[28] *Supra*, note 1 at 41-48.

PART III

THE CHARTER

9

Charter of Rights and Freedoms — The Main Provisions

1. Introduction: Fundamental Rights and Freedoms Before the Charter

In order to fully understand the relevance of the Charter, it is necessary to be aware of the status of individual rights and freedoms prior to 1982. Before the entrenchment of the Charter, there were very few restrictions on the legislative power of Parliament and of the provincial legislatures.[1] There was virtually nothing to prevent either level of government from enacting discriminatory legislation or from violating fundamental rights and freedoms.

Some attempts were made by the courts to develop an "implied bill of rights". In the *Alberta Press* case,[2] Chief Justice Duff found that there were limitations on the power of government to infringe fundamental freedoms because such freedoms were necessary to the proper functioning of a responsible government. Although the doctrine received some support,[3] it never commanded a majority and was ultimately repudiated by the Supreme Court in 1978.[4]

The *Canadian Bill of Rights*[5] was enacted by the federal government in 1960. The *Bill of Rights* does not apply to the provincial governments which were unwilling to participate in its enactment. Furthermore, because the document is not constitutionally entrenched, it has no supremacy over other federal legislation. At best, the *Canadian Bill of Rights* has been used

---

[1] Prior to the Charter, judicial review primarily involved the courts determining whether a legislative enactment violated the federal/provincial divisions of powers. The only substantive restrictions on the federal and provincial governments were ss. 93 and 133 of the *Constitution Act, 1867*. Section 93 protected minority religion education rights and s. 133 protected bilingual language rights in the Parliament and in the legislatures.

[2] *Reference re Alberta Legislation*, [1938] 2 S.C.R. 100, affirmed [1939] A.C. 117 (P.C.).

[3] *Switzman v. Elbling*, [1957] S.C.R. 285, 117 C.C.C. 129.

[4] *Canada (Attorney General) v. Dupond, (sub nom. Canada (Attorney General) v. Montreal (City))* [1978] 2 S.C.R. 770.

[5] The *Canadian Bill of Rights*, R.S.C. 1985, App. III., is still a valid statute today.

by the courts as a guide for construing other statutes and has been given an extremely narrow judicial interpretation.[6]

The experience with the *Canadian Bill of Rights* made it clear that Canada needed a constitutionally entrenched guarantee of rights and freedoms, binding both the federal and provincial governments. The result was the entrenchment of the Charter. The *Canadian Charter of Rights and Freedoms* was proclaimed in force on April 17, 1982, and is contained within Part I of the *Constitution Act, 1982.* As a constitutionally entrenched document, it has supremacy over all other federal and provincial enactments.[7] The Charter does not regulate behaviour between private individuals but regulates government action, whether legislative, executive or administrative.[8] It is intended as an instrument for the protection of individuals from abuses of state power.[9]

(a) Significance of the Entrenchment of the Charter

The entrenchment of the *Charter of Rights and Freedoms* is more effective than the *Bill of Rights* because the former is part of the Constitution of Canada, whereas the latter is merely a statute.[10] In order to amend the Charter, rigorous constitutional amendment procedures must be followed, whereas the *Bill of Rights* could be repealed at any time by the federal Parliament because it is merely a statute. In addition, the Charter expressly overrides inconsistent statutes, whereas the *Bill of Rights* is not clear on this issue. Furthermore, the *Bill of Rights* applies only to the federal level of government, while the Charter applies to federal, provincial and territorial governments.

---

[6] The Supreme Court interpreted the *Canadian Bill of Rights* as merely declaratory of existing or "frozen" rights. See *Robertson v. R.*, [1963] S.C.R. 651, 41 C.R. 392, [1964] 1 C.C.C. 1 and *Canada (Attorney General) v. Lavell*, [1974] S.C.R. 1349, 23 C.R.N.S. 197. See also P. Russell, *Federalism and the Charter: Leading Constitutional Decisions* (Carleton University Press, 1990) at 347-349 and 359-364.

[7] See s. 52 of the Charter.

[8] See discussion re s. 32. See also *R.W.D.S.U., Local 580 v. Dolphin Delivery Ltd.*, [1986] 2 S.C.R. 573 at 598-599; *Blainey v. Ontario Hockey Assn.* (1986), 54 O.R. (2d) 513, 26 D.L.R. (4th) 728 (C.A.), leave to appeal to S.C.C. refused (1986), 58 O.R. (2d) 274 (headnote) (S.C.C.).

[9] See *Canada (Director of Investigation & Research, Combines Investigation Branch) v. Southam Inc.*, [1984] 2 S.C.R. 145 at 156, 41 C.R. (3d) 97, (sub nom. *Hunter v. Southam Inc.*) 14 C.C.C. (3d) 97 and *R. v. Edwards Books & Art Ltd.*, [1986] 2 S.C.R. 713 at 779, 55 C.R. (3d) 193, (sub nom. *R. v. Edward Books & Art Ltd.*; *R. v. Nortown Foods Ltd.*) 30 C.C.C. (3d) 385.

[10] P.W. Hogg, *Constitutional Law of Canada*, 2d ed. (Carswell, 1985) at 650-651.

(b) Courts' Expanded Power of Review

Before 1982, judicial review was largely confined to federalism issues. Since the entrenchment of the Charter, however, judicial review has expanded to include Charter grounds.[11] Charter cases seem to out-number federalism cases because the former are more policy-laden and Charter rights are expressed in vague terms.[12] It is inevitable that the judges will be influenced by their own social, economic and political values when giving meaning to the Charter provisions. This clearly gives the judiciary enormous power.

(c) Documents Relating to the Charter

(i) *Canadian Bill of Rights*

As previously discussed, the *Canadian Bill of Rights* is merely a statutory instrument which did not apply to the provinces and had little impact in protecting the rights it encompassed. The Charter of Rights is a more effective instrument at protecting civil liberties because of its entrenchment into the Constitution and its application to both the federal and provincial levels. The enactment of the Charter did not, however, repeal the *Bill of Rights*. Furthermore, there are two guarantees in the *Bill of Rights* that are not substantially replicated in the Charter.[13] Section 1(*a*) of the *Bill of Rights* protects property rights through a "due process" clause, and s. 2(*e*) guarantees the right to a fair hearing.[14] Therefore, these two provisions can still be relied upon notwithstanding the Charter.

(ii) *Human Rights Codes*

The provincial legislatures started enacting Human Rights Codes during the Second World War. The reason for this was to prohibit discrimination by landlords and employers on grounds such as race, national origin, colour, religion, sex or age.[15] The adoption of the Charter has not diminished the importance of these provincial Codes. This is largely because the Codes regulate the behaviour of private individuals and companies, as well as government bodies. As discussed above, the Charter applies

---

[11] *Ibid.* at 652.
[12] *Ibid.* at 653.
[13] *Ibid.* at 645.
[14] *Ibid.*
[15] *Ibid.* at 632.

only to restrict government action.[16] Furthermore, these Human Rights Codes are informal and less expensive than Charter adjudication.

(d) Process of Charter Adjudication

There are three types of applications that can be made under the Charter.[17] First, an application can be made pursuant to s. 24(1) which provides a remedy to a person whose rights or freedoms under the Charter have been infringed or denied. Second, a s. 24(2) application can be made to exclude evidence which was obtained in a manner that infringed or denied any rights or freedoms guaranteed by the Charter and which would bring the administration of justice into disrepute. Finally, s. 52(1) provides that the Constitution of Canada is the supreme law of the land and any law that is inconsistent with the provisions of the Constitution is of no force or effect. Therefore, courts are permitted to invalidate legislation that breaches provisions of the Act.

(e) Influence of American Bill of Rights

The American *Bill of Rights* had an important impact in the development of the Charter. Since the Charter's drafters adopted language similar to that found in the American *Bill of Rights*, the Canadian courts have been willing to give some consideration to American jurisprudence when interpreting the Charter. This is, however, done with appropriate caution because there are significant differences in the histories and governments of both countries. Furthermore, there are differences in the structural necessities of each Constitution. For example, the American *Bill of Rights* lacks an equivalent to the Charter's s. 1 limitation clause or s. 32 application clause.[18]

2. Doctrines Relating to the *Charter of Rights and Freedoms*

(a) Purposive Approach[19]

According to the Supreme Court of Canada, the *Canadian Charter of Rights and Freedoms* is a purposive document and must be interpreted

---

[16] *Ibid.* at 633.
[17] G.L. Gall, *The Canadian Legal System*, 2d ed. Carswell, 1983) at 62.
[18] Hogg, *supra*, note 10 at 661.
[19] See S.R. Peck, "An Analytical Framework for the Application of the Canadian Charter of Rights and Freedoms" (1987) 25 Osgoode Hall L.J. 1.

as such.[20] This means that each section of the Charter must be interpreted in light of its larger purpose and the interests which the section was designed to protect. In *R. v. Big M Drug Mart*,[21] Chief Justice Dickson discussed the manner in which the courts will determine the purpose of the particular right or freedom:

> [T]he purpose of the right or freedom in question is to be sought by reference to the character and the larger objects of the *Charter* itself, to the language chosen to articulate the specific right or freedom, to the historical origins of the concepts enshrined, and where applicable, to the meaning and purpose of the other specific rights and freedoms with which it is associated within the text of the *Charter*.[22]

A purposive approach to the Charter also calls for a generous interpretation rather than a legalistic one. The goal must be to fulfill the purpose of the section and secure the full benefit of the Charter's protection. At the same time, the Supreme Court has warned against overshooting the actual purpose of the right or freedom in question.[23]

(b) Contextualism

The factual context of each case is relevant in determining the purpose and comparative value of competing rights and freedoms. According to Justice Wilson in *Edmonton Journal*,

> a particular right or freedom may have a different value depending on the context. It may be, for example, that freedom of expression has greater value in a political context than it does in the context of disclosure of the details of a matrimonial dispute. The contextual approach attempts to bring into sharp relief the aspect of the right or freedom which is truly at stake in the case as well as the relevant aspects of any values in competition with it. . . . [T]he importance of the right or freedom must be assessed in context rather than in the abstract and its purpose must be ascertained in context.[24]

The use of this contextual approach was further expanded in *R. v. Keegstra*, where Chief Justice Dickson made clear that the factual context of the case must be considered in undertaking a s. 1 analysis.[25]

---

[20] *Southam Inc., supra*, note 9 at 156 (S.C.R.).
[21] [1985] 1 S.C.R. 295, 18 C.C.C. (3d) 385.
[22] *Ibid.* at 344 (S.C.R.).
[23] *Ibid.*
[24] *Edmonton Journal (The) v. Alberta (Attorney General)*, [1989] 2 S.C.R. 1326 at 1355-1356.
[25] [1990] 3 S.C.R. 697, 1 C.R. (4th) 129 at 163, 61 C.C.C. (3d) 1.

(c) Unconstitutional Purpose or Effect

Either the purpose or the effects of an impugned government action can violate a Charter right or freedom. In *Big M Drug Mart*, the Court found that the first step is to determine whether the legislation has a constitutionally valid purpose.[26]

In identifying the purpose of impugned government legislation and determining its validity, it is not possible to argue that the purpose of the legislation has shifted or been transformed over time by changing social conditions. "Purpose is a function of the intent of those who drafted and enacted the legislation at the time, and not of any shifting variable."[27] Even if there is a constitutional purpose, it is still possible for a litigant to argue that the government action is unconstitutional because of its effects.

3. Steps in Analyzing a Charter Problem[28]

(a) Does the Charter Apply?

(i) *Is the Conduct of the Alleged Infringer Restricted by the Charter?*

The Charter is not intended to limit or restrict the behaviour of private parties. By virtue of s. 32 and the Supreme Court decision in *McKinney*,[29] the Charter applies primarily to restrict the conduct of government actors. It should be noted that, although it is rarely done, it is possible for a government to override certain sections of the Charter through the use of the s. 33 "notwithstanding" provision.

(ii) *Is the Complainant Entitled to Claim the Protection of a Particular Charter Provision?*

Some Charter sections apply to every person in Canada, including corporate persons.[30] Other sections, however, are explicitly restricted to per-

---

[26] *Big M Drug Mart, supra,* note 21 at 334 (S.C.R.).

[27] *Ibid.* at 334-335.

[28] See discussion in *Ford c. Québec (Procureur général),* [1988] 2 S.C.R. 712 at 766 regarding the steps involved in a Charter analysis.

[29] *McKinney v. University of Guelph,* [1990] 3 S.C.R. 229.

[30] See *Big M Drug Mart, supra,* note 21 at 312 (S.C.R.) and *R. v. Wholesale Travel Group Inc.,* [1991] 3 S.C.R. 154 at 157-158, 8 C.R. (4th) 145, 67 C.C.C. (3d) 193, dealing with the issue of whether corporations are entitled to have their interests protected under the Charter.

sons who meet some particular criteria or requirement set out in the Charter section in question.[31]

(b) Has a Charter Provision Been Infringed?

The party seeking the Charter protection must prove a *prima facie* violation of a Charter right or freedom. The court will examine the purpose and/or the effect of an impugned statute or government conduct against the content of the Charter right or freedom. If there is no violation, the inquiry ends here.

(c) If There is an Infringment, is the Infringement Justified Under Section 1 of the Charter?

Once a *prima facie* violation has been established, the burden shifts to the party seeking to uphold the violation to prove on a balance of probabilities that the violation is reasonable and justifiable under s. 1.

4. Main Provisions of the Charter

(a) Guarantee and Limitation of Rights and Freedoms: Section 1[32]

Section 1 guarantees the rights and freedoms contained in the Charter "subject only to such reasonable limits prescribed by law as can be demonstrably justified in a free and democratic society." This section recognizes that rights and freedoms are not absolute. It also provides a starting point for discussions as to what limits on those rights and freedoms are reasonable and justified.[33]

Once a complainant has established that a Charter right or freedom has been violated, the onus shifts to the party seeking to uphold the viola-

---

[31] Some examples include the following: the right to vote under s. 3 applies only to Canadian citizens; the mobility rights of s. 6(1) apply only to Canadian citizens, while s. 6(2) applies to permanent residents as well as citizens; the rights under s. 10 arise only upon "arrest or detention"; the legal rights in s. 11 become effective only when a person has been "charged with an offence".

[32] For a general discussion of section 1 see: J.E. Magnet, *Constitutional Law of Canada: Cases, Notes and Materials* (Yvon Blais, 1989), vol. 2, "Note on the Operation of Section One" at 194-200; P.W. Hogg, "Section 1 Revisited" (1991) 1 N.J.C.L. 1; A. Lokan, "The Rise and Fall of Doctrine Under Section 1 of the *Charter*" (1992) 24 Ottawa L. Rev. 163.

[33] D. Gibson, *The Law of the Charter: General Principles* (Carswell, 1986) at 134.

tion to establish a s. 1 justification.[34] The following issues must be considered in the s. 1 analysis.

(i) *Is the Limitation of the Charter Right or Freedom "Prescribed by Law"?*

Any Charter violation which is not "prescribed by law" cannot be upheld under s. 1. In determining if a limit has been "prescribed by law", the question that must be addressed is whether the government action provides an "intelligible standard for the judiciary to work with", or whether it is so vague that it is impossible to apply.[35] Where there is no intelligible standard, and where the legislature has given a "plenary discretion", there can be no limit prescribed by law.

In assessing whether an act provides such an intelligible standard, the courts will give consideration to the manner in which the provision has been judicially interpreted. "If the judicial interpretation of an otherwise uncertain term provides an intelligible standard, the threshold test for s. 1 is met."[36]

(ii) *Is the Violation a "Reasonable Limit"?*

In *R. v. Oakes*,[37] the Supreme Court developed a test for determining whether a Charter violation is a reasonable limit under s. 1. Essentially, the party seeking to uphold the violation must establish that the infringing act or legislation seeks to address a pressing and substantial concern, and that the means used are proportionate to this goal. More specifically, the *Oakes* test can be stated as follows:

1. Does the impugned state action have an objective of pressing and substantial concern?
2. If so, is this objective proportional to the impugned measure?

---

[34] According to the Supreme Court in *Southam Inc., supra*, note 9 at 169 (S.C.R.), the onus of proof shifts to the party seeking to uphold the violation because of the language in s. 1.

[35] *Irwin Toy Ltd. v. Québec (Procureur général)*, [1989] 1 S.C.R. 927 at 983.

[36] For example, see *R. v. Butler*, [1992] 1 S.C.R. 452, 11 C.R. (4th) 137, 70 C.C.C. (3d) 129, where the Court held that the meaning of "undue" in the *Criminal Code* pornography provision provided an "intelligible standard" in light of the judicial interpretation of the word. See also *Canada v. Pharmaceutical Society (Nova Scotia)*, [1992] 2 S.C.R. 606, 15 C.R. (4th) 1, 74 C.C.C. (3d) 289, 93 D.L.R. (4th) 36 at 44-52.

[37] [1986] 1 S.C.R. 103, 50 C.R. (3d) 1, 24 C.C.C. (3d) 321.

a. Is it rationally connected to the objective?[38]
b. Does it impair the right or freedom as little as possible?[39]
c. Is there a proportionality between the objective and the effects of the measure which limits the right or freedom?[40]

Failure at any stage of the analysis will mean that the impugned government action cannot be upheld as a reasonable limit under s. 1.

In *Oakes*, the Court originally stated that this test must be stringently applied, with clear and cogent proof required at every stage of the analysis.[41] More recently, the standard of proof required under the *Oakes* test would appear to have become more flexible.[42] In fact, the Supreme Court has expressly stated that *Oakes* should be treated more as a guideline or analytical framework than as a rigid test with high evidentiary requirements.[43]

---

[38] The measure adopted must be carefully designed to achieve the pressing and substantial objective. The legislation must not be arbitrary, unfair or based on irrational considerations. See *Oakes, ibid.* at 139 (S.C.R.).

[39] The "minimal impairment" branch of the proportionality test has been the most difficult hurdle of the *Oakes* test. Under strict scrutiny standards, courts require the legislative provision to be carefully tailored to the objective such that no less intrusive alternative method was available. This standard has, however, been made less stringent in a number of recent cases which suggest a preference for a "reasonable basis" of scrutiny. For example, see *Edwards Books & Art, supra*, note 9.

[40] According to Wilson J. in *Lavigne v. O.P.S.E.U.*, [1991] 2 S.C.R. 211, 81 D.L.R. (4th) 545 at 612, application for re-hearing refused (1991), 4 O.R. (3d) xii (note) (S.C.C.), "[t]he point of this branch of the proportionality test is to ensure that laws which otherwise pass constitutional muster should not be struck down where the unconstitutional effects they produce are 'trivial' or 'insubstantial.'" See also *Butler, supra*, note 36 at 455-456 (S.C.R.) where the issue was worded as "[whether] the effects of the law do not so severely trench on a protected right that the legislative objective is outweighed by the infringement."

[41] See *Oakes, supra*, note 37 at 136 (S.C.R.).

[42] For example, see *Edwards Books & Art, supra*, note 9. See also Magnet, *supra*, note 32 at 195; P. Monahan & A. Petter, "Developments in Constitutional Law: The 1986-87 Term" (1988) 10 Supreme Court L.R. 61.

[43] See *Canada (Canadian Human Rights Commission) v. Taylor*, [1990] 3 S.C.R. 892, 75 D.L.R. (4th) 577 at 598. Dickson C.J.C. states that "the various categories of the *Oakes* approach to proportionality are simply intended to provide an analytical framework. The rigid compartmentalization of these categories is illogical . . . and no bright line separates one from the other."

(iii) *Can the Limit be "Demonstrably Justified in a Free and Democratic Society?"*

The words "free and democratic society" in s. 1 underlie the very purpose of the Charter and embody various fundamental beliefs and principles.[44] In assessing whether an impugned limitation can be "demonstrably justified in a free and democratic society", the courts may consider evidence of international community standards, the standards of other free and democratic countries and other Charter provisions such as ss. 15, 27 and 28.[45]

(b) Fundamental Freedoms: Section 2

Section 2 of the Charter states that everyone has the following fundamental freedoms:

(a) freedom of conscience and religion;
(b) freedom of thought, belief, opinion and expression, including freedom of the press and other media of communication;
(c) freedom of peaceful assembly; and
(d) freedom of association.

(i) *Freedom of Conscience and Religion: Section 2(a)*[46]

In *Big M Drug Mart*[47] and *Edwards Books & Art*,[48] the Supreme Court defined the purpose of the freedom of conscience and religion. The Court held that:

> The purpose of s. 2(a) is to ensure that society does not interfere with profoundly personal beliefs that govern one's perception of oneself, humankind, nature, and, in some cases, a higher or different order of being.[49]

---

[44] For example, the words "free and democratic" embody such principles as: respect for human dignity; commitment to social justice and equality; accommodation for a wide variety of beliefs; respect for cultural and group dignity; and faith in social and political institutions. See *Oakes, supra,* note 37 at 136 (S.C.R.).

[45] For example, see *Butler, supra,* note 34; *Keegstra, supra,* note 25; and *Taylor, supra,* note 43.

[46] See M. Brundrett, "Demythologizing Sunday Shopping: Sunday Retail Restriction and the Charter" (1992) 50 U.T. Fac. L. Rev. 1.

[47] *Supra,* note 21.

[48] *Supra,* note 9.

[49] *Ibid.* at 759 (S.C.R.).

[E]very individual [must] be free to hold and to manifest whatever beliefs and opinions his or her conscience dictates, provided *inter alia* only that such manifestations do not injure his or her neighbours or their parallel right to hold and manifest beliefs and opinions of their own.[50]

The content of s. 2(*a*) has been developed in light of this purpose. Freedom of religion under s. 2(*a*) has at least two aspects. First, there is a positive freedom to hold and manifest religious beliefs. If the purpose or effect of a statute is to prevent conduct that is integral to the practice of an individual's religion, s. 2(*a*) will have been violated.[51]

The second aspect of s. 2(*a*) is the freedom *from* coerced conformity to religious doctrine or practice. This "freedom from religion" is more limited than the positive freedom to engage in religious belief or practice.[52] According to the Supreme Court, s. 2(*a*) only protects an individual's freedom from religion in circumstances where the impugned government action was motivated by a religious purpose. It is not enough that the *effect* of the impugned action coerces religious conformity. In other words, the state cannot, *for a religious purpose*, coerce an individual to affirm a specific religious belief or to manifest a specific religious practice.[53]

It should also be noted that s. 2(*a*) not only protects religious freedom, but also protects an individual's freedom to hold and manifest conscientious beliefs which are not religiously motivated.[54]

(ii) *Freedom of Expression: Section 2(b)*

Freedom of expression has long been considered an essential element in the development of the social, educational and political foundations of Western society.[55] The Supreme Court has held that the purpose of this freedom is to ensure that thoughts and feelings may be conveyed in non-violent ways without fear of censure.[56] The *Irwin Toy* test outlines the basic approach which the courts will take in analyzing a claim under s. 2(*b*).[57] The test can be stated as follows.

---

[50] *Big M Drug Mart, supra*, note 21 at 346 (S.C.R.).

[51] *Edwards Books & Art, supra*, note 9.

[52] *Ibid.* at 760 (S.C.R.).

[53] *Big M Drug Mart, supra*, note 21 and *Edwards Books & Art, ibid.* at 790.

[54] *R. v. Morgentaler*, [1988] 1 S.C.R. 30 at 179, 62 C.R. (3d) 1, 37 C.C.C. (3d) 449.

[55] See *Edmonton Journal, supra*, note 24 at 1336. See also *Cherneskey v. Armadale Publishers Ltd.*, [1979] 1 S.C.R. 1067 at 1096, and K. Greenawalt, "Free Speech Justification" (1989) 89 Columbia L. Rev. 119.

[56] *Butler, supra*, note 36.

[57] *Irwin Toy, supra*, note 35 at 967-977.

(A) *Is the Activity an "Expression" that Falls Within the Meaning of Section 2(b)?*

- If the activity has expressive content, and it is in a protected form, it will be "expression" within the meaning of s. 2(*b*).
- *Content*: The activity will have expressive content if it conveys or attempts to convey meaning. Any expressive content will suffice — no expression will be excluded from the protection of s. 2(*b*) because of the nature of the meaning conveyed.[58]
- *Form*: Expression in a violent form is not protected.[59] However, threats of violence or expression which is analogous to violence are still protected under s. 2(*b*).[60]

(B) *Does the Government Action, in Purpose or Effect, Restrict Freedom of Expression?*

- *Purpose*: To determine the purpose of the impugned action, the courts will ask what was the mischief addressed by the government action. If the mischief being addressed is in the physical consequences of the expression, then its purpose is aimed only at the physical consequences and such a purpose will not violate s. 2(*b*). If the mischief is in the meaning being conveyed or its influence, then the purpose is to control or restrict expression. In this case, there is a *prima facie* violation of s. 2(*b*).
- *Effects:* Even if the purpose of the government action does not violate freedom of expression, its effects may still do so. If the effect is to restrict attempts to convey meaning and the meaning being restricted contributes to one of the three main values underlying freedom of expression, then s. 2(*b*) will be violated.[61] The values underlying this freedom have been identified as: (i) the pursuit of truth; (ii) political and social participation; and (iii) self-fulfillment and human flourishing.

---

[58] For example, s. 2(*b*) protects, among other forms of expression: commercial expression and advertising (*Ford, supra*, note 28, and *Rocket v. Royal College of Dental Surgeons (Ontario)*, [1990] 2 S.C.R. 232); freedom from coerced expression (*Slaight Communications v. Davidson*, [1989] 1 S.C.R. 1038); non-violent picketing (*Dolphin Delivery, supra*, note 8).

[59] *Dolphin Delivery, ibid.*, holding that non-violent picketing is "expression" within the meaning of s. 2(*b*). Violent picketing would be a form of expression excluded form the section.

[60] *Keegstra, supra*, note 25 and *Taylor, supra*, note 43. See generally: L.E. Weinrib, "Hate Promotion in a Free and Democratic Society: *R. v. Keegstra*" (1991) 36 McGill L.J. 1416; D. Bottos, "*Keegstra* and *Andrews*: A Commentary on Hate Propaganda and The Freedom of Expression" (1989) 27 Alta. L. Rev. 461.

[61] *Irwin Toy, supra*, note 35 at 976 (S.C.R.).

An interesting question arises under s. 2(*b*) in regard to the extent that the section will protect freedom of expression in a public place. In such circumstances, the freedom to express oneself in public must be balanced against the interests of government and of the citizenry as a whole. In *Committee for the Commonwealth of Canada v. Canada*,[62] the members of the divided Court suggested two possible approaches to this type of situation.

Chief Justice Lamer's "compatibility with function" approach, concurred with by Justices Sopinka and Cory, is connected to the form of the restricted activity. Under this approach, an individual will only be free to communicate in a public place if the form of expression is compatible with the principal function or intended purpose of the place.[63] If the form of the expression is inconsistent with this function, then such a form of expression falls outside the protection of s. 2(*b*).[64]

An alternative put forth by Justice McLachlin is related to the government purpose in imposing the forum restriction. Under this approach, to determine if the individual's freedom of expression in that public forum has been violated, the court would ask whether the government's purpose in imposing the forum restriction is to regulate the content of the expression or merely its consequences, regardless of its content.[65]

- *Content-Based Restriction*: If the restriction on forum is aimed at the content of the expression, there would be an infringement of s. 2(*b*).
- *Content-Neutral Restriction:* If the restriction on forum is merely aimed at avoiding the undesirable consequences of the expression, the claimant may establish a violation of s. 2(*b*) by showing that the expression *in that forum* is related to one of the purposes underlying the guarantee of free expression identified in *Irwin Toy*.[66]

---

[62] [1991] 1 S.C.R. 139, 77 D.L.R. (4th) 385, application for re-hearing refused (May 8, 1991), Doc. 20334 (S.C.C.). See also M. Kanter, "Balancing Rights Under S. 2(b) of the Charter: Case Comment on *Committee for the Commonwealth of Canada v. Canada*" (1992) 17 Queen's L.J. 489.

[63] *Committee for the Commonwealth of Canada, ibid.* at 395 (D.L.R.).

[64] *Ibid.* at 395-396.

[65] *Ibid.* at 456.

[66] The three main values or purposes underlying freedom of expression were outlined in *Irwin Toy, supra,* note 35 at 976. These values, as previously mentioned, are: (i) the pursuit of truth; (ii) political and social participation; and (iii) self-fulfillment and human flourishing.

(iii) *Freedom of Peaceable Assembly: Section 2(c)*

Setting the limits on freedom of peaceable assembly involves the balancing of this individual freedom with the need for public order.[67] For example, s. 2(c) has been held not to guarantee unlimited freedom of assembly to prison inmates.[68]

An analogy has sometimes been made between freedom of assembly and freedom of expression. Pre-Charter cases held that demonstrations were a form of collective action which did not pertain to freedom of speech. Under the Charter, however, non-violent picketing was ruled to be a form of expression which was entitled to protection under s. 2(b).[69]

(iv) *Freedom of Association: Section 2(d)*[70]

The purpose and scope of s. 2(d) has been primarily limited to the protection of the collective exercise of various individual freedoms. In the *Alberta Labour Reference*,[71] the Supreme Court held that freedom of association must at least include the following *individual* freedoms:

1. the freedom to establish, belong to and maintain an association;
2. the freedom to collectively exercise the constitutional rights and freedoms of an individual; and
3. the freedom to collectively exercise the lawful rights of the individual.

There is also support for the notion that s. 2(d) protects an individual's freedom from compelled association. For example, several members of the Supreme Court in *Lavigne* found that, while some degree of compelled association is unavoidable, s. 2(d) will be violated when an individual is compelled to contribute to causes which are beyond the immediate concerns of the bargaining unit to which he/she belongs. "When the association extends itself outside the realm of the common interest which

---

[67] K. Norman, "Freedom of Peaceful Assembly and Freedom of Association (Section 2(c) and (d))" in G. Beaudoin & E. Ratushny, eds., *The Canadian Charter of Rights and Freedoms*, 2d ed. (Carswell, 1989) at 227-228.

[68] *Butler v. R.* (1983), 5 C.C.C. (3d) 356 (Fed. T.D.).

[69] *Dupond, supra*, note 4; *Dolphin Delivery, supra*, note 8.

[70] See generally S. Renouf, " 'One More Battle to Fight': Trade Union Rights and Freedom of Association in Canada" (1989) 27 Alta. L. Rev. 226.

[71] *Reference re Public Service Employee Relations Act (Alberta)*, [1987] 15 C.R. 313, 51 Alta. L.R. (2d) 97.

justified its creation, it interferes with the individual's right to refrain from association."[72]

Freedom of association is not a collective freedom.[73] The Supreme Court has held freedom of association to be

> a freedom belonging to the individual and not to the group formed through its exercise. . . . [T]he group can exercise only the constitutional rights of its individual members on behalf of those members. If the right asserted is not found in the Charter for the individual, it cannot be implied for the group merely by the fact of association.[74]

Section 2(*d*) does not, therefore, protect the freedom to engage in an activity solely because that activity is essential to the meaningful existence of an association.[75] More specifically, s. 2(*d*) does not protect a right to strike[76] or a right to bargain collectively.[77]

(c) Democratic Rights: Sections 3, 4 and 5

Section 3 of the Charter constitutionally entrenches the right of every Canadian citizen to vote. According to the Supreme Court, the purpose of this section is to guarantee effective representation to all citizens.[78] The right to vote under s. 3 is not absolute and may be subject to reasonable restrictions such as requirements of mental capacity, age, residence or registration.[79] Section 3 has been held not to apply to municipal elections,[80] nor does it guarantee a right to vote in a referendum.[81]

Under s. 4, unless special circumstances exist, no House of Commons or Legislative Assembly is to continue for more than five years. Section

---

[72] *Lavigne, supra*, note 40 at 627 (D.L.R.). See also B. Etherington, "*Lavigne* v. *OPSEU*: Moving Toward or Away from a Freedom to Not Associate?" (1991) 23 Ottawa L. Rev. 533.

[73] *Alberta Labour Reference, supra*, note 71. See also *Lavigne, ibid*.

[74] *Alberta Labour Reference, ibid.* at 158-159 (Alta. L.R.).

[75] *Ibid.* at 167.

[76] *Ibid.* and *P.S.A.C.* v. *Canada*, [1987] 1 S.C.R. 424.

[77] See *P.I.P.S.* v. *Northwest Territories (Commissioner)*, [1990] 2 S.C.R. 367, 72 D.L.R. (4th) 1. See also the *Alberta Labour Reference, supra*, note 71 at 158 (Alta. L.R.).

[78] *Reference re Provincial Electoral Boundaries*, [1991] 2 S.C.R. 158. Note that s. 3 guarantees effective representation but not equality of voting power *per se*.

[79] *Scott* v. *British Columbia (Attorney General)* (1986), 29 D.L.R. (4th) 544 (B.C. S.C.). See also P.W. Hogg, *Constitutional Law of Canada*, 3d ed. (Supp.) (Carswell, 1992), vol. 2 at 42-2; G. Beaudoin, "Democratic Rights (Sections 3, 4 and 5)" in Beaudoin & Ratushny, *supra*, note 67 at 268.

[80] *Jones* v. *Ontario (Attorney General)* (1992), 89 D.L.R. (4th) 11 (Ont. C.A.).

[81] *Haig* v. *Canada (Chief Electoral Officer)*, [1993] 2 S.C.R. 995.

5 of the Charter further provides that Parliament and the legislatures must sit at least once each year.

(d) Mobility Rights: Section 6

(i) *Mobility Rights of Citizens: Section 6(1)*

Section 6(1) provides that "every citizen of Canada has the right to enter, remain in and leave Canada." This section imposes no positive duty on the government to assist Canadians stranded in a foreign country, nor does it grant the right to live anywhere one chooses within Canada. The federal government may still impose travel restrictions on citizens seeking to visit certain countries. The extradition of Canadians, though in violation of s. 6(1), has been upheld under s. 1.[82] Only Canadian citizens are entitled to the protection of s. 6(1). Non-citizens have no rights under this section and may be refused entry or have conditions imposed on their entry or stay in Canada.[83]

(ii) *Rights to Move and Gain Livelihood: Sections 6(2)(a) and (b)*

Unlike s. 6(1), the rights in s. 6(2) are not limited to Canadian citizens but apply to permanent residents as well. Under s. 6(2)(*a*), a person has the right "to move and take up residence in any province." While this allows individuals to live within their province of choice, it does not prohibit the provinces from placing restrictions on the location *within* the province where an individual may reside.

Under s. 6(2)(*b*), a person has the right "to pursue the gaining of a livelihood in any province." This section must be read within the context of mobility rights and does not guarantee an independent right to work.[84] Section 6(2)(*b*) does not, however, require a person to become a resident of a province before acquiring a right to gain a livelihood in that province. For example, a transprovincial border commuter need not establish residence within a province in order to have a right to work under s. 6(2)(*b*).[85]

---

[82] *Cotroni c. Centre de Prévention de Montréal*, [1989] 1 S.C.R. 1469, (*sub nom. United States v. Cotroni*) 48 C.C.C. (3d) 193. For a discussion on extradition of Canadian citizens, see J.-G. Castel & S. Williams, "The Extradition of Canadian Citizens and Sections 1 and 6(1) of the Canadian Charter of Rights and Freedoms" (1987) 25 Can. Y.B. Int'l L. 263.

[83] Hogg, *supra*, note 79 at 43-2. See also P. Blache, "Mobility Rights (Section 6)" in Beaudoin & Ratushny, *supra*, note 67.

[84] *Skapinker v. Law Society (Upper Canada)*, [1984] 1 S.C.R. 357 at 382, 11 C.C.C. (3d) 481.

[85] *Black v. Law Society (Alberta)*, [1989] 1 S.C.R. 591 at 615.

(iii) *Limitations on Mobility Rights: Sections 6(3)(a) and (b)*

The mobility rights guaranteed by s. 6(2) are subject to any valid, non-discriminatory provincial laws of general application, as well as any laws imposing reasonable residency requirements as a condition for the receipt of social assistance.[86]

(e) Legal Rights: Sections 7 to 14

Sections 7 to 14 of the Charter outline a series of constitutionally entrenched legal rights designed primarily to protect persons subject to the criminal process. Most of the rights provided for in these sections existed prior to the Charter at common law or were codified in the *Canadian Bill of Rights*. Entrenchment in a constitutional document, however, has given much more force to these rights and prevents Parliament from overriding them by legislation.

(i) *Life, Liberty and Security of the Person: Section 7*[87]

Section 7 provides that "[e]veryone has the right to life, liberty and security of the person and the right not to be deprived thereof except in accordance with the principles of fundamental justice."

This section applies to everyone who is physically within the country so that even persons who are in Canada illegally are entitled to its protection.[88] Because of the human nature of the rights to "life, liberty and security of the person", s. 7 does not apply *per se* to corporations. Corporate persons are, however, entitled to rely on this section when challenging a government action which may also violate the s. 7 rights of individual persons.[89]

In the *B.C. Motor Vehicle Reference*, Lamer J. discussed the purpose and general interpretive approach required under s. 7:

---

[86] See ss. 6(3)(*a*) and (*b*). See also *Black*, *ibid.* at 617-618.

[87] See, generally, P. Garant, "Fundamental Freedoms and Natural Justice (Section 7)" in W. Tarnopolsky & G. Beaudoin, eds., *The Canadian Charter of Rights and Freedoms: Commentary* (Carswell, 1982) 258; Justice D. McDonald, *Legal Rights in the Canadian Charter of Rights and Freedoms*, 2d ed. (Carswell, 1989) at 105; J.M. Evans, "The Principles of Fundamental Justice: The Constitution and the Common Law" (1991) 29 Osgoode Hall L.J. 51; E. Colvin, "Section Seven of the Canadian Charter of Rights and Freedoms" (1989) 68 Can. Bar Rev. 560.

[88] *Singh v. Canada (Minister of Employment & Immigration)*, [1985] 1 S.C.R. 177 at 201-202.

[89] *Wholesale Travel Group*, *supra*, note 30.

In the framework of a purposive analysis, designed to ascertain the purpose of the s. 7 guarantee and the "interests it was meant to protect" . . . , it is clear to me that the interests which are meant to be protected . . . are the life, liberty and security of the person. The principles of fundamental justice . . . are not a protected interest, but rather a qualifier of the right not to be deprived of life, liberty and security of the person.[90]

In light of this interpretation, it is first necessary to determine whether the individual has been denied the right to life, liberty *or* security of the person. It is not necessary to prove that all three aspects of this right have been denied in order to bring the individual within the protection of s. 7.[91] A denial of any one of those rights will suffice.

While the full scope of the words "life, liberty and security of the person" has not yet been fully explored by the courts, these words generally relate to one's physical or mental integrity.[92]

"Liberty" has been defined as "the right to pursue one's goals free of governmental constraint."[93] The "liberty" interest in s. 7 is not limited to freedom from physical harm or restraint, but also guarantees a degree of personal autonomy over important decisions intimately affecting the private lives of individuals.[94] According to Wilson J., liberty includes the

freedom of the individual to develop and realize his potential to the full, to plan his own life to suit his own character, to make his own choices for good or ill, to be non-conformist, idiosyncratic and even eccentric.[95]

The right to "security of the person" has also been broadly interpreted and means more than a right to one's physical security.[96] "Security of the person" extends to protection against serious psychological stress[97] imposed by the state and "must at least encompass freedom from the threat of physical punishment or suffering as well as freedom from punishment itself."[98]

There has been little judicial discussion as to the meaning of the word "life"[99] in s. 7.

---

[90] *Reference re s. 94(2) of Motor Vehicle Act (British Columbia)*, [1985] 2 S.C.R. 486 at 501, 48 C.R. (3d) 289, 23 C.C.C. (3d) 289.

[91] *Singh, supra*, note 88.

[92] *Morgentaler, supra*, note 54 at 54 (S.C.R.).

[93] *Canada v. Operation Dismantle Inc.*, [1985] 1 S.C.R. 441 at 448.

[94] *Morgentaler, supra*, note 54 at 179 (S.C.R.).

[95] *R. v. Jones*, [1986] 2 S.C.R. 284 at 318, 28 C.C.C. (3d) 513, holding that "liberty" extends to the freedom to educate one's children as one sees fit.

[96] *Singh, supra*, note 88 at 206-207. See also I. Johnstone, "Section 7 of the Charter and Constitutionally Protected Welfare" (1988) 46 U.T. Fac. L. Rev. 1.

[97] *Morgentaler, supra*, note 54 at 56 (S.C.R.).

[98] *Singh, supra*, note 88 at 207.

[99] See McDonald, *supra*, note 87 at 106. The question of the right to "life" would certainly be an issue if Parliament attempted to reintroduce capital punishment in Canada.

Once it has been established that the individual's right to life, liberty, or security of the person has been denied, it is then necessary to determine whether the denial was made in accordance with the principles of fundamental justice. Only if the denial was *not* made in accordance with these principles will there be a violation of s. 7.

The Supreme Court has given a broad interpretation to the meaning of the words "principles of fundamental justice". The nature of these principles are illustrated by the other legal rights in ss. 8 to 14 of the Charter.[100] "Fundamental justice" is not synonymous with the narrow procedural concept of "natural justice". To give the term this interpretation would "strip the protected interests of much, if not most, of their content and leave the right to life, liberty and security of the person in a sorely emaciated state."[101] Furthermore, the principles of fundamental justice are not limited to procedural guarantees but include substantive guarantees as well. This means that s. 7 protects against government actions which are either procedurally *or* substantively unjust.[102]

(ii) *Unreasonable Search and Seizure: Section 8*[103]

Section 8 provides that "[e]veryone has the right to be secure against unreasonable search or seizure." The primary purpose of this section is "to protect individuals from unjustified state intrusions upon their privacy".[104]

Section 8 applies only where there has actually been a "search or seizure". The section protects against searches *or* seizures whether or not they are made in connection with one another.[105]

---

[100] *B.C. Motor Vehicle Reference, supra*, note 89 at 501 (S.C.R.).

[101] *Ibid.*

[102] For further discussion, see L. Tremblay, "Section 7 of the Charter: Substantive Due Process?" (1984) 18 U.B.C. L. Rev. 201; P.J. Monahan & A. Petter, "Developments in Constitutional Law: The 1985-86 Term" (1987) 9 Supreme Court L.R. 69; R.A. Macdonald, "Procedural Due Process in Canadian Constitutional Law: Natural Law and Fundamental Justice" (1987) 39 U. Fla. L. Rev. 217; B. Chapman, "Criminal Law Liability and Fundamental Justice: Toward a Theory of Substantive Judicial Review" (1986) 44 U.T. Fac. L. Rev. 153.

[103] See generally R.W. Wood, "Search, Seizure and the Canadian Charter of Rights" (1986) 15 Anglo-Am. L. Rev. 37; G. Luther, "The Search and Seizure of Motor Vehicles: Learning From an American Mistake" (1988) 12 Queen's L.J. 239; N. Finkelstein, "Constitutional Law — Search and Seizure after *Southam*" (1985) 63 Can. Bar Rev. 178.

[104] See *Southam, supra*, note 9 at 160 (S.C.R.). See also *R. v. Dyment*, [1988] 2 S.C.R. 417, 66 C.R. (3d) 348, 45 C.C.C. (3d) 244.

[105] *Dyment, ibid.*, illustrates that an unreasonable seizure can violate s. 8 even though it was not the result of a search.

Within the meaning of s. 8, a "search" occurs when a government action invades an individual's reasonable expectation of privacy,[106] and a "seizure" is "the taking of a thing from a person by a public authority without that person's consent."[107] The line between

a seizure and a mere finding of evidence [is to be drawn] logically and purposefully at the point at which it can reasonably be said that the individual had ceased to have a privacy interest in the subject-matter allegedly seized.[108]

Once it has been established that a search or seizure has taken place, it is necessary to determine whether or not it was "reasonable".[109] Only an unreasonable search or seizure will be in violation of s. 8. The standard of reasonableness will vary depending on the degree of privacy which an individual should be able to expect in a given situation.[110] For example, the standard of reasonableness may be lower where the intrusion on privacy is fairly common and expected.[111] On the other hand, a higher standard may be required where state security is involved[112] or where an individual's bodily integrity is seriously interfered with.[113]

The reasonableness of a search or seizure under s. 8 is determined by balancing the interests of the parties involved. The question is essentially whether the public's interest in being left alone by government must give way to the government's interest in intruding on the individual's privacy in order to advance its goals, notably those of law enforcement.[114]

In *Southam*, the Supreme Court outlined the following three basic criteria which should be considered in balancing these interests:

---

[106] *R. v. Wise*, [1992] 1 S.C.R. 527 at 533, 11 C.R. (4th) 253, 70 C.C.C. (3d) 193.

[107] *Dyment, supra*, note 104 at 431 (S.C.R.). See also McDonald, *supra*, note 87 at 315, suggesting that the courts have given a very restricted interpretation to "seizure" within the meaning of s. 8. For example, the expropriation of real property was held not to be a "seizure" in *Becker v. Alberta* (1983), 148 D.L.R. (3d) 539 at 546 (Alta. C.A.); and the taking of a person was held not to be a "seizure" in *R. v. Parton* (1983), 9 C.C.C. (3d) 295 (Alta. Q. B.).

[108] *Ibid.* at 435.

[109] See generally K. Murray, "The Reasonable Expectation of Privacy Test and the Scope of Protection Against Unreasonable Search and Seizure Under s. 8 of the Charter of Rights and Freedoms" (1985) 17 U. Ottawa L. Rev. 25; R.T.H. Stone, "The Inadequacy of Privacy: *Hunter v. Southam* and the Meaning of 'unreasonable' in Section 8 of the *Charter*" (1989) 34 McGill L.J. 685.

[110] See Hogg, *supra*, note 79 at 45-15 and McDonald, *supra*, note 87 at 236-237. See also *Wise, supra*, note 106 at 534 and 538 (S.C.R.).

[111] For example, police stop-checks in *R. v. Hufsky*, [1988] 1 S.C.R. 621, 63 C.R. (3d) 14, 40 C.C.C. (3d) 398.

[112] *Southam, supra*, note 9 at 168 (S.C.R.).

[113] *Dyment, supra*, note 104.

[114] *Southam, supra*, note 9 at 159-160 (S.C.R.).

1. Where possible, the search must have been approved by prior authorization.
2. The person authorizing the search need not be a judge but must act in a judicial manner.
3. There must be reasonable and probable grounds, established upon oath, to believe that an offence has been committed and that evidence of this is to be found at a particular place.[115]

Where there has been a warrantless search or seizure, it is presumed to have been unreasonable and in violation of section 8.[116]

(iii) *Arbitrary Detention or Imprisonment: Section 9*

Section 9 of the Charter guarantees that "[e]veryone has the right not to be arbitrarily detained or imprisoned." It is first necessary to determine whether the accused has actually been "detained or imprisoned" within the meaning of s. 9. Generally, "there must be some form of compulsion or coercion to constitute an interference with liberty or freedom of action that amounts to a detention."[117] A compulsory constraint of liberty need not be physical, but can be psychological as well.[118]

If it is established that there has been an imprisonment or detention, it is then necessary to determine whether it was "arbitrary". An impugned government action may be "arbitrary" even if it is within the scope of a statutorily created discretion. For example, in the circumstances in *Hufsky*, a random police stop-check was held to be an arbitrary detention:

> Although authorized by statute and carried out for lawful purposes, the random stop for the purposes of the spot check procedure nevertheless resulted . . . in an arbitrary detention because there were no criteria for the selection of the drivers to be stopped and subjected to the spot check procedure. The selection was in the absolute discretion of the police officer. *A discretion is*

---

[115] *Southam, ibid.* at 160-165. See also *R. v. Simmons*, [1988] 2 S.C.R. 495, 66 C.R. (3d) 297, 45 C.C.C. (3d) 296, and *R. v. Collins*, [1987] 1 S.C.R. 265 at 278, 56 C.R. (3d) 193, 33 C.C.C. (3d) 1. For further discussion, see McDonald, *supra*, note 87 at 236-237.

[116] *Southam, ibid.* at 161; *Collins, ibid.* at 278 (S.C.R.).

[117] *R. v. Therens*, [1985] 1 S.C.R. 613 at 641-642, 45 C.R. (3d) 97, 18 C.C.C. (3d) 481. Note that the doctrine relating to the meaning of "detention" under s. 10 is applied to s. 9 as well. See *Hufsky, supra*, note 111 at 632 (S.C.R.) where the Court found there was no reason not to apply the s. 10 definition of "detention" from *Therens* to s. 9.

[118] For example, see *Therens, ibid.* at 642 (S.C.R.) where a police stop-check was a "detention" within the meaning of s. 9 because "[the] police officer [assumed] control over the movement of [the appellant] by a demand or direction which may have significant legal consequence."

> *arbitrary if there are no criteria, express or implied, which govern its exercise.*[119] [Emphasis added.]

If the imprisonment or detention is found to be arbitrary, then s. 9 will have been violated.

(iv) *Rights on Arrest or Detention: Section 10*

The rights guaranteed by ss. 10(*a*) to (*c*) arise only "on arrest or detention". As with s. 9, a "detention" occurs when a police officer or other agent of the state assumes control over the movement of a person by a demand or direction which may have significant legal consequence and which prevents or impedes the person's access to counsel.[120] A detention can either be a physical or psychological restriction of liberty.[121]

(A) *Right to Reasons: Section 10(a)*

Upon arrest or detention, a person is entitled to be informed promptly of the reasons for the arrest or detention. The purpose behind s. 10(*a*) is to permit the person to take prompt and appropriate action in response to the arrest. This means that sufficient information must be provided so that he/she will be able to initiate the necessary immediate steps to deal with the arrest or detention.[122]

(B) *Right to Counsel: Section 10(b)*[123]

Under s. 10(*b*), police cannot question an arrested or detained person until that person understands that he/she has a right to counsel.[124] Police

---

[119] *Hufsky, supra*, note 111 at 633 (S.C.R.).

[120] *Therens, supra*, note 117 at 642 (S.C.R.). See also *R. v. Thomsen*, [1988] 1 S.C.R. 640 at 649, 63 C.R. (3d) 1, 40 C.C.C. (3d) 411 for a review of the essentials for a "detention" under s. 10.

[121] *Therens, ibid.* at 644.

[122] Magnet, *supra*, note 32 at 579. Note the difference between the s. 10(*a*) right to reasons arising upon arrest or detention and the s. 11(*a*) right when charged with an offence to be informed without unreasonable delay of the specific offence. Different information must be given under each section. For example, under s. 10(*a*), the reason for arrest need not be technically precise or even accurately reflect the charge that will be laid. Section 11(*a*), however, requires more precise information about the specific charge.

[123] See generally P.B. Michalyshyn, "The Charter Right to Counsel: Beyond *Miranda*" (1987) 25 Alta. L. Rev. 190; D.M. Paciocco, "The Development of *Miranda*-Like Doctrines Under the Charter" (1987) 19 Ottawa L. Rev. 49; D.M. Paciocco, "More on *Miranda* — Recent Developments Under Subsection 10(b) of the Charter" (1987) 19 Ottawa L. Rev. 573.

[124] *R. v. Evans*, [1991] 1 S.C.R. 869, 4 C.R. (4th) 144, 63 C.C.C. (3d) 289.

may also have a duty to inform a detainee of the availability of legal aid or duty counsel.[125] It should be noted, however, that police do not have to provide the opportunity to contact counsel unless and until it is actually requested.[126]

Once the accused expresses the desire to contact a lawyer, police must provide him/her with a "reasonable opportunity" to exercise this right without delay.[127] Until the right has been fully exercised, police should not continue to question the detainee[128] or place him/her in a line-up.[129]

While the detained or arrested person is entitled to seek the services of a preferred lawyer, there is no constitutional right under s. 10(b) to obtain the lawyer of choice.[130] The detainee must be "reasonably diligent" in his/her attempt to contact counsel and cannot needlessly delay the investigation process.[131]

The right to counsel may be waived by the arrested or detained person. For the waiver to be effective, it must be "clear and unequivocal that the person is waiving the procedural safeguard and is doing so with full knowledge of the rights the procedure was enacted to protect and of the effect the waiver will have on those rights in the process."[132] If the individual was intoxicated and could not appreciate the effect of waiving the right to counsel, s. 10(b) is breached and any statements made may be inadmissible.[133] Furthermore, a statement by the detainee that he/she cannot afford a lawyer does not amount to a valid waiver. In such a case, the police may have to inform the individual as to the availability of legal aid or duty counsel.[134]

---

[125] *R. v. Brydges*, [1990] 1 S.C.R. 190, 74 C.R. (3d) 129, 53 C.C.C. (3d) 330.

[126] See *R. v. Baig*, [1987] 2 S.C.R. 537, 61 C.R. (3d) 97, 37 C.C.C. (3d) 181, citing with approval *R. v. Anderson* (1984), 39 C.R. (3d) 193, 10 C.C.C. (3d) 417 (Ont. C.A.).

[127] Hogg, *supra*, note 79 at 47-9.

[128] *R. v. Manninen*, [1987] 1 S.C.R. 1233, 58 C.R. (3d) 97, 34 C.C.C. (3d) 385.

[129] *R. v. Leclair*, [1989] 1 S.C.R. 3, 67 C.R. (3d) 209, (*sub nom. R. v. Ross*) 46 C.C.C. (3d) 129.

[130] Hogg, *supra*, note 79 at 47-11.

[131] *R. v. Smith*, [1989] 2 S.C.R. 368, 71 C.R. (3d) 129, 50 C.C.C. (3d) 308, where an arrested person who refused to contact his lawyer outside of office hours was held not to have been "reasonably diligent" in contacting counsel. The police were able to question him without violating s. 10(b).

[132] See *Korponey v. Canada (Attorney General)*, [1982] 1 S.C.R. 41 at 49, 26 C.R. (3d) 343, 65 C.C.C. (2d) 65, and *R. v. Clarkson*, [1986] 1 S.C.R. 383 at 394, 50 C.R. (3d) 289, 25 C.C.C. (3d) 207.

[133] *Clarkson, ibid.*

[134] See *Brydges, supra*, note 125.

(C) *Right to* Habeas Corpus*: Section 10(c)*

Section 10(*c*) provides that, upon arrest or detention, everyone has the right "to have the validity of the detention determined by way of *habeas corpus* and to be released if the detention is not lawful."

Traditionally at common law, the remedy of *habeas corpus* would only apply where: (1) there was a deprivation of liberty, and (2) the *complete* liberty of the applicant was sought. It would not, therefore, apply where the applicant merely sought a transfer from one form of detention to another.[135]

In *Miller*,[136] the availability of *habeas corpus* was expanded so that an inmate could rely on the remedy to challenge the validity of a transfer to a more restrictive and severe part of the penitentiary. Under s. 10(*c*), therefore, it is not essential that an applicant for *habeas corpus* seeks complete liberty. Furthermore, it is accepted that an incarcerated person can still be subject to a new deprivation of liberty within the prison system.[137]

(v) *Rights on Being Charged: Section 11*

The rights enumerated in ss. 11(*a*) to (*i*) only become effective once a person has been "charged with an offence". The meaning of these words must be applied uniformly to all the rights in s. 11.[138] An individual will have been "charged with an offence" within the meaning of s. 11 if he/she is subject to proceedings which are either criminal or quasi-criminal "by nature" *or* which give rise to "true penal consequences".[139]

Proceedings which are criminal or quasi-criminal "by nature" are those which deal with matters "of a public nature, intended to promote

---

[135] *R. v. Miller*, [1985] 2 S.C.R. 613 at 634, 49 C.R. (3d) 1, 23 C.C.C. (3d) 97. See also *Dumas c. Centre de détention Leclerc de Laval, (sub nom. Dumas v. Leclerc Institute)* [1986] 2 S.C.R. 459 at 463, (*sub nom. Dumas v. Leclerc Institute of Laval*) 55 C.R. (3d) 83, 30 C.C.C. (3d) 129. For an example of the traditional approach to *habeas corpus* when the applicant sought a transfer to a different form of detention, see *R. v. Wandsworth Prison (Governor); Ex parte Silverman* (1952), 96 Sol. J. 853.

[136] *Miller, ibid.* at 638 (S.C.R.). The Court accepted the application of the *habeas corpus* remedy "to release a prisoner from an unlawful form of detention within a penitentiary into normal association with the general inmate population of the penitentiary."

[137] *Ibid.* at 640-641.

[138] *R. v. Schmidt, (sub nom. Canada v. Schmidt)* [1987] 1 S.C.R. 500 at 519, 58 C.R. (3d) 1, 33 C.C.C. (3d) 193: the words "any person charged with an offence" contained in the opening sentence of s. 11 "must have a constant meaning throughout, one that harmonizes with the various paragraphs of the section."

[139] *R. v. Wigglesworth*, [1987] 2 S.C.R. 541 at 558, 60 C.R. (3d) 193, 37 C.C.C. (3d) 385. For a discussion on Wilson J.'s "by nature" and "true penal consequence" tests, see McDonald, *supra*, note 87 at 544-546.

public order and welfare within a public sphere of activity."[140] Similarly, "a true penal consequence which would attract the application of s. 11 is imprisonment or a fine which by its magnitude would appear to be imposed for the purpose of redressing the wrong done to society at large."[141]

Other less serious "offences" are subject only to the more flexible criteria of "fundamental justice" in s. 7.[142] For example, purely regulatory or disciplinary proceedings are not generally considered criminal or quasi-criminal "by nature" and s. 11 rights will not apply unless the proceedings involve the imposition of "true penal consequences".[143]

(A) *Right to be Informed of the Specific Offence: Section 11(a)*

Section 11(*a*) provides that a person charged with an offence has the right to be informed without unreasonable delay of the specific offence. This guarantees the fundamental right not to be prosecuted except for an offence charged in a formal accusation. There are three important corollaries of that right: first, the right to be informed of the charge; second, the right to specificity in the allegation of the offence; and third, the right to be informed without unreasonable delay.[144]

(B) *Right to Trial Within Reasonable Time: Section 11(b)*[145]

Section 11(*b*) provides that a person charged with an offence has the right to be tried within a reasonable time. According to the Supreme Court, the broad purpose of this section is to ensure the individual rights guaranteed to the accused in s. 7 of the Charter.[146] More specifically, s. 11(*b*) seeks:

1. to protect the right to security of the person by minimizing the anxiety and stigma associated with a criminal charge;

---

[140] *Wigglesworth, ibid.* at 560 (S.C.R.).

[141] *Ibid.* at 561.

[142] *Ibid.* at 558.

[143] *Ibid.* See also *Trimm v. Durham Regional Police Force,* [1987] 2 S.C.R. 582, 37 C.C.C. (3d) 120, holding that s. 11 rights did not apply to disciplinary proceedings under the *Police Act.*

[144] Magnet, *supra*, note 32 at 578.

[145] See generally S.G. Coughlan, "R. v. Askov — A Bold Step Not Boldly Taken" (1991) 33 Crim. L.Q. 247; L.N. Ledgerwood, "The Dangers of *R. v. Askov*" (1992) 1 N.J.C.L. 395.

[146] See *R. v. Morin,* [1992] 1 S.C.R. 771 at 786, 12 C.R. (4th) 1, 71 C.C.C. (3d) 1, and *R. v. Askov,* [1990] 2 S.C.R. 1199 at 1219, 79 C.R. (3d) 273, 59 C.C.C. (3d) 449.

2. to protect the right to liberty by minimizing the length of restrictions on liberty due to pre-trial incarceration and restrictive bail conditions; and

3. to protect the right to a fair trial by ensuring that evidence is available and fresh at the proceedings.[147]

The Supreme Court has also recognized the important societal interests associated with ensuring that accused persons come to trial within a reasonable time:

> Although it must be recognized that the primary goal of s. 11(*b*) is the protection of the individual's interest in fundamental justice, nevertheless that same section contains a secondary and inferred societal interest that should not be ignored.[148]

Essentially, society has an interest in law enforcement and in seeing that accused persons are treated humanely and fairly.[149]

In *Askov* and *Morin*, the Supreme Court set out a test for determining the "reasonableness" of the delay in advancing a case to trial.[150] This test requires a number of factors to be considered and weighed as follows:

1. Length of delay — This is measured from the time when a person is charged[151] to the end of the trial. The length of the delay may be shortened by subtracting periods of delay which have been waived by the accused.[152] The longer the delay is, the more difficult it will be to excuse as reasonable.[153]

2. Waivers — Any waiver of a Charter right must be clear and unequivocal. It must also be made with full knowledge of the rights the procedure was enacted to protect and of the effect which the waiver will have on those rights. Silence or lack of objection cannot constitute a

---

[147] *Morin, ibid.* at 786 (S.C.R.).

[148] *Askov, supra*, note 146 at 1222 (S.C.R.).

[149] *Morin, supra*, note 146 at 786-787 (S.C.R.).

[150] For early cases relevant to the development of this test, see *R. v. Mills*, [1986] 1 S.C.R. 863, 52 C.R. (3d) 1, 26 C.C.C. (3d) 481, and *R. v. Rahey*, [1987] 1 S.C.R. 588, 57 C.R. (3d) 289, 33 C.C.C. (3d) 289. The test was first formulated in *Askov, supra*, note 146, and was summarized therein at 1231-1232 (S.C.R.). The Court revisited the issue in *Morin, supra*, note 146, and the test was slightly varied. The test outlined here is that set out in *Morin*.

[151] The time of charge is the date on which an information is sworn or an indictment is preferred. Pre-charge delay is not considered in determining the length of time which is at issue. See *Morin, supra*, note 146 at 789 (S.C.R.).

[152] *Morin, ibid.* at 788.

[153] *Askov, supra*, note 146 at 1233 (S.C.R.).

lawful waiver.[154] Consent to a trial date can, however, give rise to an inference of a waiver.[155]

3. Reasons for delay — These include:
   (a) Inherent time requirements of the case: Inevitably, some delay is necessary for both sides to make discoveries and generally prepare the case. More complex cases will have a longer inherent delay than simpler ones.
   (b) Actions by the accused: Legitimate voluntary actions by the accused which cause delay will be considered, as well as any deliberate delaying tactics by the accused. Factors which are beyond the control of the accused will not, however, be taken into account against him/her.
   (c) Actions by the Crown: This includes the time required for adjournments requested by the Crown, delay in disclosure or change of venue motions. Such delays, though valid, cannot be relied upon by the Crown to explain away delay which is otherwise unreasonable.[156]
   (d) Limits on institutional resources: In large part, systemic delays have been due to insufficient resources and increased caseloads. Assessing the reasonableness of institutional delays requires a non-mechanical comparison with the institutional delays in other comparable jurisdictions. This is an exercise of judicial discretion and involves "taking into account the evidence of the limitations on resources, the strain imposed on them, statistics from other comparable jurisdictions and the opinions of other courts and judges, as well as any expert opinion."[157] The determination must be made on a case-by-case basis and there is no maximum length of time beyond which institutional delays are not reasonable.
   (e) Other reasons for delay: Any other reasons for the delay which do not fit into the above categories should also be considered.[158]
4. Prejudice to the accused — Prejudice to an accused can either be inferred from a prolonged delay[159] or may be demonstrated or contradicted by evidence adduced by either party.[160]

The onus of persuasion is primarily on the accused because the inquiry under s. 11(*b*) is usually triggered by the accused's application under

---

[154] *Ibid.* at 1228. See also *Morin, supra,* note 146 at 790 (S.C.R.).
[155] *Morin, ibid.*
[156] *Ibid.* at 794.
[157] *Ibid.* at 797.
[158] An example would be the repeated adjournments called by the Judge in *Rahey, supra,* note 150.
[159] *Morin, supra,* note 146 at 801 (S.C.R.).
[160] *Ibid.*

s. 24(1) of the Charter.[161] If the court, after assessing all the various factors, decides that there has been an unreasonable delay, s. 11(*b*) will have been violated.

(C) *Right of Non-Compellability: Section 11(c)*

Section 11(*c*) provides that "[a]ny person charged with an offence has the right . . . not to be compelled to be a witness in proceedings against that person in respect of the offence." This right applies only to proceedings dealing with the same particular offence with which the accused has been charged.

In *R. v. Dubois*,[162] the prosecution was prohibited from reading into evidence at a retrial the testimony which was given by the accused at his first trial. According to the Court,

> [t]o allow the prosecution to use, as part of its case, the accused's previous testimony would, in effect, allow the Crown to do indirectly what it is estopped from doing directly by s. 11(*c*), *i.e.* to compel the accused to testify.[163]

Despite s. 11(*c*), however, a person charged as an accessory to a crime may be compelled to testify at the trial of the principal,[164] several co-accused who are being tried separately may be compelled to testify at each other's trials,[165] and an accused may be compelled to testify as a witness at a civil trial against that accused arising on the same set of facts as the criminal trial.[165]

(D) *Presumption of Innocence: Section 11(d)*[167]

Section 11(*d*) provides that any person charged with an offence has the right "to be presumed innocent until proven guilty according to law in a fair and public hearing by an independent and impartial tribunal." The rights expressed in this section are fundamental to our criminal justice system.

The Supreme Court of Canada has held that the right to be presumed innocent until proven guilty requires that s. 11(*d*) contain, at minimum,

---

[161] *Ibid.* at 788-789.

[162] *R. v. Dubois*, [1985] 2 S.C.R. 350, 48 C.R. (3d) 193, 22 C.C.C. (3d) 513.

[163] *Ibid.* at 365 (S.C.R.).

[164] *R. v. Bleich* (1983), 7 C.C.C. (3d) 176, 150 D.L.R. (3d) 600 (Man. Q.B.).

[165] *R. v. Crooks* (1982), 39 O.R. (3d) 193, 2 C.C.C. (3d) 157 (H.C.), affirmed (1982), 39 O.R. (3d) 193n, 2 C.C.C. (3d) 57 at 64n (C.A.).

[166] *Saccomanno v. Swanson* (1987), 34 D.L.R. (4th) 462 (Alta. Q.B.).

[167] R. Mahoney, "The Presumption of Innocence: A New Era" (1988), 67 Can. Bar Rev. 1.

the following three elements: first, an individual must be proven guilty beyond a reasonable doubt; second, the state must bear the burden of proof; and third, the criminal prosecutions must be carried out in accordance with lawful procedures and fairness.[168]

As every accused is innocent until proven guilty beyond a reasonable doubt, reverse onus provisions will be in conflict with s. 11(*d*). According to the Supreme Court in *Oakes*, any burden on an accused which makes it possible to have a conviction despite the presence of a reasonable doubt contravenes s. 11(*d*) of the Charter.[169]

(E) *Right to Reasonable Bail: Section 11(e)*

Under s. 11(*e*), "[a]ny person charged with an offence has the right . . . not to be denied reasonable bail without just cause." This implies that unreasonable pre-trial terms and conditions can be imposed where a court believes there is "just cause" for so doing. For example, just cause may exist if the detention is necessary to protect the public interest or to ensure the accused's attendance in court.

The onus is usually on the Crown to "show cause" for detention except when the accused has been charged with certain offences such as murder, or the accused has already been released on an indictable charge.[170]

(F) *Right to Trial by Jury: Section 11(f)*

Section 11(*f*) provides that "[a]ny person charged with an offence has the right . . . to the benefit of trial by jury where the maximum punishment for the offence is imprisonment for five years or a more severe punishment." This section guarantees an accused the "benefit" of a jury trial when, in the opinion of the accused, this is in his/her best interest.[171]

The right to the benefit of a trial by jury can be waived by an accused. This does not, however, prevent a jury trial from being imposed on an unwilling accused. In *Turpin*, for example, a provision of the *Criminal Code* made a jury trial mandatory for a murder charge. While the accused was entitled to waive the right to the benefit of a trial by jury, this did not invalidate the Code provision. In other words, the ability to waive

---

[168] *Oakes, supra,* note 37 at 121 (S.C.R.).
[169] See *ibid.* at 132-133. See also *R. v. Holmes,* [1988] 1 S.C.R. 914, 64 C.R. (3d) 97, 41 C.C.C. (3d) 497; *R. v. Whyte,* [1988] 2 S.C.R. 3, 64 C.R. (3d) 123, 42 C.C.C. (3d) 97; *R. v. Schwartz,* [1988] 2 S.C.R. 443, 66 C.R. (3d) 251, 45 C.C.C. (3d) 97.
[170] Hogg, *supra,* note 79 at 48-17 to 48-18.
[171] *R. v. Turpin,* [1989] 1 S.C.R. 1296, 69 C.R. (3d) 97, 48 C.C.C. (3d) 8.

the right to a jury trial does not entitle the accused to demand a trial without a jury.[172]

(G) *Retroactive Offences: Section 11(g)*

Section 11(*g*) provides that "[a]ny person charged with an offence has the right . . . not to be found guilty on account of any act or omission unless, at the time of the act or omission, it constituted an offence under Canadian or international law." This protects individuals from being punished for an act or omission which was not a criminal offence at the time it was committed.

(H) *Double Jeopardy: Section 11(h)*

Under s. 11(*h*), a person charged with an offence has the right "if finally acquitted of the offence, not to be tried for it again and, if finally found guilty and punished for the offence, not to be tried or punished for it again." Section 11(*h*) prevents an accused from being prosecuted more than once for the same offence. It does not, however, prevent an accused from being charged with several offences arising from a single act.[173]

For s. 11(*h*) to apply, it is necessary that the accused was "finally acquitted" or "finally found guilty and punished"[174] for the offence. It is clear that s. 11(*h*) does not prevent an appeal from a decision on a matter for which there has not been a final disposition. An appeal by trial *de novo* has been held to be a new trial rather than a true appeal: "The fact that a proceeding is called 'appeal' is not sufficient to make it a true appeal and so prevent the accused from relying on s. 11(*h*) of the *Canadian Charter*."[175]

---

[172] *Ibid.* at 1313 (S.C.R.).

[173] *Wigglesworth, supra,* note 139.

[174] Note that the accused must be "finally found guilty" but may not need to be "finally" punished in order to receive the benefit of this section. In *R. v. R. (T.)* (1983), 28 Alta. L.R. (2d) 383 (Q.B.), the Court held that s. 11(*h*) prevented new charges from being laid where punishment was being served but had not been completed.

[175] *Corp. professionnelle des médecins (Québec) v. Thibault,* [1988] 1 S.C.R. 1033 at 1045, 63 C.R. (3d) 273, 42 C.C.C. (3d) 1.

(I) *Right to the Lesser Punishment: Section 11(i)*[176]

Section 11(*i*) provides that a person charged with an offence has the right "if found guilty of the offence and if the punishment for the offence has been varied between the time of commission and the time of sentencing, to the benefit of the lesser punishment." If the punishment for an offence changes between the time when the offence is committed and the time of sentencing, the accused is entitled to the lesser of the two penalties.[177] If, however, the penalty is reduced while the person is already serving a sentence, he/she will not be eligible for the reduction.[178]

(vi) Right to be Free from Cruel and Unusual Punishment: Section 12

Section 12 provides that "[e]veryone has the right not to be subjected to any cruel and unusual treatment or punishment." The court must determine what would have been an appropriate punishment or treatment under the circumstances. This is then weighed against the effects of the actual treatment or punishment imposed.[179] In making this determination, a court would ask whether the punishment prescribed is so excessive as to outrage the standards of decency. To answer this, the following must be considered:[180]

1. What range of sentences would have been appropriate in order to punish, rehabilitate or deter this offender or to protect society from this offender? The appropriate sentence is determined by considering the following factors: (i) the gravity of the offence; (ii) the personal characteristics of the offender; (iii) the particular circumstances of the case.
2. Was the effect of the actual punishment grossly disproportionate to the sentence that would have been appropriate? Some punishments or treatments will always be grossly disproportionate and will always outrage society's standards of decency.[181] Other forms of punishment may be found to be grossly disproportionate after the following factors are taken into account: (i) was the punishment necessary to achieve a valid

---

[176] F. Chevrette, "Protection Upon Arrest or Detention and Against Retroactive Penal Law (Sections 8, 9, 10(c), 11(e), (g), and (i))" in Beaudoin & Ratushny, *supra*, note 67 at 445.

[177] See McDonald, *supra*, note 87 at 556.

[178] See *R. v. Milne*, [1987] 2 S.C.R. 512 at 527, (*sub nom. Milne v. Canada (Government)*) 61 C.R. (3d) 55.

[179] *R. v. Smith*, [1987] 1 S.C.R. 1045, 58 C.R. (3d) 193, 34 C.C.C. (3d) 97.

[180] *Ibid* at 1072 (S.C.R.).

[181] *Ibid.* at 1073-1074. Some examples offered by the court are the lobotomization of dangerous offenders, castration or corporal punishment.

penal purpose; (ii) was it founded on recognized sentencing principles; and (iii) were there alternatives to the punishment imposed.[182]

If the actual sentence is found to be "grossly disproportionate" to the sentence that should have been imposed, then s. 12 will have been violated.

(vii) *Right Against Self-Incrimination: Section 13*[183]

Section 13 provides that "[a] witness who testifies in any proceedings has the right not to have any incriminating evidence so given used to incriminate that witness in any other proceedings." This section essentially prevents testimony made at one formal proceeding from being used to incriminate the witness or accused at a subsequent proceeding. Section 13 must be viewed in light of the s. 11(*c*) right of non-compellability and the s. 11(*d*) presumption of innocence. These sections are closely related and, without the protection of s. 13, it would be impossible to fully guarantee these other rights.[184]

The right under s. 13 applies only to protect against the subsequent use of "incriminating evidence". Any evidence tendered by the Crown against the accused will be presumed to be incriminating.[185] It is not necessary that the incriminating nature of the evidence be apparent at the time of the first proceeding, though it must be apparent by the time of the second proceeding.[186]

For s. 13 to apply, the evidence must have been given at a formal proceeding and must be sought to be subsequently introduced at another formal proceeding.[187] Section 13 is not, however, limited to the criminal context.[188] Furthermore, "any other proceedings" includes a retrial of an offence for which the accused previously chose to testify.[189] If this were

---

[182] *Ibid.* at 1074. See also W.S. Tarnopolsky, "Just Desserts or Cruel and Unusual Treatment or Punishment? Where Do We Look for Guidance?" (1978) 10 Ottawa L. Rev. 1.

[183] See generally D.M. Paciocco, "Self-Incrimination: Removing the Coffin Nails" (1989) 35 McGill L.J. 73.

[184] *Dubois, supra*, note 162 at 356-357 (S.C.R.).

[185] *Ibid.* at 364.

[186] *Ibid.* at 363.

[187] There has also been some extension of the right against self-incrimination under s. 7 of the Charter. In some circumstances, s. 7 protects the accused's right to silence where the original incriminating statement was made to the authorities after detention but not in the context of a formal proceeding. See *R. v. Hebert*, [1990] 2 S.C.R. 151, 77 C.R. (3d) 145, 57 C.C.C. (3d) 1.

[188] *Dubois, supra*, note 162 at 377 (S.C.R.). See, for example, *Donald v. Law Society (British Columbia)*, [1985] 2 W.W.R. 671 (B.C. C.A.), leave to appeal to S.C.C. refused (1984), 55 N.R. 237 (S.C.C.), regarding the use of prior testimony at a subsequent disciplinary proceeding. See also McDonald, *supra*, note 87 at 580-581.

[189] *Dubois, ibid.* at 365-366.

not so, the Crown would be able to do indirectly under s. 13 that which it is prohibited from doing directly under ss. 11(c) and (d).[190]

This does not, however, mean that an accused who chooses to testify is insulated against challenges to his/her credibility. Where an accused's prior testimony is inconsistent with that given at the subsequent proceeding, it is possible to introduce the prior inconsistent statements when the sole purpose of doing so is to challenge the credibility of the accused.[191]

(viii) *Right to an Interpreter: Section 14*

Section 14 provides that "[a] party or witness in any proceedings who does not understand or speak the language in which the proceedings are conducted or who is deaf has the right to the assistance of an interpreter." The right to an interpreter which is protected by s. 14 is an essential aspect of a fair hearing.[192] It would, for example, be impossible to have a fair hearing if a witness testifying in another language could not be understood by the trier of fact, or if a defendant did not understand the proceedings and could not effectively instruct counsel.[193]

The party or witness must request an interpreter at the time when one is needed.[194] Unless there is compelling evidence that the request has not been made in good faith, the court should not refuse the request for an interpreter.[195] Section 14 has been held to apply only to parties and witnesses, not to lawyers.[196] It has also been applied in administrative proceedings where the rules of natural justice apply.[197]

(f) Equality Rights: Section 15[198]

Section 15(1) of the Charter guarantees that

[e]very individual is equal before and under the law and has the right to the equal protection and equal benefit of the law without discrimination and,

---

[190] *Ibid.* at 365.

[191] *R. v. Kuldip*, [1990] 3 S.C.R. 618, 1 C.R. (4th) 285, 61 C.C.C. (3d) 385.

[192] *MacDonald v. Montreal (City)*, [1986] 1 S.C.R. 460 at 499, 25 C.C.C. (3d) 481.

[193] See also McDonald, *supra*, note 87 at 590-592.

[194] *R. v. Tsang* (1985), 27 C.C.C. (3d) 365 (B.C. C.A.). See also Magnet, *supra*, note 32 at 693-694.

[195] *R. v. Petrovic* (1984), 41 C.R. (3d) 275, 13 C.C.C. (3d) 416 (Ont. C.A.). See also McDonald, *supra*, note 87 at 590.

[196] *Cormier v. Fournier* (1986), 69 N.B.R. (2d) 155 (Q.B.).

[197] *Roy v. Hackett* (1987), 62 O.R. (2d) 365 (C.A.).

[198] See generally A.F. Bayefsky, "A Case Comment on the First Three Equality Rights Cases Under the Canadian Charter of Rights and Freedoms: *Andrews, Worker's Compensation Reference, Turpin*" (1990) 1 Supreme Court L.R. 503; G.M. Dickinson, "The Supreme Court of Canada and Mandatory Retirement: The Last Word?" (1993) 4 E.L.J.

in particular, without discrimination based on race, national or ethnic origin, colour, religion, sex, age or mental or physical disability.

The primary purpose of s. 15(1) is to ensure equality in the formulation and application of the law[199] and to protect against the oppression resulting from discriminatory measures which have the force of law.[200] "Equality" is a complex and elusive concept,[201] and its promotion "entails the promotion of a society in which all are secure in the knowledge that they are recognized at law as human beings equally deserving of concern, respect and consideration."[202]

The threshold requirement for the application of s. 15(1) is that the alleged discrimination must be the result of the "application or operation of law".[203] The meaning of "law" in this context includes statutes and regulations as well as all governmental exercise of statutory discretion.[204]

Once the threshold requirement is met, it is necessary to determine whether the "law" creates an inequality or distinction between different groups or individuals. The complainant must show that he/she is not receiving equal treatment before or under the law, or that the law has a differential impact on him/her in the protection or benefit afforded by the law.[205]

While each right under s. 15 is supposed to have distinct meanings, neither has been exhaustively defined.[206] The Supreme Court has, however, stated that the minimal content of "equality before the law" is that no individual is to be treated more harshly than another under the law. If one is treated more harshly, there is an unequal application of the law creating a distinction.[207]

In assessing whether one of the equality rights has been infringed, consideration must be given to the content of the law, its purpose, and its impact on those to whom it applies and on those whom it excludes.[208]

Once it is established that an inequality or distinction exists, it is then

---

349; D.M. McAllister, "Sexual Orientation and Section 15" (1992) 1 N.J.C.L. 377; M. Gold, "Comment: *Andrews* v. *Law Society of British Columbia*" (1989) 34 McGill L.J. 1063; M. Eaton, "*Andrews* v. *Law Society of British Columbia*" (1990) 4 C.J.W.L. 276.

[199] *Andrews v. Law Society (British Columbia)*, [1989] 1 S.C.R. 143 at 171.

[200] *Ibid.* at 172.

[201] *Ibid.* at 164.

[202] *Ibid.* at 171.

[203] *Ibid.* at 175 and *McKinney, supra*, note 29 at 276.

[204] Justice La Forest in *McKinney, ibid.*

[205] *Andrews, supra*, note 199 at 165-168.

[206] *Turpin, supra*, note 171 at 1325-1326 (S.C.R.).

[207] *Ibid.* at 1329.

[208] *Andrews, supra*, note 199 at 182.

necessary to determine if the distinction is one which is discriminatory.[209] This means that the complainant must show proof of some harm, prejudice or disadvantage arising from the distinction.[210] Even if the unequal operation or application of the "law" results in discrimination, s. 15 only prohibits discrimination on the basis of the grounds specifically enumerated in the section or on grounds analogous to them. "Analogous grounds" are those representing "discrete and insular minorities"[211] who are lacking in political power and are vulnerable to having their interests overlooked and their rights to equal concern and respect violated.[212]

Finally, s. 15(2) provides that the equality rights in s. 15(1) do not "preclude any law, program or activity that has as its object the amelioration of conditions of disadvantaged individuals or groups." This protects affirmative action programs from being challenged as discriminatory under s. 15(1). It is also consistent with the ultimate goal of protecting the equality rights for those groups that are systemically disadvantaged.

(g) Language Rights: Sections 16 to 22

The provisions of s. 133 of the *Constitution Act, 1867* are reaffirmed, and the principles of the *Official Languages Act*[213] are constitutionalized, in ss. 16 to 22 of the Charter.[214] The language rights in these sections apply only to the federal government and to the government of New Brunswick. The other provinces were unwilling to bind themselves to these Charter provisions.[215]

The Supreme Court has held that judicial restraint is required on questions of language rights because language rights are the product of political compromise and are therefore better left to be resolved through the political process.[216]

(i) *Official Languages: Section 16*

Section 16 provides that English and French are the official languages of Canada. Both languages have equal status, rights and privileges as to

---

[209] *Ibid.* at 174-175 and 182.

[210] *Ibid.* at 174-175.

[211] *Ibid.* at 152.

[212] Justice Wilson in *Andrews, ibid.*

[213] *Official Languages Act*, R.S.C. 1985 (4th Supp.), c. 31.

[214] Russell, *supra*, note 6 at 644. See also Justice Beetz in *Assn. of Parents for Fairness in Education, Grand Falls District 50 Branch v. Société des Acadiens du Nouveau-Brunswick Inc.*, [1986] 1 S.C.R. 549 at 572-573.

[215] See generally Russell, *ibid.*

[216] *Société des Acadiens, supra*, note 214 at 578.

their use in all the institutions of the federal and New Brunswick governments.[217]

(ii) *Parliamentary Proceedings: Section 17*

Section 17 provides that everyone has the right to use English or French in the debates and other proceedings of Parliament or of the legislature of New Brunswick. According to the Supreme Court, the language rights in this section vest in the person who is speaking, not in that person's audience. This means that, under s. 17, a person speaking in Parliament or in the New Brunswick legislature has the constitutionally protected right to speak in the official language of his/her choice. This section does not guarantee the speaker the right to be heard or understood in that language.[218]

(iii) *Parliamentary Statutes and Records: Section 18*

Under s. 18, the statutes, records and journals of Parliament and of the New Brunswick legislature must be printed and published in English and French. The section further provides that both language versions are equally authoritative.[219]

(iv) *Languages of the Courts: Section 19*

Section 19 provides that either English or French may be used in any court established by Parliament or in any court of New Brunswick. This section also protects the right to use either official language in any pleading or process issuing from these courts.[220]

Section 19 only guarantees a right to a speaker, writer or issuer of court processes a right to speak or write in the official language of choice. As with s. 17, the rights under s. 19 vest only in the speaker and there is no guaranteed right to be understood in that language.[221]

---

[217] See also A. Tremblay & M. Bastarache, "Language Rights (Sections 16 to 22)" in Beaudoin & Ratushny, *supra*, note 67 at 660. See also Magnet, *supra*, note 32 at 810.

[218] *Société des Acadiens, supra*, note 214 at 574-575.

[219] *Quebec (Attorney General) v. Blaikie*, [1981] 1 S.C.R. 312, 60 C.C.C. (2d) 524, considering the rights under s. 133 of the *Constitution Act, 1867* which are reaffirmed by s. 18 of the Charter.

[220] *Société des Acadiens, supra*, note 214 at 574.

[221] It should be noted that the right to be understood does exist in the court context, but it is based on fair hearing principles embodied in the legal rights sections, not in the narrower language rights provisions: Russell, *supra*, note 6 at 644.

(v) *Languages of Federal Institutions: Section 20*[222]

Under s. 20(1), any member of the public in Canada has the right to communicate with and to receive services in either official language from the head office of a federal government institution. With other branch offices, this right exists where there is a significant demand and where it is reasonable that bilingual service be available given the nature of the office.[223] Section 20(2) also provides that a member of the public has the right to bilingual service from any New Brunswick government office.

Unlike ss. 17 and 19 of the Charter, s. 20 guarantees the right to "communicate" in the official language of choice. This necessarily includes the right to be heard and understood in either language: "The right to communicate in either language postulates the right to be heard or understood in either language."[224]

(h) Minority Language Educational Rights: Section 23[225]

Section 23 provides protection for the anglophone minority in Quebec and for francophone minorities in other provinces who wish to have their children educated in their first language. Under ss. 23(1)(*a*) and (*b*), citizens of Canada, (1) whose first language learned and still maintained is that of the English or the French linguistic minority of the province where they live, or (2) who have received primary schooling in Canada in that minority language, have the right to have their children receive primary and secondary school instruction in that language.

Under s. 23(2), citizens of Canada who have at least one child who is or was educated in the minority language have the right to have all their children receive primary and secondary education in that language.

These rights are by no means absolute. The number of children must be sufficient to warrant providing the service with public funds.[226] The number of children will also determine the type of services which are appropriate.[227] For example, smaller numbers may have to be bussed to the proper facilities, while larger numbers may necessitate minority education within a local majority school.

---

[222] J.E. Magnet, "The Charter's Official Language Provisions: The Implications of Entrenched Bilingualism" (1982) 4 Supreme Court L.R. 163.

[223] Hogg, *supra*, note 79 at 53-21.

[224] *Société des Acadiens*, *supra*, note 214 at 575.

[225] For a discussion on the political environment and purpose of s. 23, see Russell, *supra*, note 6 at 619-621. See also M. Bastarache, "Education Rights of Provincial Language Minorities (Section 23)" in Beaudoin & Ratushny, *supra*, note 67 at 690.

[226] See s. 23(3) of the Charter. See also *Mahe v. Alberta*, [1990] 1 S.C.R. 342.

[227] *Mahe, ibid.* at 366.

These rights extend to the management and control of minority education, not merely the physical facilities in which classes are held. This includes the right to representation on a combined school board if numbers do not warrant a separate school administration.[228]

(i) Enforcement of Charter Rights: Section 24

Section 24 makes it clear that the enforcement of Charter rights is clearly the responsibility of the judiciary. Section 24(1) provides that "[a]nyone whose rights or freedoms, as guaranteed by this Charter, have been infringed or denied may apply to a court of competent jurisdiction to obtain such remedy as the court considers appropriate and just in the circumstances."

A "court of competent jurisdiction" has been defined by the Supreme Court as a court which has jurisdiction over the person and the subject-matter in question, as well as the authority to grant the remedy sought.[229]

Section 24(1) grants a wide discretionary power to the courts to remedy Charter violations with any remedy which is "appropriate and just in the circumstances".[230] The Supreme Court has recognized and accepted the scope of this discretion:

> It is difficult to imagine language which could give the court a wider and less fettered discretion. It is impossible to reduce this wide discretion to some sort of binding formula for general application in all cases, and it is not for appellate courts to pre-empt or cut down this wide discretion.[231]

Section 24(2) provides that,

> [w]here . . . a court concludes that evidence was obtained in a manner that infringed or denied any rights or freedoms guaranteed by this Charter, the evidence shall be excluded if it is established that, having regard to all the circumstances, the admission of it in the proceedings would bring the administration of justice into disrepute.

This provision is narrower than s. 24(1), especially in that the only remedy available is the exclusion of evidence. It should be noted that it is not pos-

---

[228] *Mahe, ibid.* See also R.G. Richards, "*Mahe* v. *Alberta*: Management and Control of Minority Language Education" (1991) 36 McGill L.J. 216.

[229] *Mills, supra,* note 150 at 903-904 (S.C.R.). In *Mills,* the Court held that a magistrate presiding over a preliminary hearing has no power to administer Charter remedies.

[230] See Hogg, *supra,* note 79 at 37-20.

[231] *Mills, supra,* note 150 at 965 (S.C.R.).

sible to apply for the exclusion of evidence as a remedy under the less onerous requirements of s. 24(1).[232]

An applicant under s. 24(2) must first establish that there has been a violation of a Charter right or freedom. Without such a violation, it is not possible to have evidence excluded under this section.

The next question is whether "the evidence was obtained in a manner that infringed or denied any rights or freedoms."[233] While the language of s. 24(2) clearly requires some degree of connection between the Charter violation and the obtaining of the evidence, the exact nature of the connection is uncertain.[234] Possibilities suggested range from a strict causal connection to a mere temporal link where it would be sufficient if the violation chronologically preceded the obtaining of the evidence.[235] The most recent statements by the Supreme Court on this matter make clear that a strict causal connection is not appropriate under s. 24(2). It is sufficient if the Charter violation occurred in the course of obtaining the evidence.[236] It remains to be seen exactly how this standard is to be applied.

A further requirement under s. 24(2) is that the applicant establish on a balance of probabilities that the administration of justice would[237] be brought into disrepute by the admission of the impugned evidence.[238] In *R. v. Collins*, the Supreme Court set out a number of factors which must be considered in determining whether the administration of justice could be brought into disrepute.[239] These factors are:

1. *Fairness of the Trial*: Real evidence existing prior to and irrespective of the Charter violation is not likely to render the trial unfair. Self-incriminatory evidence provided by the applicant after there has been a Charter breach is more likely to render the trial unfair.
2. *Seriousness of the Charter Breach*: If the Charter breach is more serious, the admission of the impugned evidence will be more likely to bring the administration of justice into disrepute. Factors to consider in determining the seriousness of the breach include: (i) whether the breach

---

[232] *Therens, supra*, note 117.

[233] *Ibid.* at 623-624 (S.C.R.).

[234] See B. Donovan, "The Role of Causation Under s. 24(2) of the *Charter*: Nine Years of Inconclusive Jurisprudence" (1991) 49 U.T. Fac. L. Rev. 233.

[235] See *Therens, supra*, note 117, where Justice Lamer suggests the need for a strict causal connection and Justice Le Dain suggests a temporal connection.

[236] *Brydges, supra*, note 125.

[237] *Collins, supra*, note 115 at 287 (S.C.R.). The French text of s. 24(2) states that the evidence can be excluded if it "could" bring the administration of justice into disrepute. Because this less onerous interpretation better protects the right to a fair trial, "would" is to be replaced by "could" in reading the English version of the text.

[238] *Collins, ibid.* at 280-281.

[239] *Ibid.* at 284-286.

was deliberate or flagrant; (ii) whether the government actor was acting in good faith or was acting inadvertently; and (iii) whether the breach occurred in an emergency situation, etc. It is also relevant if other investigating techniques could have been used to obtain the evidence without resulting in a Charter violation.

3. *Effect of Excluding the Evidence*: It is necessary to weigh the seriousness of the offence with which the applicant has been charged with the seriousness of the Charter breach. Depending on the circumstances, the administration of justice may be brought into disrepute either by admitting or excluding the impugned evidence.

If an examination of these factors leads the court to conclude that the administration of justice could be brought into disrepute by the admission of the impugned evidence, then the court shall exclude that evidence.

(j) Application of the Charter: Section 32

Under s. 32, the provisions of the Charter apply to the Parliament and government of Canada and to the legislature and government of each province. This means that the Charter applies as a restriction on the legislative, executive and administrative branches of government[240] and is not intended to restrict the behavior of non-governmental actors.

In determining if a given entity is a government actor to which the Charter would apply, it is not sufficient that the entity has a statutory basis for its authority. A sufficent degree of government control or interference in the day-to-day operations of the entity is necessary before it will be considered a government actor which falls within the scope of s. 32.[241]

(k) The "Notwithstanding" or Override Clause: Section 33[242]

Section 33(1) provides that "Parliament or the legislature of a province may expressly declare in an Act . . . that the Act or a provision thereof shall operate notwithstanding a provision included in section 2 or sections

---

[240] *Dolphin Delivery, supra*, note 8 at 598-599.

[241] For example, hospital held not to be a government actor (*Stoffman v. Vancouver General Hospital*, [1990] 3 S.C.R. 483, 91 C.L.L.C. 17,003); university held not to be a government actor (*McKinney, supra*, note 29); college held to be a government actor (*Douglas/Kwantlen Faculty Assn. v. Douglas College*, [1990] 3 S.C.R. 570, 91 C.L.L.C. 17,002).

[242] See generally J.D. Whyte, "On Not Standing For Notwithstanding" (1990) 28 Alta. L. Rev. 347; T. Macklem, "Engaging the Override" (1992) 1 N.J.C.L. 274; D. Greschner & K. Norman, "The Courts and Section 33" (1987) 12 Queen's L.J. 155.

7 to 15 of this Charter.'' When s. 33 is invoked, legislation may be enacted which is not bound by the limitations of s. 2 (Fundamental Freedoms), ss. 7 to 14 (Legal Rights) and/or s. 15 (Equality Rights) of the Charter.[243]

A legislative override of Charter rights may be effective for up to five years without being re-enacted.[244] Each subsequent re-enactment is then valid for another five-year maximum.[245] This system of renewal ensures that there is no extended period of rights deprivation without proper reflection by the Parliament or legislature in power. The s. 33 ''notwithstanding'' clause has been used sparingly to date.[246]

Ford c. Québec (Procureur général) is a key decision dealing with the operation of s. 33. This case involved a challenge to the validity of an override declaration in the Quebec government's *Charter of the French Language*. According to the Supreme Court in *Ford*, an override declaration must expressly declare that an Act or a provision thereof shall operate notwithstanding a provision included in s. 2 or ss. 7 to 15 of the Charter.[247] It is not necessary to include in the legislation the full text of the Charter provision which is to be overridden.[248] Instead, a s. 33 declaration is deemed to be sufficiently express if it refers to the number of the section, subsection or paragraph which contains the provisions to be overridden.[249] It is also unnecessary for the legislature to provide a justification for its decision to override a right or freedom.[250]

The Court in *Ford* also held that s. 33 permits more than one Charter section to be overridden at the same time;[251] and it upheld Quebec's ''omnibus'' or blanket use of the override as a valid exercise of s. 33. The Court held ''the validity of its enactment is not affected by the fact that it was introduced into all Quebec statutes enacted prior to a certain date by a single enactment.''[252] The Supreme Court did, however, find the Quebec legislature's attempt to invoke the override retrospectively to be an improper and invalid application of s. 33.[253]

---

[243] See s. 33(2) of the Charter.

[244] See s. 33(3) of the Charter.

[245] See ss. 33(4) and (5) of the Charter.

[246] From 1982 to 1987, the Quebec National Assembly attached an override clause to all its existing legislation. This blanket use of s. 33 was upheld by the Supreme Court in *Ford, supra*, note 28. The Quebec government later attached s. 33 to its French-only sign legislation in order to override s. 2(*b*). Saskatchewan also used the override in legislation ordering striking civil servants back to work. See Russell, *supra*, note 6 at 5, n. 5.

[247] *Ford, supra*, note 28 at 741.

[248] *Ibid.* at 738.

[249] *Ibid.* at 741.

[250] *Ibid.*

[251] *Ibid.*

[252] *Ibid.* at 742-743.

[253] *Ibid.* at 743.

(l) The Constitution as Supreme Law: Section 52

Section 52(1) provides that "[t]he Constitution of Canada is the supreme law of Canada, and any law that is inconsistent with the provisions of the Constitution is, to the extent of the inconsistency, of no force or effect." The supremacy clause formally provides for the supremacy of the Constitution over all federal and provincial legislation.

Section 52 of the *Constitution Act, 1982* is not actually part of the Charter and applies more broadly to the "Constitution of Canada" as defined in s. 52(2).[254] Provincial constitutions not listed in s. 52(2) are not included as part of the Constitution within the meaning of this section.[255] Furthermore, statutes codifying constitutional conventions retain their status as ordinary legislation and are not automatically entrenched in the Constitution.[256]

Section 52 is engaged when a law itself, as opposed to an action taken under that law, is held to be unconstitutional. Once it has been engaged, three questions must be addressed by the court.[257]

First, what was "the extent of the inconsistency" between the "law"[258] and the Constitution? If the legislation was unconstitutional because of its purpose, the extent of the inconsistency will usually encompass the legislation as a whole. If the legislation fails to meet some other requirement under s. 1, the extent of the inconsistency will be defined more flexibly and narrowly.

Second, can the inconsistency be dealt with by severance or by reading in, or are other parts of the legislation inextricably linked to it? Severance or reading in should only be used where it is clearly appropriate. It should be done in a manner which is consistent with or in furtherance of the legislative objective. Furthermore, there should be no significant judicial intrusion into legislative budgetary decisions as a result of the severance or reading in.

Third, should the declaration of invalidity be temporarily suspended? The purpose of doing this would be to give Parliament or the legislature the opportunity to remedy the unconstitutional legislation. This approach is warranted where striking down legislation would result in danger to the public or where persons other than those whose Charter rights had been violated would be denied benefits to which they were already entitled under the legislation.

---

[254] *Southam, supra*, note 9 at 148 (S.C.R.).

[255] *Maclean v. Nova Scotia (Attorney General)* (1987), 35 D.L.R. (4th) 306 (N.S. S.C.).

[256] *Osborne v. Canada (Treasury Board)*, [1991] 2 S.C.R. 69.

[257] *Schacter v. Canada*, [1992] 2 S.C.R. 679, 93 D.L.R. (4th) 1.

[258] For discussions on the meaning of the word "law" within the context of s. 52, see *Operation Dismantle, supra*, note 93 at 459, *McKinney, supra*, note 29 at 386, and *Schacter, ibid*.

PART IV

AMENDING THE CONSTITUTION

10

The Constitutional Amending Procedures

1. Introduction

In 1867, when the British Parliament enacted the *Constitution Act, 1867*, Canada was a Dominion of the United Kingdom. The British Parliament was expected to, and did, make all major constitutional amendments.[1] Minor amendments were made by the Canadian Parliament and provincial legislatures. Some provisions of the *Constitution Act, 1867*, by their wording, contained their own amending procedures. For example, s. 35, which relates to the number of senators needed for a quorum, begins with the words "[u]ntil the Parliament of Canada otherwise provides." A number of other provisions contained similar wording. Most, if not all, such provisions have been superceded by Acts of Parliament or the legislatures.

In addition, s. 92(1) of the *Constitution Act, 1867* originally provided that provincial legislatures could amend their own provincial Constitutions except as regards the office of the Lieutenant Governor. This provision was repealed in 1982 and a similar provision re-enacted as s. 45 of the *Constitution Act, 1982*.

Canada attained independence from Britain in 1931,[2] but the British Parliament continued to make all major constitutional amendments. Convention operated to ensure that amendments were only made at the request of the Canadian Parliament. The Canadian Parliament finally obtained a limited power of amendment by the *British North America (No. 2) Act, 1949*[3] which added a new s. 91(1) to the *Constitution Act, 1867*. Like the provincial amending power, this provision was repealed and re-enacted during the patriation of the Constitution. The power is now in a similar form in s. 44 of the *Constitution Act, 1982*.

The leading case on amending procedures prior to the patriation of

---

[1] For the history of amending procedures see P.W. Hogg, *Constitutional Law of Canada* 3d ed. (Toronto: Carswell, 1992) at 61-69.

[2] The *Statute of Westminster, 1931* (U.K.), 22 Geo. 5, c. 4 removed the effects of s. 129 of the *Constitution Act, 1867* which had prevented the Canadian Parliament from altering or repealing certain laws of the United Kingdom which were in force in Canada.

[3] (U.K.), 13 Geo. 6, c. 81.

the Constitution is *Re Resolution to Amend the Constitution*.⁴ This case arose when the federal government decided to patriate the Constitution unilaterally over the objections of some provinces. The Supreme Court said that where provincial powers were affected, a convention existed which required a substantial degree of provincial consent to the amendment. The Court also said that, from a purely legal perspective, Parliament could proceed unilaterally. Politics at the time dictated that a compromise had to be reached and changes were made to the reform package. All provinces except Quebec eventually supported patriation.

2. The Amending Procedures

In 1982, the patriation package added a comprehensive set of procedures for amending the Constitution. There are five main amending formulae.⁵ These procedures are contained in Part V (ss. 38 to 49) of the *Constitution Act, 1982*. Section 52(3) of the Act says that amendments to the "Constitution of Canada" can only be made in accordance with the authority contained in the "Constitution of Canada". This is somewhat circular and raises the question as to whether there are still amending procedures independent of Part V in some other provisions of the Constitution Acts.⁶

An important point to remember is that the various amending formulae in Part V make subtle distinctions in relation to the bodies authorized to carry out amendments. For example, there is an important difference between the provincial "legislative assemblies",⁷ which participate in amendments under s. 38, and provincial "legislatures",⁸ which make amendments under s. 45. There is also a difference between the legal document which makes the amendment under s. 38, namely a proclamation issued by the Governor General, and the legal document which makes an amendment under s. 45, namely an Act passed by the provincial legislature. Similarly, the "House of Commons" and "Senate" are distinct from the "Parliament of Canada".⁹

---

⁴ *Manitoba (Attorney General) v. Canada (Attorney General)*, [1981] 1 S.C.R. 753.

⁵ These five are referred to in this Chapter as: (1) the General Formula; (2) the Unanimity Formula; (3) the One-or-More-but-not-all Formula; (4) the Unilateral Federal Formula; and (5) the Unilateral Provincial Formula.

⁶ See, for example, the *Constitution Act, 1886* (U.K.), 49-50 Vict., c. 35, and the *Constitution Act, 1871* (U.K.), 34-35 Vict., c. 28.

⁷ This is the body of elected representatives alone.

⁸ The legislature is constituted as the Lieutenant Governor and the legislative assembly. See, for example, s. 69 of the *Constitution Act, 1867*.

⁹ Section 17 of the *Constitution Act, 1867* says Parliament is made up of three distinct institutions: the Queen, the House of Commons and the Senate.

Section 46 says that for all those amending formulae that require resolutions as part of their procedure, any of the Senate, House of Commons or provincial legislative assemblies can initiate the amending process by adopting a resolution. In practice, resolutions calling for constitutional amendments would likely only be initiated after intergovernmental discussions had revealed a substantial level of support for a proposed amendment.

3. The General Formula[10]

The s. 38 procedure is commonly called the "General Formula" or the "7 and 50" Formula.[11] The formula is set out in s. 38, but ss. 39, 40, 42, 46, and 48 are important to its operation. The General Formula is the most complicated of the five formulae.

The actors involved in amendments under the General Formula are the House of Commons, Senate, provincial legislative assemblies, and the Governor General. This formula is used for amendments to the "Constitution of Canada".[12] It applies to general matters that are not caught by other formulae, as well as to a specific list of matters set out in s. 42. The only body with a veto under this formula is the House of Commons. In fact, the support of the House of Commons is required for all amending procedures, except the Unilateral Provincial Formula set out in s. 45. The Senate's role, by contrast, is circumscribed by s. 47 which says in effect that the Senate alone cannot prevent an amendment. An amendment may be made without a Senate resolution if, within 180 days after a resolution is adopted by the House of Commons, the Senate has not adopted a resolution and if, at any time after the expiration of the 180 days, the House

---

[10] The amendments made to the Constitution of Canada following the 1983 Constitutional Conference on Aboriginal Matters used this Formula. See Chapter 8, "Rights of Aboriginal Peoples of Canada".

[11] The Formula actually calls for resolutions from "two-thirds" of the provinces. Territories are not given a role in any of the amending formulae, even where territories may be directly affected by an amendment. Two-thirds of 10 is six and two-thirds, but it is rounded up to seven. The Formula requires that if only seven provinces eventually support an amendment, those seven must contain 50% of the total population "of all the provinces". The drafters seem to have inadvertently overlooked the population of the two territories. In theory, the House of Commons would probably be seen as representing territorial interests under this Formula and one might have expected the section to say 50% of the population of "Canada". See also *Penikett v. R.*, [1988] 2 W.W.R. 481, (*sub nom. Penikett v. Canada*) 45 D.L.R. (4th) 108 (Y.T. C.A.), leave to appeal to S.C.C. refused [1988] 6 W.W.R. lxix (note) (S.C.C.) and *Sibbeston v. Northwest Territories (Attorney General)*, [1988] 2 W.W.R. 501, (*sub nom. Sibbeston v. Canada (Attorney General)*) 48 D.L.R. (4th) 691 (N.W.T. S.C.), leave to appeal to S.C.C. refused [1988] 6 W.W.R. lxix (note) (S.C.C.).

[12] See the definition of "Constitution of Canada" in s. 52(2) of the *Constitution Act, 1982*.

of Commons adopts the resolution again. This second resolution of support from the House of Commons would then satisfy the requirements of the General Formula and a proclamation could issue.

At first glance, the formula appears to create a simple two-step approach: (1) resolutions are adopted by the House of Commons and Senate, and at least seven provincial legislative assemblies which combined represent at least 50 per cent of the population of Canada, and then, (2) the Governor General issues a proclamation making the amendment. However, it gets a bit more complicated.

One factor that must be considered is timing. The first issue of timing arises from s. 39(1). For example, suppose seven provinces have adopted supporting resolutions within some period less than a year, and they happen to have 50 per cent, or more, of the total population. In this example, the requisite support for the amendment has been obtained, but three provincial legislative assemblies presumably still have not considered the matter. In such a case, s. 39(1) requires the Governor General to wait for a period of one year before issuing a proclamation. The period starts to run from the day the first supporting resolution is adopted. There is, however, an exception: a proclamation can be issued within the year if every provincial legislative assembly has considered the amendment and has either opposed it or adopted it in a resolution.

A second time limit also affects amendments under the General Formula. For any amendment to occur, the House of Commons, Senate, and provincial assemblies must pass resolutions within three years.[13] The period starts to run from the day the first supporting resolution is passed. The Governor General can only issue a proclamation if the required number of resolutions are passed within this three-year period.[14]

Depending on the nature of a particular proposed amendment, another factor that has to be considered is the internal level of support for an amendment in the provincial legislative assemblies, and in the House of Commons and Senate. If an amendment will alter provincial powers, proprietary rights, or other provincial rights or privileges, s. 38(2) requires that a supporting resolution must be approved by "a majority of the members". In other words, a supporting resolution in the House of Commons, which has 295 members, would require 148 votes to be adopted whether

[13] See s. 39(2) of the *Constitution Act, 1982.*

[14] The constitutional amendments contemplated by the Meech Lake Accord expired because of this three-year requirement. The Meech Lake Accord raises questions about the timing requirements of the various amending procedures. In the Accord, the First Ministers agreed politically to treat the proposed amendments as a package which would require unanimous agreement. However, some of the amendments contemplated by the package could have been made under the General Formula. Others in the package required the Unanimity Formula which has no three-year time limit. The Meech Lake Accord seemed to create a hybrid formula by political agreement: a unanimity formula with a three-year time limit.

or not some members were absent from the House on the day the vote was taken.[15]

By contrast, other amendments under the General Formula only require resolutions to be adopted by *a majority of those voting*. If, for example, 15 members were absent from the House on the day of voting for an amendment that did *not* affect provincial powers or rights, 141 votes would be needed to adopt it.

Under the General Formula, even if an amendment is eventually made it may not apply to all the provinces. Section 38(3) allows a province to opt out of the application of any amendment affecting provincial powers, proprietary rights, or other provincial rights or privileges. A "majority of members" in the provincial legislative assembly is required for the adoption of an opting out resolution. The opting out resolution has to be adopted before the Governor General issues a proclamation. A province cannot decide to opt out after the amendment has already been made. If a province is planning to opt out it has to be mindful of timing. For example, if a year has passed and the House of Commons, Senate and six provinces have adopted supporting resolutions, things could move quickly once a seventh province supports the amendment: s. 48 requires the Governor General to issue a proclamation "forthwith" once the necessary number of approvals are in place.

A variation on the opting out approach under the General Formula is found in s. 40. Suppose a proposed amendment will transfer provincial power over education or other cultural matters to Parliament. A province decides to retain these powers and passes a resolution to opt out of the amendment. Under s. 40, the federal government then has to pay "reasonable" compensation to a province which has opted out. This raises questions as to what would constitute reasonable compensation. Up to three provinces could opt out of an amendment, provided their total population was less than 50 per cent of the total population. This provision has not been used to date.

Finally, the General Formula is also used for amendments in relation to a specific list of issues. Section 42(1) says the General Formula has to be used where an amendment relates to:

(*a*) the principle of proportionate representation of the provinces[16] in the House of Commons. . .;

(*b*) the powers of the Senate and method of selecting Senators;

---

[15] Note s. 49 of the *Constitution Act, 1867* which says the Speaker of the House of Commons does not vote on "questions arising in the House" unless there is a tie.

[16] The effect of territorial representation on the principle of proportionate representation in the House does not appear to be covered by s. 42(1)(*a*). The *Constitution Act, 1886* allows Parliament alone to provide for House of Commons representation for territories. The *Constitution Act (No.1), 1975* amended s. 51(2) of the *Constitution Act, 1867* to provide two seats for the Northwest Territories and one seat for the Yukon.

(c) the number of members by which a province is entitled to be represented in the Senate and the residence qualifications of Senators;[17]

(d) [with some exceptions], the Supreme Court of Canada;

(e) the extension of existing provinces into the territories; and

(f) notwithstanding any other law or practice, the establishment of new provinces.

Section 42(2) says that provincial legislative assemblies cannot opt-out of any amendments in relation to the matters listed in s. 42(1). In addition, the resolutions for amendments referred to in s. 42(1) only require a majority of those voting.

4. The Unanimity Formula

The "Unanimity Formula", as it is commonly called, is found in s. 41. This formula is relatively straight forward when compared to the General Formula. The Unanimity Formula applies to a specific list of matters set out in the section. The actors involved are the Governor General, Senate, House of Commons and provincial legislative assemblies. The procedure requires resolutions followed by a proclamation. As the name implies, the support of all 10 provincial assemblies and the House of Commons is required for an amendment. The Senate only has a 180-day "suspensory veto" and cannot ultimately block an amendment that has been supported by all the other actors.

There is no one-year waiting period at the front end of the procedure, nor is there a three-year outside limit on the issue of a proclamation. One unusual element of this formula is paragraph 41(d) which says that the Unanimity Formula applies to an amendment to the "Constitution of Canada" in relation to "the composition of the Supreme Court of Canada". Unfortunately, the Supreme Court of Canada is not set out in the Constitution of Canada. It is governed by an ordinary statute, the *Supreme Court Act*.[18] Opinions differ as to whether all, or part, or none of the *Supreme Court Act* has been boot-strapped into the Constitution and thus entrenched.[19]

---

[17] The number of Senators for each province and territory is set out in a variety of constitutional Acts which have amended the original s. 22 of the *Constitution Act, 1867*. Qualifications of Senators are set out in s. 23 of that Act. The *Constitution Act (No.2), 1975* defines the word "province" in s. 23 to include the Northwest Territories and Yukon. It is not clear whether this interpretive provision in the *Constitution Act (No.2), 1975* would have any relevance to the interpretation of the word "province" in s. 42(1)(c) of the *Constitution Act, 1982*.

[18] R.S.C. 1985, c. S-26.

[19] For a discussion of this point, see Hogg, *supra*, note 1 at 72, n. 52.

The Unanimity Formula also covers amendments to the Constitution of Canada in relation to:

1. the office of the Queen, Governor General and Lieutenant Governor of a province;
2. the "Senate floor rule" which says a province must have at least as many members in the House of Commons as it has members in the Senate; this rule is based on the number of senators a particular province had in 1982;
3. with some exceptions, the use of English and French; and
4. an amendment to any of the provisions in Part V (*i.e.*, the amending procedures themselves).

This formula has not been used to date.

5. The One-or-More-but-not-all Formula

This Formula is set out in s. 43. The actors are the Governor General, Senate, House of Commons and provincial legislative assemblies. The procedure requires resolutions followed by a proclamation. As the name implies, this Formula is used when "any provision" to be amended applies to one or more but not all of the provinces. If it did apply to all provinces, either the General Formula or Unanimity Formula would be required. The use of the expression "any provision" in s. 43 is unclear. It could mean that this formula is only to be used when an amendment is being made to a matter which is already the subject of a provision of the Constitution of Canada. On the other hand, can it also be used to give new powers to one province, but not to the others? Probably not. Section 43 lists two examples of the sort of amendments that would be covered:

1. any alteration to boundaries between provinces, and
2. amendment to a provision that relates to the use of English or French within a province.

This procedure is generally seen as a bilateral formula. New Brunswick and Canada used this Formula in 1993 to amend provisions of the *Canadian Charter of Rights and Freedoms* in relation to official languages in New Brunswick.[20]

---

[20] See *Constitution Amendment Proclamation, 1993*, SI/93-54 (*New Brunswick Act*).

6. The Unilateral Federal Formula

This Formula is set out in s. 44 and covers amendments to the "Constitution of Canada" in relation to the federal executive, or the Senate and the House of Commons, provided that the amendments do not fall within the category of amendments caught by the General Formula or the Unanimity Formula. The actor in this Formula is "Parliament" in its law-making capacity. The procedure requires an Act of Parliament, rather than a resolution from each of the House of Commons and Senate. No proclamation is issued by the Governor General.

7. The Unilateral Provincial Formula

This Formula is found in s. 45. The actor is the provincial "legislature" in a law-making capacity, rather than the "legislative assembly" adopting a resolution. No proclamation is issued by the Governor General. This Formula covers amendments in relation to the "constitution of the province", except matters covered by the Unanimity Formula, for example the office of Lieutenant Governor. What is covered by the expression "constitution of the province" and how is this different from the "Constitution of Canada"?[21] In some cases the Constitution of a province and the Constitution of Canada appear to be the same thing. It must be remembered that Part V of the *Constitution Act, 1867* is entitled "Provincial Constitutions", and that the Schedule to the *Constitution Act, 1982* lists several Acts and Orders in Council which could be described as the "constitution of a province".[22] These Acts and Orders are defined as the "Constitution of Canada" by s. 52(2) of the *Constitution Act, 1982*.

8. Review of Amending Formulae

Section 49 contains a requirement for a "constitutional conference" composed of the Prime Minister and Premiers to discuss the amending

---

[21] This issue has been dealt with indirectly in cases involving electoral boundaries and the right to vote under s. 3 of the *Canadian Charter of Rights and Freedoms*. In *Wilson v. Cowichan Co-op Services* (1986), 34 D.L.R. (4th) 620 (B.C. C.A.), the Court said the Charter of Rights could be used to strike down a provision of the British Columbia Constitution which was a provincial Act. The Supreme Court of Canada also seemed to take the same approach in the case of *Reference re Provincial Electoral Boundaries*, [1991] 2 S.C.R. 158. However, the courts have not used the Charter to strike down any provision of the Constitution of Canada on the rationale that one part of the Constitution cannot be used to overturn another.

[22] See the Schedule to the *Constitution Act, 1982*, the *Manitoba Act, Alberta Act, Saskatchewan Act, British Columbia Terms of Union, Prince Edward Island Terms of Union* and *Newfoundland Act.*

procedures. The section says this must occur by April 17, 1997. Opinion varies as to whether this requirement has already been met by the Meech Lake Accord negotiations and the Charlottetown Accord negotiations,[23] both of which proposed changes to the amending formulae.

On a literal reading of s. 49, the composition of a conference is limited to the Prime Minister and provincial Premiers. At past constitutional conferences, territorial governments and national aboriginal organizations have participated; however, at present neither territorial governments nor aboriginal peoples have a direct role in the amending procedures set out under Part V.

9. Conclusion

Reform of the Constitution dominated the national agenda for a significant part of the 1980s and early 1990s. As previous Chapters have indicated, the written Constitution is extremely flexible and has undergone significant change since 1867 as a result of conventions, judicial interpretation and administrative arrangements. There is reason to believe the Constitution could continue to evolve by these means without major constitutional amendments. However, there is also reason to believe that further constitutional amendments will be sought in relation to Quebec and aboriginal peoples in particular. The Constitution is subject to widely divergent interpretations and, while some see it as open and flexible, others see it as narrow and confining. In the end, to make a constitution work, we must all expect a little less from our Constitution and a little more of ourselves.

---

[23] See Chapter 1.

APPENDICES

Constitution Act, 1867

U.K., 30 & 31 Victoria, c. 3.

. . .

VI. DISTRIBUTION OF LEGISLATIVE POWERS.

Powers of the Parliament.

Legislative Authority of Parliament of Canada.

91. It shall be lawful for the Queen, by and with the Advice and Consent of the Senate and House of Commons, to make Laws for the Peace, Order, and good Government of Canada, in relation to all Matters not coming within the Classes of Subjects by this Act assigned exclusively to the Legislatures of the Provinces; and for greater Certainty, but not so as to restrict the Generality of the foregoing Terms of this Section, it is hereby declared that (notwithstanding anything in this Act) the exclusive Legislative Authority of the Parliament of Canada extends to all Matters coming within the Classes of Subjects next hereinafter enumerated; that is to say, —

1. Repealed.
1A. The Public Debt and Property.
2. The Regulation of Trade and Commerce.
2A. Unemployment insurance.
3. The raising of Money by any Mode or System of Taxation.
4. The borrowing of Money on the Public Credit.
5. Postal Service.
6. The Census and Statistics.
7. Militia, Military and Naval Service, and Defence.
8. The fixing of and providing for the Salaries and Allowances of Civil and other Officers of the Government of Canada.
9. Beacons, Buoys, Lighthouses, and Sable Island.
10. Navigation and Shipping.
11. Quarantine and the Establishment and Maintenance of Marine Hospitals.
12. Sea Coast and Inland Fisheries.
13. Ferries between a Province and any British or Foreign Country or between Two Provinces.
14. Currency and Coinage.
15. Banking, Incorporation of Banks, and the Issue of Paper Money.
16. Savings Banks.
17. Weights and Measures.
18. Bills of Exchange and Promissory Notes.
19. Interest.
20. Legal Tender.
21. Bankruptcy and Insolvency.
22. Patents of Invention and Discovery.
23. Copyrights.

24. Indians, and Lands reserved for the Indians.
25. Naturalization and Aliens.
26. Marriage and Divorce.
27. The Criminal Law, except the Constitution of Courts of Criminal Jurisdiction, but including the Procedure in Criminal Matters.
28. The Establishment, Maintenance, and Management of Penitentiaries.
29. Such Classes of Subjects as are expressly excepted in the Enumeration of the Classes of Subjects by this Act assigned exclusively to the Legislatures of the Provinces.

And any Matter coming within any of the Classes of Subjects enumerated in this Section shall not be deemed to come within the Class of Matters of a local or private Nature comprised in the Enumeration of the Classes of Subjects by this Act assigned exclusively to the Legislatures of the Provinces.

Exclusive Powers of Provincial Legislatures.

Subjects of exclusive Provincial Legislation.
92.   In each Province the Legislature may exclusively make Laws in relation to Matters coming within the Classes of Subject next hereinafter enumerated; that is to say, —

1. Repealed.
2. Direct Taxation within the Province in order to the raising of a Revenue for Provincial Purposes.
3. The borrowing of Money on the sole Credit of the Province.
4. The Establishment and Tenure of Provincial Offices and the Appointment and Payment of Provincial Officers.
5. The Management and Sale of the Public Lands belonging to the Province and of the Timber and Wood thereon.
6. The Establishment, Maintenance, and Management of Public and Reformatory Prisons in and for the Province.
7. The Establishment, Maintenance, and Management of Hospitals, Asylums, Charities, and Eleemosynary Institutions in and for the Province, other than Marine Hospitals.
8. Municipal Institutions in the Province.
9. Shop, Saloon, Tavern, Auctioneer, and other Licences in order to the raising of a Revenue for Provincial, Local, or Municipal Purposes.
10. Local Works and Undertakings other than such as are of the following Classes: —
    (*a*) Lines of Steam or other Ships, Railways, Canals, Telegraphs, and other Works and Undertakings connecting the Province with any other or others of the Provinces, or extending beyond the Limits of the Province;
    (*b*) Lines of Steam Ships between the Province and any British or Foreign Country;
    (*c*) Such Works as, although wholly situate within the Province, are before or after their Execution declared by the Parliament of Canada

to be for the general Advantage of Canada or for the Advantage of Two or more of the Provinces.

11. The Incorporation of Companies with Provincial Objects.
12. The Solemnization of Marriage in the Province.
13. Property and Civil Rights in the Province.
14. The Administration of Justice in the Province, including the Constitution, Maintenance, and Organization of Provincial Courts, both of Civil and of Criminal Jurisdiction, and including Procedure in Civil Matters in those Courts.
15. The Imposition of Punishment by Fine, Penalty, or Imprisonment for enforcing any Law of the Province made in relation to any matter coming within any of the Classes of Subjects enumerated in this Section.
16. Generally all Matters of a merely local or private Nature in the Province.

Non-Renewable Natural Resources, Forestry Resources and Electrical Energy.

Laws respecting non-renewable natural resources, forestry resources and electrical energy.

92A. (1) In each province, the legislature may exclusively make laws in relation to

(*a*) exploration for non-renewable natural resources in the province;

(*b*) development, conservation and management of non-renewable natural resources and forestry resources in the province, including laws in relation to the rate of primary production therefrom; and

(*c*) development, conservation and management of sites and facilities in the province for the generation and production of electrical energy.

Export from provinces of resources.

(2) In each province, the legislature may make laws in relation to the export from the province to another part of Canada of the primary production from non-renewable natural resources and forestry resources in the province and the production from facilities in the province for the generation of electrical energy, but such laws may not authorize or provide for discrimination in prices or in supplies exported to another part of Canada.

Authority of Parliament.

(3) Nothing in subsection (2) derogates from the authority of Parliament to enact laws in relation to the matters referred to in that subsection and, where such a law of Parliament and a law of a province conflict, the law of Parliament prevails to the extent of the conflict.

Taxation of resources.

(4) In each province, the legislature may make laws in relation to the raising of money by any mode or system of taxation in respect of

(*a*) non-renewable natural resources and forestry resources in the province and the primary production therefrom, and (*b* sites and facilities in the province for the generation of electrical energy and the production therefrom,

whether or not such production is exported in whole or in part from the province, but such laws may not authorize or provide for taxation that differentiates between production exported to another part of Canada and production not exported from the province.

"Primary production".

(5) The expression "primary production" has the meaning assigned by the Sixth Schedule.

Existing powers or rights.

(6) Nothing in subsections (1) to (5) derogates from any powers or rights that a legislature or government of a province had immediately before the coming into force of this section.

Education.

93. In and for each Province the Legislature may exclusively make Laws in relation to Education, subject and according to the following Provisions: —

(1) Nothing in any such Law shall prejudicially affect any Right or Privilege with respect to Denominational Schools which any Class of Persons have by Law in the Province at the Union:

(2) All the Powers, Privileges, and Duties at the Union by Law conferred and imposed in Upper Canada on the Separate Schools and School Trustees of the Queen's Roman Catholic Subjects shall be and the same are hereby extended to the Dissentient Schools of the Queen's Protestant and Roman Catholic Subjects in Quebec:

(3) Where in any Province a System of Separate or Dissentient Schools exists by Law at the Union or is thereafter established by the Legislature of the Province, an Appeal shall lie to the Governor General in Council from any Act or Decision of any Provincial Authority affecting any Right or Privilege of the Protestant or Roman Catholic Minority of the Queen's Subjects in relation to Education:

(4) In case any such Provincial Law as from Time to Time seems to the Governor General in Council requisite for the due Execution of the Provisions of this Section is not made, or in case any Decision of the Governor General in Council on any Appeal under this Section is not duly executed by the proper Provincial Authority in that Behalf, then and in every such Case, and as far only as the Circumstances of each Case require, the Parliament of Canada may make remedial Laws for the due Execution of the Provisions of this Section and of any Decision of the Governor General in Council under this Section.

. . .

Old Age Pensions.

Legislation respecting old age pensions and supplementary benefits.

94A. The Parliament of Canada may make laws in relation to old age pensions and supplementary benefits, including survivors, and disability benefits irrespective of age, but no such law shall affect the operation of any law present or future of a provincial legislature in relation to any such matter.

Agriculture and Immigration.

Concurrent Powers of Legislation respecting Agriculture, etc.

95. In each Province the Legislature may make Laws in relation to Agriculture in the Province, and to Immigration into the Province; and it is hereby declared that the Parliament of Canada may from Time to Time make Laws in relation to Agriculture in all or any of the Provinces, and to Immigration into all or any of the Provinces; and any Law of the Legislature of a Province relative to Agriculture or to Immigration shall have effect in and for the Province as long and as far only as it is not repugnant to any Act of the Parliament of Canada.

. . .

General Court of Appeal, etc.

101. The Parliament of Canada may, notwithstanding anything in this Act, from Time to Time provide for the Constitution, Maintenance, and Organization of a General Court of Appeal for Canada, and for the Establishment of any additional Courts for the better Administration of the Laws of Canada.

. . .

Appropriation from Time to Time.

106. Subject to the several Payments by this Act charged on the Consolidated Revenue Fund of Canada, the same shall be appropriated by the Parliament of Canada for the Public Service.

. . .

Treaty Obligations.

132. The Parliament and Government of Canada shall have all Powers necessary or proper for performing the Obligations of Canada or of any Province thereof, as Part of the British Empire, towards Foreign Countries, arising under Treaties between the Empire and such Foreign Countries.

Constitution Act, 1871

. . .

34-35 Victoria, c. 28 (U.K.)

Parliament of Canada may establish new Provinces and provide for the constitution, etc., thereof

2. The Parliament of Canada may from time to time establish new Provinces in any territories forming for the time being part of the Dominion of Canada, but not included in any Province thereof, and may, at the time of such establishment, make provision for the constitution and administration of any such Province, and for the passing of laws for the peace, order, and good government of such Province, and for its representation in the said Parliament.

Alteration of limits of Provinces

3. The Parliament of Canada may from time to time, with the consent of the Legislature of any Province of the said Dominion, increase, diminish, or otherwise alter the limits of such Province, upon such terms and conditions as may be agreed to by the said Legislature, and may, with the like consent, make provision respecting the effect and operation of any such increase or diminution or alteration of territory in relation to any Province affected thereby.

Parliament of Canada may legislate for any territory not included in a Province

4. The Parliament of Canada may from time to time make provision for the administration, peace, order, and good government of any territory not for the time being included in any Province.

. . .

Limitation of powers of Parliament of Canada to legislate for an established Province

6. Except as provided by the third section of this Act, it shall not be competent for the Parliament of Canada to alter the provisions of the last-mentioned Act of the said Parliament in so far as it relates to the Province of Manitoba, or of any other Act hereafter establishing new Provinces in the said Dominion, subject always to the right of the Legislature of the Province of Manitoba to alter from time to time the provisions of any law respecting the qualification of electors and members of the Legislative Assembly and to make laws respecting elections in the said Province.

Constitution Act, 1982
Schedule B to Canada Act 1982 (U.K.)

PART I

CANADIAN CHARTER OF RIGHTS AND FREEDOMS

Whereas Canada is founded upon principles that recognize the supremacy of God and the rule of law:

Guarantee of Rights and Freedoms

Rights and freedoms in Canada

1. The *Canadian Charter of Rights and Freedoms* guarantees the rights and freedoms set out in it subject only to such reasonable limits prescribed by law as can be demonstrably justified in a free and democratic society.

Fundamental Freedoms

Fundamental freedoms

2. Everyone has the following fundamental freedoms:

(*a*) freedom of conscience and religion;

(*b*) freedom of thought, belief, opinion and expression, including freedom of the press and other media of communication;

(*c*) freedom of peaceful assembly; and

(*d*) freedom of association.

Democratic Rights

Democratic rights of citizens

3. Every citizen of Canada has the right to vote in an election of members of the House of Commons or of a legislative assembly and to be qualified for membership therein.

Maximum duration of legislative bodies

4. (1) No House of Commons and no legislative assembly shall continue for longer than five years from the date fixed for the return of the writs at a general election of its members.

Continuation in special circumstances

(2) In time of real or apprehended war, invasion or insurrection, a House of Commons may be continued by Parliament and a legislative assembly may be continued by the legislature beyond five years if such continuation is not opposed by the votes of more than one-third of the members of the House of Commons or the legislative assembly, as the case may be.

Annual sitting of legislative bodies
    5. There shall be a sitting of Parliament and of each legislature at least once every twelve months.

Mobility Rights

Mobility of citizens
    6. (1) Every citizen of Canada has the right to enter, remain in and leave Canada.

Rights to move and gain livelihood
    (2) Every citizen of Canada and every person who has the status of a permanent resident of Canada has the right
    (*a*) to move and take up residence in any province; and
    (*b*) to pursue the gaining of a livelihood in any province.

Limitation
    (3) The rights specified in subsection (2) are subject to
    (*a*) any laws or practices of general application in force in a province other than those that discriminate among persons primarily on the basis of province of present or previous residence; and
    (*b*) any laws providing for reasonable residency requirements as a qualification for the receipt of publicly provided social services.

Affirmative action programs
    (4) Subsections (2) and (3) do not preclude any law, program or activity that has as its object the amelioration in a province of conditions of individuals in that province who are socially or economically disadvantaged if the rate of employment in that province is below the rate of employment in Canada.

Legal Rights

Life, liberty and security of person
    7. Everyone has the right to life, liberty and security of the person and the right not to be deprived thereof except in accordance with the principles of fundamental justice.

Search or seizure
    8. Everyone has the right to be secure against unreasonable search or seizure.

Detention or imprisonment
    9. Everyone has the right not to be arbitrarily detained or imprisoned.

Arrest or detention
    10. Everyone has the right on arrest or detention
    (*a*) to be informed promptly of the reasons therefor;
    (*b*) to retain and instruct counsel without delay and to be informed of that right; and

(*c*) to have the validity of the detention determined by way of *habeas corpus* and to be released if the detention is not lawful.

Proceedings in criminal and penal matters

11. Any person charged with an offence has the right

(*a*) to be informed without unreasonable delay of the specific offence;

(*b*) to be tried within a reasonable time;

(*c*) not to be compelled to be a witness in proceedings against that person in respect of the offence;

(*d*) to be presumed innocent until proven guilty according to law in a fair and public hearing by an independent and impartial tribunal;

(*e*) not to be denied reasonable bail without just cause;

(*f*) except in the case of an offence under military law tried before a military tribunal, to the benefit of trial by jury where the maximum punishment for the offence is imprisonment for five years or a more severe punishment;

(*g*) not to be found guilty on account of any act or omission unless, at the time of the act or omission, it constituted an offence under Canadian or international law or was criminal according to the general principles of law recognized by the community of nations;

(*h*) if finally acquitted of the offence, not to be tried for it again and, if finally found guilty and punished for the offence, not to be tried or punished for it again; and

(*i*) if found guilty of the offence and if the punishment for the offence has been varied between the time of commission and the time of sentencing, to the benefit of the lesser punishment.

Treatment or punishment

12. Everyone has the right not to be subjected to any cruel and unusual treatment or punishment.

Self-crimination

13. A witness who testifies in any proceedings has the right not to have any incriminating evidence so given used to incriminate that witness in any other proceedings, except in a prosecution for perjury or for the giving of contradictory evidence.

Interpreter

14. A party or witness in any proceedings who does not understand or speak the language in which the proceedings are conducted or who is deaf has the right to the assistance of an interpreter.

Equality Rights

Equality before and under law and equal protection and benefit of law

15. (1) Every individual is equal before and under the law and has the right to the equal protection and equal benefit of the law without discrimination and, in particular, without discrimination based on race, national or ethnic origin, colour, religion, sex, age or mental or physical disability.

Affirmative action programs

(2) Subsection (1) does not preclude any law, program or activity that has as its object the amelioration of conditions of disadvantaged individuals or groups including those that are disadvantaged because of race, national or ethnic origin, colour, religion, sex, age or mental or physical disability.

Official Languages of Canada

Official languages of Canada

16. (1) English and French are the official languages of Canada and have equality of status and equal rights and privileges as to their use in all institutions of the Parliament and government of Canada.

Official languages of New Brunswick

(2) English and French are the official languages of New Brunswick and have equality of status and equal rights and privileges as to their use in all institutions of the legislature and government of New Brunswick.

Advancement of status and use

(3) Nothing in this Charter limits the authority of Parliament or a legislature to advance the equality of status or use of English and French.

English and French linguistic communities in New Brunswick

16.1 (1) The English linguistic community and the French linguistic community in New Brunswick have equality of status and equal rights and privileges, including the right to distinct educational institutions and such distinct cultural institutions as are necessary for the preservation and promotion of those communities.

Role of the legislature and government of New Brunswick

(2) The role of the legislature and government of New Brunswick to preserve and promote the status, rights and privileges referred to in subsection (1) is affirmed. SI/93-54.

Proceedings of Parliament

17. (1) Everyone has the right to use English or French in any debates and other proceedings of Parliament.

Proceedings of New Brunswick legislature

(2) Everyone has the right to use English or French in any debates and other proceedings of the legislature of New Brunswick.

Parliamentary statutes and records

18. (1) The statutes, records and journals of Parliament shall be printed and published in English and French and both language versions are equally authoritative.

New Brunswick statutes and records

(2) The statutes, records and journals of the legislature of New Brunswick shall be printed and published in English and French and both language versions are equally authoritative.

Proceedings in courts established by Parliament

19. (1) Either English or French may be used by any person in, or in any pleading in or process issuing from, any court established by Parliament.

Proceedings in New Brunswick courts

(2) Either English or French may be used by any person in, or in any pleading in or process issuing from, any court of New Brunswick.

Communications by public with federal institutions

20. (1) Any member of the public in Canada has the right to communicate with, and to receive available services from, any head or central office of an institution of the Parliament or government of Canada in English or French, and has the same right with respect to any other office of any such institution where

(*a*) there is a significant demand for communications with and services from that office in such language; or

(*b*) due to the nature of the office, it is reasonable that communications with and services from that office be available in both English and French.

Communications by public with New Brunswick institutions

(2) Any member of the public in New Brunswick has the right to communicate with, and to receive available services from, any office of an institution of the legislature or government of New Brunswick in English or French.

Continuation of existing constitutional provisions

21. Nothing in sections 16 to 20 abrogates or derogates from any right, privilege or obligation with respect to the English and French languages, or either of them, that exists or is continued by virtue of any other provision of the Constitution of Canada.

Rights and privileges preserved

22. Nothing in sections 16 to 20 abrogates or derogates from any legal or customary right or privilege acquired or enjoyed either before or after the coming into force of this Charter with respect to any language that is not English or French.

Minority Language Educational Rights

Language of instruction

23. (1) Citizens of Canada

(*a*) whose first language learned and still understood is that of the English or French linguistic minority population of the province in which they reside, or

(*b*) who have received their primary school instruction in Canada in English or French and reside in a province where the language in which they received that instruction is the language of the English or French linguistic minority population of the province,

have the right to have their children receive primary and secondary school instruction in that language in that province.

Continuity of language instruction

(2) Citizens of Canada of whom any child has received or is receiving primary or secondary school instruction in English or French in Canada, have the right to have all their children receive primary and secondary school instruction in the same language.

Application where numbers warrant

(3) The right of citizens of Canada under subsections (1) and (2) to have their children receive primary and secondary school instruction in the language of the English or French linguistic minority population of a province

(*a*) applies wherever in the province the number of children of citizens who have such a right is sufficient to warrant the provision to them out of public funds of minority language instruction; and

(*b*) includes, where the number of those children so warrants, the right to have them receive that instruction in minority language educational facilities provided out of public funds.

Enforcement

Enforcement of guaranteed rights and freedoms

24. (1) Anyone whose rights or freedoms, as guaranteed by this Charter, have been infringed or denied may apply to a court of competent jurisdiction to obtain such remedy as the court considers appropriate and just in the circumstances.

Exclusion of evidence bringing administration of justice into disrepute

(2) Where, in proceedings under subsection (1), a court concludes that evidence was obtained in a manner that infringed or denied any rights or freedoms guaranteed by this Charter, the evidence shall be excluded if it is established that, having regard to all the circumstances, the admission of it in the proceedings would bring the administration of justice into disrepute.

General

Aboriginal rights and freedoms not affected by Charter

25. The guarantee in this Charter of certain rights and freedoms shall not be construed so as to abrogate or derogate from any aboriginal, treaty or other rights or freedoms that pertain to the aboriginal peoples of Canada including

(*a*) any rights or freedoms that have been recognized by the Royal Proclamation of October 7, 1763; and

(*b*) any rights or freedoms that now exist by way of land claims agreements or may be so acquired. SI/84-102.

Other rights and freedoms not affected by Charter

26. The guarantee in this Charter of certain rights and freedoms shall not be construed as denying the existence of any other rights or freedoms that exist in Canada.

Multicultural heritage

27. This Charter shall be interpreted in a manner consistent with the preservation and enhancement of the multicultural heritage of Canadians.

Rights guaranteed equally to both sexes

28. Notwithstanding anything in this Charter, the rights and freedoms referred to in it are guaranteed equally to male and female persons.

Rights respecting certain schools preserved

29. Nothing in this Charter abrogates or derogates from any rights or privileges guaranteed by or under the Constitution of Canada in respect of denominational, separate or dissentient schools.

Application to territories and territorial authorities

30. A reference in this Charter to a province or to the legislative assembly or legislature of a province shall be deemed to include a reference to the Yukon Territory and the Northwest Territories, or to the appropriate legislative authority thereof, as the case may be.

Legislative powers not extended

31. Nothing in this Charter extends the legislative powers of any body or authority.

Application of Charter

Application of Charter

32. (1) This Charter applies

(*a*) to the Parliament and government of Canada in respect of all matters within the authority of Parliament including all matters relating to the Yukon Territory and Northwest Territories; and

(*b*) to the legislature and government of each province in respect of all matters within the authority of the legislature of each province.

Exception

(2) Notwithstanding subsection (1), section 15 shall not have effect until three years after this section comes into force.

Exception where express declaration

33. (1) Parliament or the legislature of a province may expressly declare in an Act of Parliament or of the legislature, as the case may be, that the Act or a provision thereof shall operate notwithstanding a provision included in section 2 or sections 7 to 15 of this Charter.

Operation of exception

(2) An Act or a provision of an Act in respect of which a declaration made

under this section is in effect shall have such operation as it would have but for the provision of this Charter referred to in the declaration.

Five year limitation
(3) A declaration made under subsection (1) shall cease to have effect five years after it comes into force or on such earlier date as may be specified in the declaration.

Re-enactment
(4) Parliament or the legislature of a province may re-enact a declaration made under subsection (1).

Five year limitation
(5) Subsection (3) applies in respect of a re-enactment made under subsection (4).

Citation

Citation
34. This Part may be cited as the *Canadian Charter of Rights and Freedoms.*

PART II
RIGHTS OF THE ABORIGINAL PEOPLES OF CANADA

Recognition of existing aboriginal and treaty rights
35. (1) The existing aboriginal and treaty rights of the aboriginal peoples of Canada are hereby recognized and affirmed.

Definition of "aboriginal peoples of Canada"
(2) In this Act, "aboriginal peoples of Canada" includes the Indian, Inuit and Métis peoples of Canada.

Land claims agreements
(3) For greater certainty, in subsection (1) "treaty rights" includes rights that now exist by way of land claims agreements or may be so acquired.

Aboriginal and treaty rights are guaranteed equally to both sexes
(4) Notwithstanding any other provision of this Act, the aboriginal and treaty rights referred to in subsection (1) are guaranteed equally to male and female persons. SI/84-102.

Commitment to participation in constitutional conference
35.1 The government of Canada and the provincial governments are committed to the principle that, before any amendment is made to Class 24 of section 91 of the *"Constitution Act, 1867"*, to section 25 of this Act or to this Part,
(a) a constitutional conference that includes in its agenda an item relating to the proposed amendment, composed of the Prime Minister of Canada and the first ministers of the provinces, will be convened by the Prime Minister of Canada; and

(*b*) the Prime Minister of Canada will invite representatives of the aboriginal peoples of Canada to participate in the discussions on that item. SI/84-102.

. . .

PART V

PROCEDURE FOR AMENDING CONSTITUTION OF CANADA

General procedure for amending Constitution of Canada

38. (1) An amendment to the Constitution of Canada may be made by proclamation issued by the Governor General under the Great Seal of Canada where so authorized by

(*a*) resolutions of the Senate and House of Commons; and

(*b*) resolutions of the legislative assemblies of at least two-thirds of the provinces that have, in the aggregate, according to the then latest general census, at least fifty per cent of the population of all the provinces.

Majority of members

(2) An amendment made under subsection (1) that derogates from the legislative powers, the proprietary rights or any other rights or privileges of the legislature or government of a province shall require a resolution supported by a majority of the members of each of the Senate, the House of Commons and the legislative assemblies required under subsection (1).

Expression of dissent

(3) An amendment referred to in subsection (2) shall not have effect in a province the legislative assembly of which has expressed its dissent thereto by resolution supported by a majority of its members prior to the issue of the proclamation to which the amendment relates unless that legislative assembly, subsequently, by resolution supported by a majority of its members, revokes its dissent and authorizes the amendment.

Revocation of dissent

(4) A resolution of dissent made for the purposes of subsection (3) may be revoked at any time before or after the issue of the proclamation to which it relates.

Restriction on proclamation

39. (1) A proclamation shall not be issued under subsection 38(1) before the expiration of one year from the adoption of the resolution initiating the amendment procedure thereunder, unless the legislative assembly of each province has previously adopted a resolution of assent or dissent.

Idem

(2) A proclamation shall not be issued under subsection 38(1) after the expiration of three years from the adoption of the resolution initiating the amendment procedure thereunder.

Compensation

40. Where an amendment is made under subsection 38(1) that transfers provincial legislative powers relating to education or other cultural matters from provincial legislatures to Parliament, Canada shall provide reasonable compensation to any province to which the amendment does not apply.

Amendment by unanimous consent

41. An amendment to the Constitution of Canada in relation to the following matters may be made by proclamation issued by the Governor General under the Great Seal of Canada only where authorized by resolutions of the Senate and House of Commons and of the legislative assembly of each province:

(*a*) the office of the Queen, the Governor General and the Lieutenant Governor of a province;

(*b*) the right of a province to a number of members in the House of Commons not less than the number of Senators by which the province is entitled to be represented at the time this Part comes into force;

(*c*) subject to section 43, the use of the English or the French language;

(*d*) the composition of the Supreme Court of Canada; and

(*e*) an amendment to this Part.

Amendment by general procedure

42. (1) An amendment to the Constitution of Canada in relation to the following matters may be made only in accordance with subsection 38(1):

(*a*) the principle of proportionate representation of the provinces in the House of Commons prescribed by the Constitution of Canada;

(*b*) the powers of the Senate and the method of selecting Senators;

(*c*) the number of members by which a province is entitled to be represented in the Senate and the residence qualifications of Senators;

(*d*) subject to paragraph 41(*d*), the Supreme Court of Canada;

(*e*) the extension of existing provinces into the territories; and

(*f*) notwithstanding any other law or practice, the establishment of new provinces.

Exception

(2) Subsections 38(2) to (4) do not apply in respect of amendments in relation to matters referred to in subsection (1).

Amendment of provisions relating to some but not all provinces

43. An amendment to the Constitution of Canada in relation to any provision that applies to one or more, but not all, provinces, including

(*a*) any alteration to boundaries between provinces, and

(*b*) any amendment to any provision that relates to the use of the English or the French language within a province,

may be made by proclamation issued by the Governor General under the Great Seal of Canada only where so authorized by resolutions of the Senate and House of Commons and of the legislative assembly of each province to which the amendment applies.

Amendments by Parliament

44. Subject to sections 41 and 42, Parliament may exclusively make laws amending the Constitution of Canada in relation to the executive government of Canada or the Senate and House of Commons.

Amendments by provincial legislatures

45. Subject to section 41, the legislature of each province may exclusively make laws amending the constitution of the province.

Initiation of amendment procedures

46. (1) The procedures for amendment under sections 38, 41, 42 and 43 may be initiated either by the Senate or the House of Commons or by the legislative assembly of a province.

Revocation of authorization

(2) A resolution of assent made for the purposes of this Part may be revoked at any time before the issue of a proclamation authorized by it.

Amendments without Senate resolution

47. (1) An amendment to the Constitution of Canada made by proclamation under section 38, 41, 42 or 43 may be made without a resolution of the Senate authorizing the issue of the proclamation if, within one hundred and eighty days after the adoption by the House of Commons of a resolution authorizing its issue, the Senate has not adopted such a resolution and if, at any time after the expiration of that period, the House of Commons again adopts the resolution.

Computation of period

(2) Any period when Parliament is prorogued or dissolved shall not be counted in computing the one hundred and eighty day period referred to in subsection (1).

Advice to issue proclamation

48. The Queen's Privy Council for Canada shall advise the Governor General to issue a proclamation under this Part forthwith on the adoption of the resolutions required for an amendment made by proclamation under this Part.

Constitutional conference

49. A constitutional conference composed of the Prime Minister of Canada and the first ministers of the provinces shall be convened by the Prime Minister of Canada within fifteen years after this Part comes into force to review the provisions of this Part.

Selected Bibliography

Abel, Albert S., ed. *Laskin's Canadian Constitutional Law*. 4th rev. ed. Carswell, 1975.

Banks, Margaret A. *Understanding Canada's Constitution*. University of Western Ontario, 1991.

Bayefsky, Anne and Mary Eberts, eds. *Equality Rights and the Canadian Charter of Rights and Freedoms*. Carswell, 1985.

Beaudoin, Gerald and Edward Ratushny, eds. *The Canadian Charter of Rights and Freedoms*. 2d ed. Carswell, 1989.

Davis, Louis B.Z. *Canadian Constitutional Law Handbook*. Canada Law Book, 1985.

Finkelstein, Neil, ed. *Laskin's Canadian Constitutional Law*. 5th ed. Carswell, 1986.

Finkelstein, Neil and Brian M. Rogers, eds. *Charter Issues in Civil Cases*. Carswell, 1988.

Fogarty, Hon. Kenneth H. *Equality Rights and Their Limitations in the Charter*. Carswell, 1987.

Gibson, Dale. *The Law of the Charter: Equality Rights*. Carswell, 1990.

Gibson, Dale. *The Law of the Charter: General Principles*. Carswell, 1986.

Heard, Andrew. *Canadian Constitutional Conventions: The Marriage of Law and Politics*. Oxford University Press, 1991.

Hogg, Peter W. *Constitutional Law of Canada*. 3d ed. 2 volumes, supp. Carswell, 1992.

Magnet, Joseph P. *Constitutional Law of Canada: Cases, Notes and Materials*. 2 volumes. 4th ed. Yvon Blais, 1989.

McDonald, Hon. David C. *Legal Rights in the Canadian Charter of Rights and Freedoms*. 2d ed. Carswell, 1989.

Monahan, Patrick. *Politics and the Constitution: The Charter, Federalism and the Supreme Court of Canada*. Carswell, 1987.

Paciocco, David M. *Charter Principles and Proof in Criminal Cases*. Carswell, 1987.

Schneiderman, David, ed. *Freedom of Expression and the Charter.* Carswell, 1991.

Sharpe, Robert J., ed. *Charter Litigation.* Butterworths, 1987.

Stuart, Don. *Charter Justice in Canadian Criminal Law.* Carswell, 1991.

Van Loon, Richard and Michael Whittington. *The Canadian Political System.* McGraw-Hill Ryerson, 1987.

Varcoe, Frederick P. *The Constitution of Canada.* 2d ed. Carswell, 1965.

Whitley, Stuart J. *Criminal Justice and the Constitution.* Carswell, 1989.

Whyte, John, William R. Lederman and Donald Bur. *Canadian Constitutional Law: Cases, Notes and Materials.* 3d ed. Butterworths, 1992.

Index

[All references are to page numbers of the text.]